Also by Author, Barbara Roose Cramer

CHILD OF DREAMS,
Trafford Publishing, 2014

A PINCH OF DRY MUSTARD,
Trafford Publishing, 2009

THE BARRELMAN, History of the Denver Bronco Football Club
Kendall Hunt Publishing, 1992

BROKEN SOULS

with
Rebecca Harrison

BARBARA ROOSE CRAMER

Order this book online at www.trafford.com
or email orders@trafford.com

Most Trafford titles are also available at major online book retailers.

Cover Design: Steven G. Cramer

Print information available on the last page.

ISBN: 978-1-4907-7640-8 (sc)
ISBN: 978-1-4907-7642-2 (hc)
ISBN: 978-1-4907-7641-5 (e)

Library of Congress Control Number: 2016913712

Trafford rev. 09/09/2016

 www.trafford.com

North America & international
toll-free: 1 888 232 4444 (USA & Canada)
fax: 812 355 4082

"I am not what happened to me, I am
what I choose to become."

Carl Gustaf Jung

Broken Souls is a fictional story based in part on the true story of four sisters whose lives were completely destroyed by supposedly, loving, adoptive parents.

Broken Souls is dedicated to all of those broken souls who have been kidnapped, brainwashed, abandoned or killed, experienced living in an orphanage or raised in foster care or have been adopted by the wrong families for all the wrong reasons… those whose voices may not or will never be heard…this book is for you. *

"Although I have not experienced a broken home, or lived in an orphanage or in a foster home, I have great respect for the foster care program (my husband and I were foster parents), and the adoption system (my granddaughter and God-daughter are both adopted). I agree with Ms. Harrison that the systems are not perfect, and that the writings in this book, although horrific and at times unbelievable, can and do happen. I agreed completely with Ms. Harrison to write this book."
Barbara Roose Cramer

"I am telling this story for my sisters, and for all the wounded and broken souls who cannot or will not speak for themselves."
Rebecca Harrison

INTRODUCTION

Driving my 1985 rusted out, green Buick in the middle lane on Greenwood Boulevard at rush hour, in a city as big as Dawson, Colorado, is either one of the more stupid things I've ever done or I have the "need to die young", syndrome. In this case, I need to get to a really important appointment at this un-godly time of the evening on the east side of Dawson. You got it—it's stupidity.

First of all, I'm a sometimes paid, most of the time not paid or underpaid, close to middle-age, advocate—an advocate for those people who seem to have no money, no family, no vehicle, no job and no one to turn to in time of crisis, that is, except for me. I'm self-employed (which is another mistake I made early on in life), advisor and beggar for those who need a voice; those who have no voice of their own. I have two years of a 4-year law degree from the University of Dawson law school, several classes in sociology and biology under my belt, and a certificate that reads "how to succeed in life without really trying". However, that never got me the position I really wanted in life...my own law firm. So, here I am, a self-employed private eye/advocate/ caring Christian woman who has a heart as big as New York City, but who's always broke.

So, this week after having visited this client previously, and after yet another tearful, no, sobbing telephone call from this desperate young woman needing assistance, and after my already frustrating day, I am making the drive in rush hour, on Greenwood Boulevard. This part of Greenwood Boulevard however, makes for a beautiful drive. The boulevard is lined with tall evergreen trees, beautiful white, purple or pink lilac bushes and massive amounts of pink, white and red azaleas—all due to the landscaping artistry of the well-known Dawson Country Club (dream on lady). The beauty around me changes my outlook a little, and I think I've got it together enough to talk with this frustrated client.

As I drive my old Buick with a right handed gas control (my one leg is paralyzed), held together with duck tape, my thirty-year-old manual E&J wheelchair in the back seat (just in case I get too tired to walk), and one sad looking crutch, I notice the two-day-old blueberry muffin setting on the dashboard. "If I only had a cup of hot steamy Starbucks." I think to myself.

Well, anyway, let me share with you in the next few chapters what I believe could be or should be a life-changing story. This is the kind of story that should make you take a look at the REAL world we are living in. If it doesn't make you stop and think, or at least stop and thank the good Lord for what you have, or perhaps makes you stop and pray for the world we live in today, well then perhaps **you** ought to give me a call too!

BOOK
ONE

CHAPTER ONE

The Country Club

The Dawson Country Club has been a landmark in Colorado since the early 1900's. It was built for those persons with greater financial status than I'll ever know, and who needed a place to meet, dine and even live. Most of the members made their money from mining, real estate, cattle or other related business ventures and although several books have been written about the Dawson Country Club, many in the know, feel that many truths were left out; that there was too much written about golf and not enough about the club being blatantly racist.

Evidently, this Country Club area (as the area came to be called), became a Mecca for the elite. It was and is a private club, located on the southern boundary of an exclusive, historic part of Dawson. There were and still are, parties, golf, fine dining, a place to mingle, beautiful black tie galas and balls held almost every weekend, and because of the elite area, housing boomed with beautifully built and now historic homes, which currently are on the real estate market for millions of dollars.

The Dawson Country Club is a private club and is located on the southern boundary of this exclusive, historic part of Dawson, and this is where our story of those with broken souls begins.

Chapter Two

Melissa Jane Baker

There were numerous puffy white clouds in the western Colorado sky and the sun, which was about to set, displayed a golden glow around many of them. Sunsets are always beautiful in Colorado. Folks who live here, claim that God is a local football team fan, as sunsets seem to be more orange than gold, and are often surrounded with just a touch of blue. I agree. I stare up at those clouds for just a moment, realizing that football season is about to begin; but only for a moment, as I definitely don't want to take my eyes off the road—road rage you know—it can happen to anyone on this section of Greenwood Boulevard.

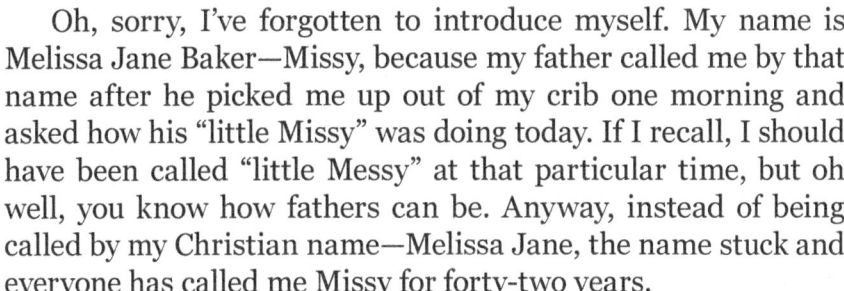

Oh, sorry, I've forgotten to introduce myself. My name is Melissa Jane Baker—Missy, because my father called me by that name after he picked me up out of my crib one morning and asked how his "little Missy" was doing today. If I recall, I should have been called "little Messy" at that particular time, but oh well, you know how fathers can be. Anyway, instead of being called by my Christian name—Melissa Jane, the name stuck and everyone has called me Missy for forty-two years.

I am one of six children, two girls and four boys. My mother is a stay-at-home mom, although she could have been about anything she wanted to be. She could sew, bake, cook, remodel the house, mow the lawn, plant petunias, bake ten dozen cookies for a church bake sale, all the while, stitching up a huge cut on Rocky's (our big, black Labrador Retriever), ear and she could can twenty-four quarts of green beans—all in one day. My dad on the other hand, was laid back at home playing ball with his kids in the back yard, maybe washing a dish or vacuuming a carpet once in awhile, or restoring old pick-up trucks in his back yard. He was also one of the meanest, junkyard type detectives the state of Colorado had ever seen. He was a scrapper and not just with old pick up trucks. He was noted for putting away more shoddy customers than any other detective had in the past twenty-five years on the force. He never took on a case that he didn't think he could solve, and me, his baby girl, "little Missy", grew up to be just like him. The only difference being, daddy got paid, and paid well, and little Missy, well, she did a lot of work, saved a lot of people, helped put away a lot of bad guys, and all for pert-near nothing!

I honk at the driver, who, without signaling, swiftly pulls his immense, red, Chevrolet truck out in front of my old green Buick, just missing my right front fender. Out of his driver's side window, he gives me the "Hawaiian good luck" sign when he hears me honking my horn. Because he's paying no attention to the traffic and he's intent on giving me the finger, he almost rear-ends the dark blue Lincoln town car in front of him. He slams on his brakes. I slam on my brakes, but the driver in the car behind me and my old Buick doesn't brake in time, and I'm the one who gets rear-ended, while the guy who started this entire fiasco drives away, hand out the driver's side window, waving back at all of us, once again, with the "Hawaiian good luck" sign.

I'm angry, no doubt about it, but anger doesn't help you in a situation like this. Once I grabbed my crutch, exited my old Buick, checked out the damage to my "rear-end" and saw that the damage was minor, I realized that my ego was injured more than my old Buick.

The man, about my age, who had rear-ended me, also exited his new, shiny, silver Cadillac, so new that it didn't even have license plates (there was a sticker over where his license plate should have been), and walked up to me.

"I'm so sorry", he said. "I really did try to stop, but I guess I was driving to close too you. Should we exchange insurance information or do you think you'll be okay?"

As we both walked over to check out my rear-end and his front-end (literally), we agreed that just in case there were "unseen" damages to either of our vehicles, we should not only exchange insurance policies and license numbers, but perhaps I suggested, we should also contact the police.

"Isn't this the middle of rush hour?" The middle-aged silver-haired fox (and still noticeably attractive), man inquired of me. "We've already got traffic jammed up behind us, and there is very little damage to either car, so I don't think there is a need to call the police."

I didn't agree. There was something about this silver-haired, evidently elite member of East Dawson's community, that didn't settle well with me. I insisted that we call the police, and I did. After all, I'm a detective's daughter and a Private Investigator.

After fifteen minutes, a squad car managed to get through the traffic jam, lights flashing, siren blaring, and the officer pulled up behind the Caddy. He introduced himself, showed us his badge, checked out the damage, and asked that we try to move our vehicles into the parking lot—you got it, the parking lot of the infamous Dawson Country Club. I had been so busy trying to get through traffic unscathed, that I hadn't realized my location. I did as the traffic officer ordered and while he stopped traffic, both the silver-haired fox and I moved our cars—it's then that the **real** fun began.

CHAPTER THREE

Mandy and Mittens

In a rundown apartment building on East Jeremy Place, in Arribio, Colorado, a suburb of Dawson, a young woman with soft brown eyes, matted blond hair and a small tattoo of Jesus on her neck, paced back and forth across the red and pink linoleum of her kitchen floor. In one hand, she had a double shot of vodka in a yellow plastic cup to which she had added a tad bit of Sprite. In the other hand she nervously held onto a butcher knife that measured approximately seven inches in length. From her right wrist, a trickle of blood dropped onto the kitchen floor, matching the red, spilled spaghetti sauce from three days earlier. Time and again she had checked her watch, and each time she checked the time, she would walk up to and open her front door, look out, and when she saw no sign of Missy Baker, she would slam the door, and tell the mangy black cat that she was going to **do** it.

"This time, Mittens, I'm going to do it. I'm going to slash-em' good this time. Nobody cares, not even Missy. She lied to me. She said she'd be here over an hour and a half ago, and she's still not here. She's like everybody else, she lied to me".

Screaming now at the black cat, who hadn't a care in the world, except for maybe her over flowing, putrid-smelling cat box, meowed, flipped her long tail back and forth, and paid no mind to the once, beautiful young woman who was threatening to slash her wrists.

As the young woman sat down on a kitchen chair, she stretched her arm out across the dirty tablecloth, placed the sharp edge of the butcher knife across her wrist, and pulled it back, then raised it slightly before scraping her wrists again. By the time she was ready to slice her wrist for the third time, the blood was no longer a trickle, but a gushing stream of red flowing onto the tablecloth and onto the floor into the dried up spaghetti sauce and cat litter. As Mandy Sue Donnor lifted the butcher knife to start slashing her left wrist, she asked Jesus to forgive her, to please take her to Heaven, and to please watch over Mittens. The knife fell to the floor with a bang, and Mandy Sue laid her head gently onto the dirty yellow tablecloth and closed her eyes.

Missy Jane Baker was just pulling out of the Dawson Country Club's parking lot.

CHAPTER FOUR

The Silver-Haired Fox and the Cop

Missy was so happy to get away from the cop and the silver-haired moron in the country club's parking lot that she could've burned rubber in her old Buick when she pulled onto Greenwood Blvd. But she thought the better for it—the old girl would not survive that kind of burnout, plus, it was still rush hour.

The policeman had started out as a very concerned officer of the law, but after three minutes with the silver-haired-fox, he soon changed his attitude to "of course you're not guilty sir, the s.o.b. in the Chevrolet truck was to blame, and ma'am you should've been more observant and got that guy's license number. This gentleman, uh, Dr. Bernard Livingstone, had no chance to stop before hitting your bumper, causing just slight damage, and I think the good doctor would like to pay you for your slight damage, and for your inconvenience."

I could feel my blood beginning to boil, but held my cool, because number one, I don't cuss or swear (well, maybe once I slipped), and I believe in giving every man or woman a chance to explain every situation. More important, I was so anxious to get to my appointment on the east end, that I just wanted to get the heck out of there.

"I don't accept bribes, officer". I said in my sweet, little Missy voice, and before the officer opened his mouth to object to my accusation, and began to call "back-up" for this soon-to-be rowdy, out-of-control woman of forty-two (he looked at my license). "I don't want your money Dr. Livingstone, but I will take a business card."

"I insist that you take the money for your inconvenience, although, as the officer said, I really see no damage to your vehicle." The good doctor said, once again trying to hand me a one hundred dollar bill, and touching my hand slightly in the process. "I'm not trying to bribe you, nor is officer Jenkins here, I just have a business event to attend, I'm already late, and I would like to end this small inconvenience to you with my kind gesture."

Once again, I pushed his hand away, thanked them both for their time, and since there was no way the "fox" was going to give me his business card, I quickly got into my car, grabbed a pen and pad out of my glove box, and wrote down the doc's license plate number, and the cop's badge number. No one gets the best of Missy Jane Baker.

CHAPTER FIVE

There really is a God

Missy pulled into the parking lot of Mandy's run-down apartment building almost two hours after her promised time of arrival. She opened the door of her Buick, grabbed her purse, the pad and pencil, and walking as fast as she could on a bum leg and one crutch, hurried to Mandy's front door. She knocked on the door once, twice, and after the third time, carefully opened the door. She called out Mandy's name, and entered the dark, dungy apartment. The black cat quickly darted to another room, just as Missy noticed Mandy lying face down on the kitchen table. She called out her name, "Mandy, Mandy, Mandy Sue can you hear me?" Noticing all the blood, and the bloodied butcher knife, she began to open drawers in hopes of finding a rag or dishtowel—anything she could use to make a tourniquet, to try and stop the bleeding. Having found a couple towels, she immediately wrapped Mandy's wrist and put pressure on the artery above the slashes. She then did the same with the other wrist. Missy took the pale woman's pulse, which was very weak, took her own cell phone from her purse and called 911. She gave the dispatcher the address, told her that it was a life or death situation, and to send an ambulance immediately and hung up.

Missy found a blanket in the bedroom and covered the young woman with it. She didn't want to move her, but needed to keep her warm while she waited for the Paramedics to arrive. What seemed like an eternity but in reality was only three minutes, she heard the sirens, and met the police and fire department officers at Mandy's front door. The paramedics did what needed to be done to stablelize her, told Missy that her friend was in serious condition, loaded her onto the pram and into the back of the ambulance. Missy was told that Mandy would be taken to Dawson General Hospital, where she could check on her later.

After getting her composure back and sitting down on a rickety kitchen chair, a police officer took down Missy's name, address, telephone number, and asked why she was at the victim's home—Missy answered all of his questions, gave out any personal information she knew about Mandy, and was told she could leave, and that he would most likely be in touch.

"Does she have family close by?" The officer asked.

Missy said she had no idea, that Mandy was a new client that she was trying to help through some personal problems, and that she had no idea her client was this desperate or would try to commit suicide. Missy promised the officer, and silently promised herself, that she would do some digging and find more information on this desperate young woman and share it with the police department. "However", she thought to herself, "if I do share any more information right now, Mandy would most likely be placed in lock-down at the hospital, and could end up in jail." She would do more background checking before giving up any more information on her client to the police department.

As Missy got into her car, she laid her crutch on the seat next to her, and before putting the key into the ignition, took a deep breath, thanked God that Mandy Sue Donnor was still alive and thought back over the past few weeks.

On Monday morning, three weeks earlier, an anonymous caller had told Missy that there was a young lady in his apartment building who had been found drunk and bloodied outside of their apartment building twice that week. On one of those occasions the young woman said she had been attacked, raped and forced to drink vodka until she was completely oblivious to her surroundings. The next thing she knew she was waking up and found herself lying on the sidewalk in front of her apartment building.

At first the anonymous male caller said no one believed the young woman and to be honest, he admitted he didn't believe her either, but after the second time he and another tenant had found her—this time even bloodier—they believed her. The male caller admitted he found Missy's name in the telephone book, and took a chance that Missy could help this young woman. He refused to give his name, but Missy had a gut feeling that he was telling the truth. She got Mandy's name and address from him and had called her later that afternoon. The first time they met, Mandy denied everything, but on the second call back, Missy had convinced her to allow her to come over for an extended visit.

When Missy saw Mandy for the first time, the young woman was in serious disarray, dirty hair and clothing, and had a prominent black and blue eye, swollen the size of Texas. Mandy first said she had fallen, then, as the conversation continued, she admitted that she had been attacked about a block from her apartment, and she had made it to her front door before passing out. When Missy asked her about calling the police, she said she never thought to call the authorities because as she put it "cops don't care about people in this part of town and I know that some of the cops are bad too."

"Cops just think that I'm another prostitute, and they don't care about me or any of us that live in this dump!" She said, eyes filling up with tears. "No sense in calling the police because they're bad, Missy, and they'd just as soon wish I was dead." Then in a more composed tone of voice, the poor woman said, "You know, I used to live in a really nice house, a pretty house, with horses and grass and flowers..." Mandy stopped speaking, turned her body around, waved her arms around the "dump" she was now living in, and once again the tears flowed.

Missy did not ask if she was or was not a prostitute, nor if she actually knew a bad cop, or why she left her previous residence, but instead, asked her about her bruises and did she need to see a doctor? Did she hurt anywhere else? Could Missy help her take a shower, put on some clean clothes, and most important, when was the last time she had eaten a decent meal?

Mandy began to cry again, and admitted that she hadn't eaten in a few days, she had no money—her money had stopped— she gave no reason as to why—and yes, she would appreciate Missy helping her get cleaned up.

Careful not to overstep her boundaries, Missy asked if this frightened young woman needed help undressing and stepping in and out of the shower, and when Mandy said yes, Missy was overwhelmed at the amount of cuts and bruises that covered this poor woman's body. Missy asked her if she had been raped, and when Mandy began to weep even harder, she said that yes, she had been gang raped by three men. No, she couldn't remember where she had met them, and no, she couldn't describe any of them. However, she did remember that it was the same three men that had attacked and raped her the first time. However, that had been over two weeks ago—too late for a rape kit analysis.

As the warm water ran over Mandy's broken and bruised body, Missy laid down her crutch, sat down on the toilet seat and called her friend Jeanine Simpson at the Dawson Women's Shelter. She had no idea if these men would come back, if Mandy's rent were paid, if she needed medical assistance for her injuries, or if she could get Mandy to agree to have a rape analysis done at the local hospital, even though it was probably too late. Jeanine was unavailable, so Missy left her an in-depth message, hoping she would call back.

Missy helped Mandy dry herself off, got her into a somewhat clean pair of jeans and tee off a pile of clothes in the closet—a closet not only filled with jeans and tees, but two or three evening dresses, satin pumps in a variety of colors, and beautiful sweaters and slack sets. Missy sat her down in the kitchen and having found a tea bag in her own purse, brewed the young woman a cup of green tea, all the while wondering about this strange young woman who had evidently been beaten more than once. Mandy also suspected that this young woman was not telling her the complete truth.

"Mandy", Missy said kindly, "I need your permission to call the police, okay? Someone needs to be told about your attacks, and you also need to be taken to a local hospital to make sure you're okay."

Mandy adamantly disagreed!

"I don't need no more help, and I don't need those men seeing me walk out of here with you, they'll think I squealed on-em'. No!

I'm not going to go with you Missy. I'm afraid. I'm afraid of those men."

Thinking for a moment, Missy then asked this broken women if she knew the men who had attacked her? It sounded to Missy, as if Mandy knew a lot more than what she was telling.

"Mandy", she said softly, taking the young woman's hand in her own. "Do you know these men that hurt you? Can you tell me who they are? I promise, it will just be your and my secret. Please, Mandy let me help you."

Mandy stuttered and stammered, stood up from her chair, stumbled over the filthy cat box, and once again began to cry.

"I can't tell you, Missy. They will kill me next time, they swore they would kill me!"

Mandy sat down, took another sip of her tea, and Missy let her sit, asked her no more questions, figuring she should give this bruised and broken young woman more time. Meanwhile, Missy looked through the cupboards in the dirty kitchen and finding no food of substance anywhere, suggested that she go out and get some food for the two of them. She also wondered if it would be smarter to take Mandy along in her car to get some food, but thought the better for it. Who knew if she would be interfering in a police investigation, or if there really were men out there watching Mandy or her apartment building?

"Will you promise me that you will stay in your apartment, lock the door behind me and be here when I return with some food", she asked the young woman?

Mandy shook her head yes, and Missy holding on to her crutch, picked up her purse, and headed out the door. When she got to the front of the run-down apartment building, she looked both ways, left and right, and then checked the perimeters to make sure no one was just "hanging" around. Satisfied that it was safe, she unlocked and got into her old Buick and drove the two miles to the "Leftovers", supposedly a great place to eat in east Dawson. She purchased two veggie sandwiches, two bowls of chicken noodle soup, and within fifteen minutes was on her way back to Mandy's apartment.

When she returned, and knocked on Mandy's locked front door, there was no answer. She tried entering, but the door was locked, and being suspicious in nature, Missy immediately went to the supervisor's apartment, and told him the situation. The "super" let her in with a spare key, and as she suspected, the apartment was empty. Mandy Sue was gone.

Missy spent time sitting in her car, wondering if she should stay and eat one of the sandwiches and cartons of hot soup, or go directly to the hospital and see if Mandy had gone to the emergency room—that thought being absurd as Mandy had no way to get to a hospital. Missy thought for a few minutes more, and decided to eat something. The meal was just what she needed, and after a half an hour, she started the car and headed first to the Dawson Women's Shelter, and from there she would go to Dawson General Hospital—just in case by some miracle Mandy had gone there. First, however, she wanted to catch up with Jeanine if possible and make some plans for Mandy's care.

"She cannot live in that dump of an apartment building any longer," Missy thought to herself. "She needs to be somewhere safe until the police find her attackers. Unknown to Missy, the police and Mandy Sue already knew who the attackers were.

CHAPTER SIX

Jeanine Simpson

In a red, brick, three-story building in downtown Dawson, women of all ages, some with children in tow, waited in a long line outside the large black door for the security officer to open it and allow them entrance. It was 11:30am, and the women were lined up just in time for the hot noon meal. Most of these women were "street people". They had no homes, slept mostly in alleyways or under bridges, and stood on street corners, night and day, begging passers by for a few dollars. Some had small children, some even cradled newborns, but most of them were dirty and hungry, as were their children. If they were lucky, they could ask for and receive at least one hot meal a day, and if they were really lucky, maybe a place to sleep for a night or two.

Jeanine Simpson had been a part of this scenario for almost ten years. She had a degree in Social Work and loved her job. It was a difficult job, however, trying to get women off the street, get them some or more education, perhaps a job, a place to live, and her hardest job was to try not get too attached to the babies and small children that came with the territory. There had been a few deaths during her tenure at the shelter, and the hardest one had been a young mother of seventeen, who had given birth in an alleyway, with no one around, and both the mother and baby had succumbed to the elements. Their bodies had been found three days later. The young woman had been in to see Jeanine three times prior to her death and Jeanine was so sure she had been getting through to the young woman. She had arranged for her to receive temporary housing at the shelter while doing cleaning and laundry for her keep, but one day she just up and left. "Squealers" in the shelter had told Jeanine that an old boyfriend, possibly the baby's father, had somehow gotten in contact with the seventeen-year-old, and she had disappeared. There didn't seem to be any foul play, but in the end, Jeanine had taken this loss very hard. "Just another broken soul," Jeanine had told herself.

As the doors opened, the women and children poured into the hall where the smells of fried chicken permeated the air, The lunch guests took their seats in an orderly fashion, and after a blessing said by a local lay leader, the women once again stood up, and again, in orderly fashion, received their meal. Today's meal consisted of fried chicken, potatoes, gravy, green beans and biscuit, buffet style. Volunteers poured them either coffee or water, and children were served milk at their tables. The women knew the routine. They were fed, cleaned up their own tables, made sure their children ate their meals, and then used the bathroom facilities before exiting the building. If they were lucky, they would be given the right to go through this same routine the next day.

Missy Baker, after showing her PI credentials to the security guard at the gate, had parked her old Buick in the secured parking lot and walked into the front door just as all the guests were exiting the side door of the building. It never ceased to amaze her how orderly the meal for more than 65 women and children was handled. She noticed Jeanine speaking with an older woman volunteer at the kitchen door, and walked over to where she was standing.

Noticing her immediately, Jeanine waved her towards the kitchen, and after finishing her conversation with the volunteer, made her way to greet Missy. The two friends hugged, and then went into an office to the right of the kitchen.

"It's great to see you Missy." Jeanine said smiling and motioning for her to have a seat. "How've you been, and most of all, what brings you here?"

Knowing that Missy seldom made an appearance at the women's shelter, unless a woman was in trouble, she figured once again that she was there for a particular reason, or for information on a particular woman.

"You know me well, Jeanine. Yes, there's a young woman, Mandy Sue Donnor. Have you heard of her? I just left her all banged up from a rape, I think, at least a severe beating, but before I could get her to a hospital she disappeared on me. Do you know if she's been here, or is here now?"

"Did you call the police, Missy?" Jeanine asked first.

Missy answered yes, said that the paramedics had also seen to her, but that she had refused to go to a hospital, refused to identify her abusers and when Missy offered to get her food, she had run off.

"I think she's in some kind of trouble, Jeanine. She was very scared, and this was not the first time she'd been abused, I'm sure of it. I had an anonymous telephone call about her earlier, and when I finally made it to her apartment, she had tried to kill herself by slitting her wrists."

The two women chatted a few more minutes, and after Jeanine had looked through her files, and found no name under Donnor and assured Missy that Mandy had not been to the shelter, at least not recently, she assured Missy that if Mandy showed up Missy would be the first person she'd call.

The two women made a little more small talk, and when Missy stood up to leave, Jeanine mentioned to her something she had heard lately—that a woman who had been in the shelter months previously with four young daughters had been picked up at a local convenience store for fraudulent check cashing and shop lifting, and had left these young girls with no one at all to look after them. She shared that although this wasn't her area of expertise that when women and their children were away from the shelter and Social Services took over, she was out of the loop, but she still asked Missy if she would look into it.

"The police took the mother into custody, and I imagine the kids were dropped off at Social Services, or by this time may even be in a foster home. One of my friends at Social Services told me about this family one day at lunch, and I recognized the name immediately."

Jeanine continued. "I know the woman had no money, wasn't always homeless, and I believe she had been in jail before, but I took a liking to those little girls, and I'm just curious as to what may have happened to those little ones. I can always call Social

Services, myself, but in all of your spare time, Missy, how about looking into them?"

The two friends both chuckled, spare time; Missy had plenty of that these days. She agreed to follow up on it, and bid Jeanine goodbye with the promise of being in touch soon.

Missy left the shelter and drove to the hospital, but after only a few minutes at the emergency room, was told that no one matching Mandy's description had been brought in. Mandy Donnor was most likely out walking the streets somewhere—walking, hungry and probably scared to death. Missy expressed a short prayer for Mandy, and as she put her key into the ignition to start her car, her cell phone rang.

"Hello, this is Missy Baker", she said cheerfully.

"Missy. Missy, help me. Please Missy, help me!"

"Mandy. Mandy is that you?" Missy asked—a definite concern in her voice. "Mandy! Mandy! Talk to me Mandy! Mandy where are you?"

CHAPTER SEVEN

The Innocent

In a three story government building on the west end of downtown Dawson in the suburb of Lakewood Hills, Betty Mae Sullivan diligently went through new files that had literally been dropped on her desk in the early morning hours. Some weeks or better yet, days, at the Social Services office serving Jefferson County, were so busy, so frustrating for Betty that she wondered if it was worth it. She had always wanted to be a social worker and she loved helping those in need, especially children, but some days the work load was so heavy, and so many cases were left open without any solutions, that she could barely make it through her eight to ten hour days.

She tried to determine which case files were the most recent and/or the most important, and then realized that each and every case file was important, and each one was usually a crisis. However, as she checked the files, one after another, her eye caught one case file immediately. It had a red sticker on the top of the file, right under the name—red stickers almost always meant urgent. She moved all the other files to the side of her already cluttered desk, so she could concentrate just on this one—the one with the red sticker.

She removed the first and second formal looking papers from the top of the case file, those with names, dates, etc, and concentrated on a sheet of photos—mug shots—of an attractive, younger woman, with a Colorado State Penitentiary tag around her neck. The woman was nicely dressed, and the information included her name, date of birth, color of her hair, her complexion tone and color of her eyes. It also had a case or prison number—34162.

As Betty Mae turned the page, her heart sank as she saw photos of four young girls, one just an infant, perhaps about six months old, being held by an older girl, the oldest sister she presumed, and each child's name and age were listed as well—daughters of the now imprisoned young mother—all of them under the age of seven.

Betty Mae read further into the case file, which told of the young mother's "conspiracy to commit burglary" at a convenience store while her young children remained outside. The police had been called, the mother caught and taken away in handcuffs, her children taken away by a social worker. The young mother had been sentenced to two to six years in the state penitentiary. This had been the young mothers second offense, as she had been incarcerated previously but paroled early for good behavior.

"Oh my." Betty Mae thought to herself. "I wonder where the father is, or if there are any other family members to help with these beautiful little girls." The thought also crossed her mind, as to "who would possibly want to foster four children at one time."

As Betty Mae read further, she realized that the young girls were all being held at Dawson Human Services, and the staff was diligently looking for a foster home that would keep all of the sisters together—something that very seldom happened. DHS was always the starting point in protecting Dawson's most vulnerable clients. At least the children would be clean and fed, and receive medical attention if the need arose. But it wouldn't last long. It was only a temporary place for these children to stay. They needed foster care and soon.

No one, at least no foster parent that Betty Mae knew of could or would handle four children at once. First of all, foster homes had to have a bedroom for each foster child in their care, and most of her foster families already were assigned one or two children. She continued to page through the file, wondering how long these precious children could stay at the DHS facility, and how long it would take to find them a home—a home together. At this point it seemed like an impossible task but she would make it happen, no matter how long it took. She just had to keep these little girls together.

Betty Mae looked up at the white and chrome clock on her office wall, realizing that once again, she would miss her lunch break. There were just some things that were more important than food. She picked up her tattered address book, turned to the page with a number of telephone numbers marked "foster parents" and began to dial. She said a short prayer under her breath, and made the sign of the cross across her chest. If there ever was a God who looked after the needy, she needed Him now.

CHAPTER EIGHT

Officers For a Better America (OBA)

Officer Bryce Jenkins had sat in his police vehicle for about fifteen minutes after the incident with Missy Baker and Dr. Livingstone. He thought about going into the bar at the Dawson Country Club for a drink but thought the better of it since he was not in plain clothes and still on duty. He had frequented the country club in the past with the good doctor, but no one in the bar knew he was a cop—as that would jeopardize his relationship with his clients that he saw away from the fancy club. He placed his hand in his front pants pocket, and pulled out the three one hundred dollar bills that the doc had slipped him after his "slight" fender-bender with the feisty Ms. Baker. Bryce Jenkins smiled as he fingered the three bills, and thought of how much money the good doctor and his friends had paid him to "keep his mouth shut" or "cover up and make things disappear" over the last few years. The cover ups had always been minor, a speeding ticket here, a parking ticket there, even a few drunk driving tickets had suspiciously disappeared on Jenkins' watch. He hadn't planned on being a dirty cop, it just sort of happened one day. The Police Department of Dawson County paid fairly well, but with a wife who liked nicer than usual trinkets and only worked part time at the school where three of their kids were enrolled (and with one enrolled as a freshman at Dawson University), their paychecks never quite seemed to cover their needs and wants.

Jenkins had been approached one evening on an overtime gig by another Dawson cop, who was already on the take, and shared some of his "good deeds" for the wealthier people in his area of Dawson.

"I've made $750.00 this week already", his friend on the force had said. "I plan to hit $1K this week, and if you want a part of this, you just let me know. I can connect you with the right people."

Bryce had originally turned him down, stating that he could never be a dirty cop, but when he found out what a year's tuition at DU was going to cost him, he knew he had no choice. He wanted the best for his 18-year old daughter, and the only way she would ever become a lawyer, was if she attended law school at Dawson University. He would never be able to pay this kind of debt without help.

He and his wife Shelby had saved over $25K for their children's college education so far, but that would just be a drop in the bucket for what he needed—that amount wouldn't even cover one year's tuition at DU.

He gave the idea some serious thought, knowing that if he was caught his life would be history—no pension, probably jail time, and who knew what else. He would or could never tell Shelby how he made the extra cash week after week, but Shelby didn't care as long as she could luncheon with her friends at fancier restaurants, buy nice clothing and jewelry and have her hair and nails attended to. She also sported a new Mustang, and, well, he only thought about being dirty for a few days when he told his fellow officer that he wanted to be a part of the dirt.

"Look at it this way", his friend has said. "We're not dirty, just helping out our fellow man and getting rid of some of Dawson's worst garbage."

The first OBA meeting he attended was in a strip joint, more a dive than a strip joint, on South Colorado Blvd. He had been told to arrive at 9pm, tell the bouncer he was a friend of Tyler Morris and he would be let into the back room. Bryce did just that, and as he entered the room, he noticed at least twelve police officers in attendance, recognizing two or three of them. He also recognized a high-ranking detective and deputy sheriff from another city and county, and even a few female officers that he had been in contact with on prior police calls. His friend from the force was also seated across the darkened room from him, with a sexy, blond bombshell sitting on his lap. He waved at Bryce from across the room.

Bryce ordered a drink from the scantily dressed barmaid: rum and coke—no ice, and smiled as she tenderly touched his shoulder before heading to the bar. After everyone had been served their favorite drinks—at no charge, Tyler Morris, a large, black-haired, muscular man stood up and walked to the front of the room. He immediately had everyone's attention.

"Welcome ladies and gentleman," he said, speaking in a low bass voice with a possible Boston or New York accent. "I'm glad to see all of you here, and I hope the reason you're here is not only to help yourselves out financially, but to help our organization as well."

The large man continued speaking for over an hour, telling all in the room that they would be helping out the community by keeping those in high society in their positions of authority or professions by making traffic tickets or parking tickets disappear, solving unsolvable court cases with little white lies if asked to testify, or acquaint mistresses or ladies of the night for these "good doctors, lawyers, congressmen, etc.", upstanding American citizens. Then on a larger scale—take down those supposed Americans in good standing involved in over the border drug trafficking, gun smuggling or prostitution for their own gain. He also shared that the OBA was working very hard in Dawson currently to bust up a huge prostitution and sex trafficking ring.

"There is a prostitution and sex trafficking ring located in our eastern suburb", he continued. "The organizers" are not getting the message to clear out and in order to clean up our city, we may have to take stronger measures to rid our beautiful city of this riff-raff. Remember, our main focus is to keep our "good" people good, and rid our city of the "bad". The police department does not seem to be able to handle it without our help". He chuckled. "So we, the OBA, will help them Out a little."

He continued by strongly urging each one in attendance to keep this business to their selves.

"Do not talk to your spouses, children, neighbors, grocery clerk, gas station attendant about your "part time job". Do not speak with others in your departments, unless you are approached by one of your fellow officers who may already be involved in this program. We are known as the Officers for a Better America or OBA. You may be approached by a little or big time felon, someone at a traffic accident, someone at your favorite restaurant or church meeting asking you to help out with a situation. You may be offered cash on the spot, or you may be required to talk to me or another OBA associate first before accepting the request."

He continued by stating that he hated the word "bribe". "We are people fighting for a better country, and if a big name politician needs our help, or a doctor, or a judge, lawyer or any other professional to keep his name in tact, we're there to help. You start thinking that you're taking bribes, your mind will start playing tricks on you, and you'll not do well in your position. Remember you are OBA, and you are all about keeping the city of Dawson clean, you're the garbage pick up man or woman—you're tossing out the crap—discarding the "crap" and keeping our good citizens "good".

He continued. "Now, the most important thing to remember, other than the money you'll be making, is that you are a silent OBA member. You'll speak to NO ONE about this position with OBA, and I mean NO ONE. If you're caught, and you open your mouth, you are ON YOUR OWN! No one with OBA will have ever heard of you, and you will receive no help from any one on the OBA council, and you may also have to disappear if we can't get you out of your jam. The money is great, but the risk is even greater. AS FAR AS I'M CONCERNED, IF YOU SCREW UP, OBA DOES NOT EXIST AND NEITHER DO YOU!"

Several of those in attendance mumbled to themselves. Some asked questions. Others sat and spoke with others in the room. Some looked a little bewildered, but realized, as Bryce did, that now that they had all attended a meeting they were involved, and there was no backing out now. Once they walked in the door of this establishment they were caught up in the OBA. Bryce thought to himself "they say we're not dirty cops, that we're helping out our fellow man, but wow, I feel dirty already. I'm not sure I can do this."

While in deep thought a female officer approached him. He stood up and as she put out her hand to introduce herself and shake his hand, she asked what he thought of this whole OBA thing?

"I'm not real sure, but I guess I'm in, now that I've been to the meeting." He said. "I know I can sure use the money."

"Me too", she said smiling. "I've got a three-year old with Spinal Bifida, and her doctor bills are unbelievable. I am a single mom, and I can see no other way to help myself out. I'm in. What about you?"

Bryce looked at her, smiled, and said, "Yes, I've got some incredible debts too, and I think this is my only way out."

As he left the attractive blond female officer standing at his table, he wasn't really sure. "Just what am I getting myself into?" He asked himself quietly. "Just what am I getting myself into?"

CHAPTER NINE

Abused No More

Mandy Sue Donnor had called Missy Baker from the southeast corner of 14th Avenue and Peoria St. in Arribio, Colorado—over a mile from her apartment, She had begged a passerby for some change to use a pay telephone when she realized she had not picked up her cell phone when she fled her apartment, and had made the call to Missy.

Unknown to Missy, by the time Missy left Jeanine's down town office and made the drive to east Dawson, Mandy Sue Donnor was already dead. Mandy had left her apartment, placed the call to Missy, and as she ran from the area to hide and to wait for Missy to arrive, the men who had been following her, caught her. They had then dragged her screaming and hollering, and thrown her into the backseat of their car. There, they had beat her, stabbed her, shot her, and driven to a dump site, a short ways away from Mandy's apartment house, and dumped her body in a field.

Mandy had known that she was being followed, and had quickly called Missy hoping to tell her who they were (those who had raped and beat her previously), but she had not lived long enough to tell anyone about it. The men had been following her from the minute she had left her apartment.

Missy drove to east Dawson to the corner of 14th and Peoria, where Mandy Sue supposedly was hiding, but after a quick tour of the area found no trace of Mandy Sue. She parked her old Buick, grabbed her crutch and walked up to a telephone booth. The telephone was on the hook and there was trash all around, but no sign of Mandy. Missy leaned up against the outside of the booth, took a deep breath and wondered what could have possibly happened to her client. As she walked away from the telephone booth, a shoe caught her eye. She walked slowly to where the shoe lay, and before picking it up immediately recognized that it was Mandy's shoe—red, with blue trim, shoestring broken and dirty. She knew not to pick up the shoe without a glove or tissue, so instead, she called the Arribio Police Department, told her what she thought might have happened—a kidnapping or worse, and the officer promised to send out a patrol car immediately. Missy thought the worst.

"They've got Mandy. Whoever was beating her up, has taken her and heaven help her." Missy said silently. "I wonder what in the world she was into? Why would someone beat her, rape her, kidnap her and who knows what else? What made her so horribly frightened that she wouldn't talk to me?"

Missy had no answers.

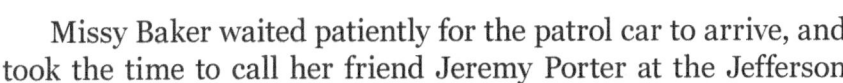

Missy Baker waited patiently for the patrol car to arrive, and took the time to call her friend Jeremy Porter at the Jefferson County Sheriff's Department to tell him her situation.

"I've not heard of any kidnapping, and no one has been on the wire about a missing person." Jeremy responded to Missy's questions. "Arribio is out of my jurisdiction, but I'll let you know if I hear anything out here. I'll call you later I promise. Plus, you owe me dinner remember?"

Missy recalled with a smile how she and Jeremy had placed a bet on a Dawson Bears Football Game, and she had lost. She wasn't a big football fan, but enjoyed a game every now and then, and when Jeremy had gotten tickets to a game, he had asked her to join him. They had also bet dinner—she would pay if the Bears lost, and he would pay if his favorite team, the Pittsburgh Steelers lost. The Steelers had romped all over the Bears, but neither one had the time to have dinner that evening. She knew that Jeremy also had a slight crush on her, and she wasn't sure she wanted to get involved with him or anyone.

"Okay", she said cheerfully. "When and where?"

Jeremy said that he had never been to Flanagan's, and would like to go there.

"Holy Cow!" Missy shouted. "You want to take my entire life savings on two dinners? That's a high falutin' place!"

Jeremy chuckled, and told her that no, he was kidding, and anywhere she suggested would be fine with him. They settled on Paradise Bar and Grill in Lakewood Hills on the west side, and they both agreed that Thursday night would work out well, as he didn't have to work on Friday this week. Missy agreed, and said she would meet him there at 8:00pm. She actually admitted to herself that she was anxious to see him again.

The patrol car pulled up just as Missy was beginning to wonder if one would ever show up. Two officers got out of their vehicle, walked over to Missy and introductions made. Missy showed her credentials, explained the situation, showed them the shoe, which they picked up and bagged, and the female officer called in to get a crime scene investigator on the scene. The three of them waited for the investigator to arrive, and when he did, and after they had roped off the area, Missy left. She hoped that her information would be enough for them to do a search for Mandy, and that they would find Mandy soon, and alive.

CHAPTER TEN

Nellie and Jim Cooper

Betty Mae looked up the telephone number for Nellie (Nell), Cooper. She stopped, took a deep breath, picked up the telephone and dialed Nell's number.

As always, Nell answered in a cheerful, although a little stressful "Hi, this is Nell and Jim Cooper's residence".

"Hi Nell", Betty Mae said sweetly. "This is Betty Mae. How are things at the Coopers this morning?"

Nell said she was fine, and after a little more small talk, Betty Mae asked after the family, and said she needed to drop by later in the day for a chat.

"...and while I'm there I'll just do a quick house check. Is it okay if I come in about an hour?"

Nell replied that everyone was fine, the house check would be okay too, and what was on Betty Mae's mind?

Nell knew before Betty Mae even answered that there must be another baby in need of a foster family, because Betty Mae loved placing babies in the Cooper home and Nell loved taking them. The Cooper's could take one more child, but three babies was their limit. This also meant that Betty Mae had to check out their home once again for safety and cleanliness, and to check on the two babies already fostered there. Given only an hour's notice was the way Social Services operated, so being prepared in one hour was not a problem for Nell. Her house was always neat and tidy, the foster children clean and healthy, and Nell always welcomed a visit from her social worker.

"I have a six-month old, Nell," She continued. "I need a home "pronto" like "yesterday", so I'll chat with you about 2:30pm okay?"

Nell shook her head, as if Betty Mae could see through the telephone, said okay to Betty Mae, thanked her for calling and hung up.

Nell immediately picked up the eleven-month old baby boy out of the old chrome high chair, wiped the baby's mouth, face and hands with a wet-wipe, kissed him, and set him down on the floor of the living room with his toys. He immediately giggled and picked up his Pooh Bear.

Charlie was a beautiful child with bright blue eyes, rosy red cheeks, golden locks, and an angelic smile that would melt even the hardest of hearts. Charlie had been placed with the Coopers two days after his birth. His mother had been an addicted street woman, and no one knew who the father might be. The baby had been taken away from the mother immediately after birth. Surprisingly, Charlie had shown no ill effects of his birth mother's addiction and Nell and Jim Cooper had planned on having him for only a few weeks. However, the adoption procedure had been complicated. The first adoptive couple had not taken the proper adoption classes and had not passed the background check. Now, the second prospective couple also had a negative in their background, so once again little Charlie was waiting for a new mommy and daddy to love. Nell didn't mind. She loved this little boy, just like all of the other little boys and girls that had come and gone through the Cooper home. After the first two or three babies, she had learned that these tiny miracles from God were not hers and Jims to keep, but just to love, nourish, care for and then pass on to another set of loving parents.

As she began to clean off the lunch table and load the dishwasher, two-year old Amy called out.

"Mama, mama". Amy called. "Mama, me come, too."

"Are you finished, sweet girl?" Nell asked pleasantly. "Let mama wash your hands and face and then you can play with Charlie, okay?"

The sweet red-headed little girl shook her head up and down, held out her hands and giggled as Nell washed them just as Amy grabbed for one more piece of peanut buttered bread still on her highchair.

"No more you little pixie." Nell said sweetly. "No more sticky fingers. You're all done for now."

She set the two-year old girl, a girl way to tiny for her age, down on the kitchen floor, and she immediately ran to play with Charlie and their toys. Nell watched with tear-filled eyes as she watched these two angels playing together. She knew, these two, would break her heart when they were finally taken away from her.

Amy had been sick her entire, short life. She had been dirty and malnourished when she was found abandoned on a church step at two months of age. The birth mother had never been found, and because of constant colds and low blood counts and being somewhat slow in the learning process, she had not been ready for placement, and most likely would not be for several more months. Amy was under constant doctor's supervision and saw a physical, occupational and speech therapist four times a month, Nell and Jim worked constantly with her to improve her motor skills, eating and sleeping habits and her all around health, but it was a slow process.

These two babies were the 8th and 9th children that had been placed in the Cooper's foster home. They had not been able to have children (although Nell still hoped for a child of her own), and so these children filled that void.

"Now, I bet Betty Mae will be bringing another little one over for us to care for." Nell thought to herself. "Yes, if God has another little one for us to look after, we will definitely do by his bidding."

With that thought, she tidied up the kitchen a bit more, and went to play with her two foster babies. Unbeknown to Nell, it wouldn't be much longer before Charlie would be placed in what should have been a very loving, adoptive home.

CHAPTER ELEVEN

A Murder Investigation

The telephone rang in the Arribio Colorado Police Department about 2:00pm. As Officer Chick Thomas answered the telephone his eye quickly scanned those sitting around waiting for booking, waiting for a family member to arrive, or waiting for God-only–knew-what.

"Arribio police." He said harshly. "Can I help you?"

"Hi, I need to speak with a detective, please." Missy Baker requested.

"In what regard?"

"I need to check on a recent missing person's report, or perhaps a kidnapping in the Arribio area." She said calmly.

"Okay, hold on ma'am". He said, more sweetly now. "I'll connect you with Detective Olson, Missing Persons.

Missy had been disheartened to think that she had not been available, or at least not available soon enough to help Mandy Sue Donnor. She wondered where she was, who had her, was she scared, what had she become involved in, and most of all was she safe? She just had to be. Missy couldn't imagine a young girl being raped, then beat up, then dumped, and now kidnapped, missing, or worse...and worst of all, Missy felt like she had failed the poor young woman.

As she continued to hold, Missy also thought about her visit with Jeanine Simpson, and the comments she had made about the young mother and the four little girls. Were those little girls safe or would they end up some day like Mandy Sue Donnor— broken and bloodied, probably damaged for life, and maybe even dead. Missy shivered at the thought. But it wasn't hard to imagine. Young girls placed in foster care, orphanages, or run-a-ways sold into prostitution...she heard about it or saw it almost every day, either in the newspapers, on television, or worse, in real life.

After ten minutes of being on hold, Missy hung up the telephone and dialed the number again

The same officer answered the telephone, and Missy gave him an ear full.

"I've been on hold for a detective Olson for the past ten minutes sir. Is he there or is he not? Can you put this call through again, or can you have him call me back. I don't intend to remain on hold for another ten minutes, as I have a life too!"

"Now hold on their missy." He said. "No need gettin' sassy with me. This is a busy place. Now, what did you need Olson for again?"

Missy reminded him again, and this time she was put through to a voice-messaging machine.

"This is the office of Detective Craig Olson, Missing Persons Division. Please leave your name and number, a brief message, and I'll try to get back to you within 24 hours."

Missy left him a "brief" message including the happenings of the last few hours, Mandy Sue's description, and her own name and telephone number. She hoped he would have some information for her directly.

Unbeknown to Missy Baker, Detective Olson was already working on Mandy Sue Donnor's case—a murder case. Three kids, ages 9 – 11, hunting for unusual rocks in the area, had found her body a few hours earlier and they had run home and called the Arribio Police Department. Since there was no identification on the body, and the girl was beaten so badly—almost to the point of being unrecognizable—the Colorado Bureau of Investigation had also been called to the scene of the murder. Detective Olsen had absolutely no leads, but, hopefully, the DNA (cells found inside the nucleus), in the tennis shoe found earlier in the day at the presumed kidnapping site, and the girl's own DNA, would give them a name by the end of the day.

The Colorado Bureau of Investigation team was now on the scene, plus three detectives, including Detective Olson, the Medical Director and his assistant and four Arribio police officers—all hoping to find the clues they needed to solve this murder.

"Jennifer? Jennifer Hayes, is that you?" Detective Olson inquired.

"Yes, yes it is." CBI team member Jennifer Hayes responded. "Wow, Olson, how long has it been? Five, six years?"

Detective Olson walked over to this petite thirty-something woman with the long black hair, took her outstretched hand, and then gave her a big bear hug.

"Wow, the Bureau must agree with you, you look great." He said letting her go and standing back now. "I guess I didn't realize that you were still in Colorado. I don't get involved with the CBI much, so, wow." He said again. "How great to see you."

The two old friends chatted for a few more minutes, then got back to the case at hand. The dead woman has been badly beaten, stabbed three or four times, then shot through the right temple.

'It looks like this murder was a grudge killing, or gang killing or perhaps she got taken out by her disgruntled Pimp. Who knows at this point? Do we have any idea who she is?" Olson asked Jennifer."

Jennifer shared with him that the investigation was just beginning, and that as soon as the body was removed and sent to the Medical Examiner's Office, they would have more answers. Until then, the Criminal Investigation Team was all over the area, the police were on it, and together, hopefully, they would find the answers.

"We got something." Another detective called out to Olson and Hayes. "Tire tracks, blood, a piece of clothing. This most likely is the murder site. We'll check out the tracks, see what kind of vehicle made them, and let you guys know. In the mean time, we'll get samples of this blood and get this piece of clothing over to the CBI lab."

All those on the scene remained there for over three hours, and when all was said and done, they would wait for the lab and autopsy results first, and the follow up on any leads that came in. The young boys that found her body would be interviewed first (with their parents of course), and then the painstaking job of finding out who this Jane Doe was, where she came from, what had she been involved in, why was she murdered, and who was responsible, would begin. Those on scene filled up bags and bottles with possible evidence, shared what they knew with the television reporter from KBDX Dawson, and the Dawson Review newspaper reporters on the scene, and left.

Craig Olson lived for these types of police cases. They were challenging, exciting, sad in a way of course, but he lived for the hunt—the hunt of sifting through the clues, interviewing those possibly involved, working with the other investigative teams. Most of all he enjoyed solving the cases he was in charge of. He always set a goal or a date to catch the bad guys, and this case would be no different. He figured to have this one solved in three weeks time—or less!

As he started his vehicle, he first checked his cell phone, picked up three messages, one being from a woman named Missy Baker.

"She can wait a few minutes." He thought. However, the more he thought about it, and when he replayed the message again, he thought that just possibly she might be talking about the case he had just taken on. She had said very little on the message machine except that she had been working with a young woman who had disappeared this morning, and that she wanted his help in finding her. Perhaps, this was the poor girl they had just found, and Ms. Baker could shed light on the case. If so, perhaps he could find his murderer or murderers in less than three weeks.

He turned off the car's motor, and dialed Missy Baker's number.

CHAPTER TWELVE

Four Little Angels

From her small cell in the Colorado State Penitentiary in Canyon City Colorado, Annamarie Meyers-Holmgruff could feel the cold coming in through the thin cement walls, and she shivered as she gently fingered the 3x5 photo of four little girls—her baby girls; Rebecca, Tabbatha, Sandra and Roseanne. As she placed the photo to her lips, and kissed the photo four separate times, one single tear dropped from her eye. She knew she had blown it this time—she would most likely never see her beautiful little girls again. She had been given a second chance, been paroled after a year in the state penitentiary for a previous felony, but with no money and no food, she had tried once again to cash a forged check—there would not be another chance this time. She had had no choice. She needed to feed her children, but this time there would be no time off for good behavior, no parole, no forgiveness, and she knew her baby girls would be taken away from her this time, forever. She closed her eyes and once again felt the cold. She remembered, the police officer placing four little girls in a car with a social worker, most likely to never to see them again.

Annamarie Meyers Holmgruff had met the love of her life, Harry Holmgruff, in Columbus Ohio, just a short six years ago— she had been 22 years of age. After dating only a few months, she gave in to his advances and became pregnant with Sandra. They were a happy family, and although Harry never proposed marriage, she knew he loved her and just a short year later, Annamarie gave birth to another daughter, Roseanne. For almost three years, Annamarie had been very happy. She loved Harry, she loved her two little girls, and life was good. However, when Harry was laid off from his job, the family agreed to move to Dawson, where Harry had family. Hopeful that he could find a job in a new city, he looked and looked, but after a few months of living with family, and still unable to find work in Dawson, as well as fighting depression and drinking heavily, Harry dumped his young family and left town. Annamarie tried her best to find work, but no one would hire a woman with two small children. Finally, Harry's younger brother Josh, who also lived in Colorado, and who had taken a liking to Annamarie, recognized her desperation, and picked up where his brother had left off. He had a good job in a department store, took very good care of her and the little girls, and after just a short time proposed to Annamarie. Needing someone to look after her young family, and after finding out she was pregnant again, this time with Tabbatha, Annamarie agreed to marry Josh. They had one more child together, Rebecca, before Josh also left her—four children were just way too much for him to handle.

Annamarie was never quite sure what the attraction had been to the Holmgruff men, and why she had allowed herself to get pregnant four times, but it was a little late to think about that now. She was in prison, her little girls were gone, and she had no one to blame but herself. As far as she was concerned, she had tried and failed, and now her life was over.

She lay down on the hard cot of her prison cell, clutching tightly to the photo of her four precious angels as tears fell from her eyes. She closed her eyes, and sobbing now, she remembered.

She had been at the convenience store where she had at times, purchased food for her girls, and where she had previously cashed forged checks without any one suspecting, or at least she thought no one had suspected. She had told Sandra, her oldest to hold Rebecca, the baby, and to wait directly outside of the store for her return. Gently touching the baby's pink cheeks, she had looked into her older daughters' eyes promising Sandra that she would only be inside for a few minutes. As she opened the door to the convenience store, she turned and looked back at her rusted out, old Ford, where Tabbatha and Roseanne sat quietly in the back seat. Upon entering the store she had picked up several items, approached the cashier, and took the forged check from her purse. Unbeknown to Annamarie, the cashier recognized her, and was prepared this time to accept the forged check but then to push the police call button underneath the counter at the same time. Before Annamarie realized what was happening around her, a police car had arrived, and two officers had entered, approached her, handcuffed her and made a quick telephone call. Within minutes, one officer placed Annamarie in the backseat of a squad car, while the other officer spoke with Sandra and checked on the other little girls. A few minutes later, a woman driving a blue station wagon pulled into the parking lot, and a woman with salt and pepper colored hair got out. She spoke with the police officer, and together they softly spoke with Sandra.

"Your mother," the officer said kindly, touching Sandra's shoulder "is being taken away because she did a very bad thing. You and your sisters will be going with Mrs. Putnam here. Can you please tell us your name, and how old you are?"

Crying now, but holding tightly on to the baby, Sandra told the two strangers that she was almost seven years old, that the baby was 6 months old, and that her two other sisters were about 4 and 2 years of age. Mrs. Putnam thanked her for the information, and gently placed Sandra and Rebecca into the front seat. Then Tabbatha and Roseanne were taken from their mother's car and placed into the back seat of the blue station wagon. Screaming now, Sandra turned, and looking out of the station wagon's side window, hollered, "Mommy, Mommy". "Mommy where are you going?" Neither she nor her sisters had any idea what was happening, nor did they have any way of knowing what a horrible journey they were all about to embark upon and all because of a mother who tried but failed.

Annamarie's cell mate yelled for her to "shut the f... up" and as the young mother turned onto her side and the photo of four young girls fell silently onto the cold, cement floor, she knew that her life as she had previously known it was over...never again would she see the blue-green, gray or blue eyes of her dark-haired beautiful little girls...never again would she hold them or kiss away the tears from those eyes.

Annamarie fell into a fitful sleep dreaming of a crying baby, but each time she reached out to calm the child there was only darkness...nothing but darkness.

CHAPTER THIRTEEN

The Prostitution Ring

In the basement of the strip club on Colorado Boulevard, late at night, the OBA was meeting once again. An impromptu meeting had been called this time. Bryce Jenkins sat in the front row with at least ten other OBA members. His face showed little or no emotion, but inside he was a wreck, an absolute, nervous wreck. He had actually helped kill someone—he—a husband, father, police officer, a good guy, never even hurt a fly kind of guy, and he had helped kill another human being. He was sick to his stomach. He wanted to vomit. He wanted to run out of this sick place away from all of these other sick people, but he couldn't. He was trapped. He had made the decision to become a "dirty" cop, to clean up his city of all the crap, to rid his city of all the pimps and prostitutes and bad politicians, and in turn, help those who were good and clean citizens of Dawson beat bad raps. He **had** been doing that, but murder, never, ever, had he thought that he would commit murder, and yet, here he sat, a murderer in the first degree. Once again, the memories made him want to vomit.

For the past several weeks, Jenkins had been working with two other OBA members to crack a prostitution and sex trafficking ring in the eastern suburb of Dawson—Arribio to be exact. A large ranch, owned and operated by the Bartlett family was known to be more than just a horse and cattle ranch, but no one had been able to prove it. The OBA was positive that there was not only prostitution involved at the ranch, but also sex trafficking, and possible money laundering. They also suspected one of Dawson's finest judges—Judge Donald Christianson of being one of the head-hotshots in the sale of young teenage girls at the ranch.

Fifty-five year old, five foot six, cute and feisty, Olivia Bartlett owned a large ranch on the outskirts of Arribio where she ran a home for run-a-way's—girls only, aged twelve to twenty-one—girls who had been tossed out by their families, had run away from abusive homes or were just bucking the systems wishing to be on their own. When their luck had run out they had found their way to the ranch, or the ranch owner had found them. Olivia wasn't breaking the law, exactly, but after taking in these girls, she never tired to find the girl's families either. Olivia and her husband, Edward, prior to his death a few years earlier, had purchased the ranch, and over the past twenty years had operated a lucrative business breeding, training and selling horses, along with offering a home for these teens. Unknown to most people of Dawson and Arribio, Olivia had trained her lost and broken souls in not only the ranching business, but had turned her young teenage girls into prostitutes. Over the years, the Bartlett's, especially Olivia, had brainwashed all of these young girls into believing that their families did not want them back, and more important, believing that their beautiful bodies were a gift from the Almighty God, and that their bodies should be used for the pleasure of men. During the daytime, the young girls would feed, train and ride the horses, clean the stables, and for at least two hours a day Olivia would home school them. Then during evening hours, they learned to use their bodies for men's pleasure. Olivia allowed each of her young girls to be with only two men per night and for no more than two hours at a time. The six or seven girls each shared a bedroom and personal bathroom, and a wardrobe of evening wear, lingerie, undergarments, powders, perfumes and colognes were at their disposal. Unknown to the girls, there was a hidden camera in their rooms. Olivia made sure her girls were treating their clients appropriately and reprimanded them severely if any client complained. The girls were brainwashed enough to believe and trust in Olivia—their mother and provider.

After receiving payment from their clients each evening, and seeing their "men" out of the secret back door where a shuttle driver would deliver them back to their vehicles across the ranch, each girl would shower and then have a "sit-down" chat with their mother and mentor—Olivia, about the evening's events. Most girls were oblivious as to what real life was really about, and did everything exactly as mother Olivia requested and most of them enjoyed their lifestyle. Olivia would buy them beautiful clothing and personal items, take them into town for lunches, and shopping sprees and on occasion to an afternoon matinee. Most of the girls were happy in the only life they now knew— most of them.

Most of Dawson knew that there was more to the Bartlett Ranch than met the eye, but the Bartlett's were great financial assets to Arribio, giving back to the community in so many ways, so no one in town ever complained about the possible goings-on at the ranch.

However, lately things had been getting out of hand at the ranch. Olivia was asking for more money per hour from her clients, and her clients were demanding more time with her "girls" for the new price, and things were beginning to boil over on her horse ranch. Some of her girls were getting older, and began complaining about the rough treatment. One or two of her girls had started poking around in the ranch business, and had seen and heard too much. Two of them had threatened to leave Olivia and go to the authorities.

The girls were allowed to make a choice when they turned twenty-one: stay on at the ranch and continue with their nightly duties, or live in a paid apartment in town, and come back to the ranch as Olivia requested them. Four of her previous girls had left the ranch when they turned twenty-one, were still prostitutes, but not for Olivia, and making it on their own—sadly, but yes, they were making a life for themselves the only way they knew how. They also knew to "keep their mouths shut" or else.

Two girls, Mandy Sue Donnor and Emily Rathburn had recently chosen to try living on their own in town. Olivia had set the two girls up in two separate apartments in a poorer part of Dawson and saw that they had groceries and some spending money. Emily had failed miserably, and because she knew too much about the ranch, Emily had been dealt with. Mandy Sue had always been one of Olivia's favorites, and Olivia was trying her best to convince Mandy to come back to the ranch, to have a better life with her. Olivia needed Mandy to keep her mouth SHUT. Olivia knew that she was not getting through to the girl, and would have to do something about it—soon.

The ranch had been under the watchful eye of police officers/ OBA members who were also clients at the ranch a time or two— Bryce Jenkins had been one of them. Just the thought of it made him even sicker to his stomach. He had never cheated on his wife, never been unfaithful, and here he was screwing around with prostitutes just to clear the streets of garbage and trash because the OBA said he had to. He played the part well, and was beginning to gather enough evidence to rid the ranch of the sex traffickers, and also getting his "kicks" from Olivia as well. Olivia, however, had no idea who Tyler Morris was, and what he was about to do to her and the ranch.

The first prostitute threatening to turn Olivia in to the authorities had been taken care of. The officers had broken into Emily's apartment late into the night, strangled her, weighted her body down and dumped her in a lake off of I-76, east of Dawson— murder number one. This last girl had given them nothing but problems. Olivia had taken a liking to Mandy Sue Donnor and wanted her to only be made uncomfortable, maybe scare her a little or rough her up a little, but when Jenkins and his three other OBA's approached her the first time, she had fought like a rabid dog, clawing, scratching and biting them. Jenkins had hit her once, then twice, and when she was knocked out cold, one OBA member had taken advantage of her...something else that had made Bryce sick to his stomach. But, the girl hadn't come to her senses and had threatened Olivia that she would go to the cops, expose her and her ranch, and ask for police protection, so Jenkins and company had gotten to her again. This time they beat her up even worse than the first time, but she refused to get the message, and they had been ordered by the OBA and Tyler Morris to "take care of her". They had done what they were told to do, and now Bryce Jenkins was a murderer.

Taking care of Mandy Sue Donnor had not been easy. She had been speaking with a private eye, and the OBA had no idea how much she had already told this PI, so after seeing the PI leave Mandy's apartment building, they had followed Mandy to a telephone booth in a park, kidnapped her and planned to shut her up once and for all. They had beat her beyond recognition, stabbed her, shot her, all to make it look like a gang or pimp had done the deed. No one would ever trace the dead woman to the ranch, or to the OBA. They were in the clear. They made sure of that. There were no clues left at the scene. There was no trace leading to the dirty cops or the OBA...or not? Bryce asked himself while riding in the backseat of the OBA vehicle—just who was the woman with the limp and the crutch? How much did this woman know? What had the murdered woman told her before they ended her life so violently? Suddenly, he felt sick all over again.

CHAPTER FOURTEEN

Doctor and Mrs. Livingstone

D r. Livingstone pulled into the driveway of his white and gray brick home in Dawson, Colorado, pushed the button on his remote and after just a few seconds drove his Cadillac into the 2-car garage attached to his beautiful, brick home. He turned off the ignition, laid his head back on the headrest and thought back to the day's events—including the traffic violation he had paid to get out of. This wasn't the first time he had paid off Officer Jenkins, or others like him. He had been stopped previously on a DUI, and that mistake had cost him almost a thousand dollars. Hell, it had been worth it. A doctor with his reputation had to have someone watching his back. After all, he couldn't let anyone know that he, Dr. Bernard Livingstone, orthopedic surgeon, rock of the community, married to Devorah, the woman who literally ran the Country Club community, might be married to a man who cavorted around, drank too much and paid off dirty cops to quiet his "sins". He smiled as he opened the car door and went to greet his socialite wife, Devorah.

Devorah LaVerne Dawkins-Livingstone, dressed in a dark, flowered black and purple skirt, white lace blouse and matching purple scarf, was in their large, stark white kitchen when Bernard entered through the garage door. Devorah was giving last minute instructions and asking questions of her housekeeper, Betsy, and her part time secretary/ personal assistant, Miriam, as to what was still needed for the Livingstone's annual "end-of-summer garden party".

"Betsy." Devorah called her name loudly. "You too Miriam! I've asked you both now twice throughout the day if the caterer has been confirmed, if the flowers have been confirmed, and how many invited guests have confirmed, and I've had no definite answers. Is everything confirmed or not?"

"Ms. Devorah" Betsy said quietly, "I've been very busy today with Katherine and I'm so sorry, but no, I've not had time today to work on final plans for the party. I asked Miriam to assist me today and I believe, Ms. Devorah, that Miriam has confirmed everything."

Looking directly into Miriam's eyes now, Devorah asked Miriam the same exact questions that she had just asked of Betsy, and Miriam responded that yes, everything had been confirmed. Fifty-six people had replied that "yes" they would be attending, and everything was in place for the event that would take place in 5 days.

Seemingly satisfied at Miriam's answers and looking directly into Betsy's eyes, Devorah asked what was so time consuming today with her daughter?

Betsy, a small boned, twenty-seven-year old, with a short pixie hairstyle, took a deep breath before answering her employer. Knowing from experience that it was better to not tell Devorah the whole truth, she said that 5-year old Katherine had come home from preschool with a stomachache. Betsy had been contacted by the school secretary to come and get her, which she had done forthright. The whole truth was that the adopted daughter, Katherine, had once again gotten into trouble at the local, elementary school; Katherine had thrown her carton of milk and dumped her plate of macaroni onto another classmate during lunch period and had been sent to the principal's office. Betsy, knowing that it was much easier to lie to the Livingstone's and that the school secretary would never actually call Bernard or Devorah anyway, chose to cover up the complete truth. Whatever disciplinary actions taken or given by the school would have to be discussed with her employer at a later time. Most likely, Devorah would never ask the real truth anyway and the school would never call her. Devorah Livingstone just flat did not care!

"Well, how is Katherine now?" Devorah inquired, smiling, a smirk on her face. "Did you see to her aches and pains properly?"

Betsy assured Devorah that yes, she had taken care of everything, and Devorah thanked Miriam for taking care of the other areas of concerns as well.

Devorah, seemingly at ease at how her two employees handled the day's activities started to leave the room, and as she went to greet her husband, turned and said to Betsy. "Have Scotch on the rocks brought to the parlor directly and see to it that Katherine receives a proper supper. Dr. and I have a dinner engagement at 7:00pm, and we will not have time to see her before we leave."

Betsy assured Mrs. Livingstone that she would see to everything and left to check on the young child.

Devorah LaVerne Dawkins-Livingstone had been born into a very prominent Dawson family, and continued her lifestyle of wealth and prominence when she married Dr. Bernard Livingstone, a well-known physician in Dawson. The only thing lacking, and the only thing money and prominence in the community could not buy for Dr. and Mrs. Livingstone was a child—Bernard was sterile. Not that Devorah would have been a good mother because to be perfectly honest, Devorah disliked children, in fact deplored children. Her mother too, had been a woman of social standing and had absolutely ignored Devorah as a child. Devorah was raised by nannies or housekeepers and Devorah swore she would never be that kind of mother—better yet, she would never become a mother and with help from Mother Nature assumed the issue was settled, until Dr. Livingstone suggested adoption. After all, being the pillar of the community that she was, and needing to put on a good front, she needed children as a part of that fasod—therefore Katherine had come into the Livingstone home directly from the local orphanage in Dawson. However, what goes around comes around, and Devorah treated her child just as badly as her mother had treated her, at least for the first years. Katherine got the love she needed from her adopted father. The worse, however, was yet to come—the Livingstone's would adopt other children, and for four of them, their lives would change forever—for the worse!

CHAPTER FIFTEEN

The Detective and the Private Eye

Missy looked at her watch, noting that it was almost five o'clock and wondered why Detective Olson had not returned her call. Knowing how busy police officers and detectives can be, she decided to not call him again. She would wait until the next day to try his number again, but she could not take her mind off of Mandy Sue Donnor. Deep down inside her very soul, she suspected the worse, that something terrible had happened to her, but she also hoped for the best. She put the key in the ignition, but did not turn the key—she wondered if she should drive on home, or go over to the police station and see if Detective Olson might actually be there. The unknown was killing her—she needed to know where Mandy Sue might be; dead or alive, she needed to know.

Detective Craig Olson, sitting in his black SUV, dialed the number Missy Baker had left on his message machine earlier in the day, and she picked up almost immediately.

"Ms. Baker?" He asked.

"Yes," Missy replied.

"Ms. Baker, this is Detective Olson. I received a message from you earlier today. How can I help you?"

Missy thanked him for calling back, asked that he call her Missy, told him that she was a Private Investigator, and shared with him her concern about a young lady whom she was afraid had gone missing or worse. After a full description of Mandy Sue, and a shortened version of how and why Missy knew her, Craig Olson shared with her his findings of the day, and that perhaps it was the same young woman, and suggested that she meet him at the Dawson City Morgue. Missy, sadly, agreed to meet him, and as they both hung up their respective telephones and started up their cars to head to down town Dawson, they both, unknown to each other, wondered where this possible murder would lead. Neither of them had any way of knowing the underlying circumstances of Mandy Sue Donnor's death or the impact it would have on both their lives.

Rush hour was horrible, as Missy suspected it would be but she made it from Arribio to down town Dawson in forty-five minutes. She parked her car, grabbed her crutch, and checked in at the clerk's desk at the Dawson City Morgue. Unlike some morgues, the entry way was bright and cheery, the after hours clerk friendly, and after introductions were made and directions given, Missy made her way down the corridor to the elevators and down to the basement. She looked right and left, found the sign stating Morgue with an arrow pointing right, and while following the arrows she saw a tall, dark haired man of about forty standing in the hallway under the Morgue signage.

Craig Olson, his shirt unbuttoned at the neck, and wearing a brown plaid sports jacket, waved at her, and as she got closer introduced himself, shook her outstretched hand, and together they walked into the morgue.

Missy was not prepared for what she saw! You could barely tell from the blood and bruising that it was Mandy, in fact, you could barely tell it was a woman. Her right eye bulged from its socket, several teeth were missing her hair was matted and bloodied from a huge hole in her head, and had it not been for the clothing she was wearing, the one missing shoe and the tattoo of Jesus on her neck, Missy may have not been able to identify her. Of course, there would still have to be a DNA test to prove it was Mandy, but Missy assured the detective that, yes, it was Mandy Sue Donnor.

Detective Olson gently and with care, pulled the white, bloodied sheet back over Mandy's body and face, and then, taking Missy's arm, led her out of the morgue and into a staff lunch room down the hall where she sat down at a black and chrome table. He asked if she would like a cup of coffee, and when she said yes, he poured her a hot, black steaming cup and one for himself, and joined her at the table.

Over coffee, Missy shared how she had come to know Mandy, how they had met, how afraid she had been for this young lady, and everything else she knew about her and her situation. No, she didn't know if Mandy had any family in the area. No, she didn't know if she worked, but feared she was a prostitute and so on. Detective Olson said how sorry he was, but continued to ask Missy questions, and take notes the entire time they were together.

At around 7:30 pm, Craig suggested they call it a day, that he would most likely be in touch with her within the next twenty-four hours, and kiddingly told her to "not leave town". As a last minute thought, Craig asked her if she were hungry, would she like to grab a sandwich at the Dawson Diner around the corner, and surprising herself and Craig, Missy said yes.

CHAPTER SIXTEEN

Father Ramsey

It only took one phone call from Betty Mae to Nellie Cooper, the foster mother in her jurisdiction, to place six-month old baby girl, Rebecca, in a loving home. Rebecca had been seen by a doctor who declared the baby girl in very good health—evidently Annamarie Holmgruff had been a good mother, feeding the baby well, keeping her clean and healthy—she just could not care for four children the way she had hoped. Placing the other three children would not be quite as easy. Most of Betty Mae's foster parents already had two or three children in their care, and there were very few homes that could take in three more children. Betty Mae did not want to split up the siblings, but she was afraid she might not have a choice.

After only four telephone calls, and taking a chance on the last of the four calls, Betty Mae had placement for the three young girls. Janice and Chet Grant, who had three of their own children but who were currently without any foster children in their care, agreed to at least speak with Betty Mae. Betty Mae scheduled an appointment for the very next day.

In the northern part of Dawson, not far from the Grant home, Father John Ramsey had just finished afternoon mass at the Church of Christ of the Resurrection, and was cleaning up the sanctuary with one of his altar boys.

"David", he asked quietly. "Would you please finish up here? I have a telephone call to make, and don't want to wait any longer to make it. If you need me, I will be in my office.

David, a 14 year-old boy, who absolutely adored Father Ramsey, and who wanted to be a priest himself one day, assured the Father that he would finish up. He gathered the delicate plates of leftover bread and two goblets used for wine, covered them with the white cloths, and proceeded to the church kitchen.

Father Ramsey entered the office located at the south end of the church and sat down at his cluttered desk. No one ever called the Father neat, but his attributes as a Catholic Priest completely outweighed his problem with neatness, and he chuckled at the sight of his messy desk as he moved papers and books aside to find his cell phone.

Father Gerald Ramsey, one of seven boys, had been raised in the Catholic faith, graduated from the local Catholic High School and the Wyoming Catholic College in Lander. Lander was a very small town, with only one Catholic church, but Father Ramsey always felt that his training and internship in Lander's small community was where he had received his greatest training in the love, caring and giving he felt for and shared with his flock and the community. He had on more than one occasion rang the bell outside of grocery stores or department stores to bring in donations for the Salvation Army or helped volunteer at rescue missions or soup kitchens when the need arose. Father Ramsey was a "peoples" priest, as so many of his peers addressed him. However, the most important part of Father Ramsey's life lately had been his involvement in the Catholic Charity Services, which included the Queen of Heaven Orphanage. His love for children was undying, but his love for the homeless child or orphan seemed to be emblazoned into the Father's heart and soul, and had been for a long time. He spent hours and hours working with Social workers, the staff at Catholic Charities Services and with the counselors, nuns and staff who were all involved in some way in the operation of the local orphanage, Queen of Heaven. It wasn't an easy position to be in, to see all of those little ones, day after day, waiting patiently for a loving family to take them in, but Father Ramsey had the patience of Job, and he passed this patience, patience given to him by God, on to the staff and children at Queen of Heaven. "There will never be a child that lives at the Queen of Heaven Orphanage his or her entire life. With patience and love, every child here will find a loving home", was the Father's decree.

The telephone rang five times, and Father Ramsey was about to leave a message when Detective Craig Olson answered.

"Craig Olson here", came the husky voice over the telephone.

"Craig, it's Gerry".

"Gerry! It's great to hear your voice. How are things at the Church of Christ? More important, how are you?"

Pleasantries completed, Father Gerald Ramsey, shared with his parishioner and friend, Craig Olson, that he had missed him at Mass on Sunday and hoped he could plan on seeing him next Sunday, but most of all, he was in need of a few officers to help out with a fundraiser coming up at the church in a few months, and with the numbers expected, he needed a little traffic control, and could Craig help him out again?

Craig chuckled. He saw the Father several times a year when his shifts allowed him Sundays off for church services, but mostly he could plan on this telephone call regularly, at least in the Spring and Fall of the year, when the Church of Christ of the Resurrection planned it's large fundraiser for the Queen of Heaven Orphanage There were almost always 500 or more cars pulling in and out of the churches huge parking lot during these two-day events, and yes, for expediting traffic flow and for safety reasons, traffic officers were required. Craig almost always saw to it that Father Ramsey had officers on site the days of the fundraiser, and most all of them would do it at no charge to the church.

Craig asked, smiling now. "What's the date, Gerry?"

The father, known to his close friends as Gerry, gave Craig the date, and Craig assured him that he would find at least four officers to help out during the fundraiser, and more if he could.

"As long as the officers are on their day off, and are willing to give up their day for you and the church, Gerry, I'll get you a few. Most likely the same officers we had in the spring will volunteer to help you again. No worries." With that, the two men hung up their telephones.

Craig Olson made a note on his calendar, figuring to call two or three officers the next day. He, too, would be there to help out Father Ramsey, as he always was.

The Churches fundraisers always took place the week prior to Easter when there was food and fun indoors, as the weather in Colorado in March or April was very unpredictable. The other fundraiser was always held in the fall of the year. The fall event always brought in the larger amounts of people, and when the church raised the most money; it was not unusual for the church to raise several thousands of dollars at the fall event. There would be events throughout the daytime hours for the young and old alike, but on the second night of the fundraiser, Mrs. Bernard Livingstone, known for her delightful and successful fundraisers, would host a large gala, including gourmet food and drink and dancing to a full orchestra. It was one of Dawson's most well known events. The Dawson police department had always been a part of this event, and would be again this year.

Craig Olson checked the date once again on his note pad, scribbled it onto his wall calendar, and in a fleeting moment thought of Missy Baker. He wondered if she would like to go out to dinner one evening, soon, and if that date went well, maybe they could see each other again. Perhaps, she would like to accompany him to the churches event in September. 'Whoa!' He said to himself. "Slow it down here, Detective, you're getting a little ahead of yourself." He made another quick note on his note pad—a reminder to call her tomorrow for sure.

CHAPTER SEVENTEEN

New Homes

Nell Cooper answered the knock on the door with a little apprehension, but with a smile on her face and hope in her heart. She loved children, but having a third little one under the age of two years might prove to be a bit challenging. She and Jim had discussed it thoroughly, and they were ready to take in yet another small soul needing their love and attention.

"Hi Nell." Betty Mae said cheerfully. "I have another little bundle of joy for you today. Are you ready for little Rebecca?"

Nell reached out to greet Betty Mae and as she did, she also took the six-month old baby girl from Betty Mae's arms. She seemed to never tire from accepting a new foster child into her care, and always took them lovingly and graciously from her social worker's arms. The little girl, wrapped in a soft yellow receiving blanket, smiled up at Nell as Nell spoke in soft motherly tones to this tiny, motherless, child.

"I have her room all ready." Nell told Betty Mae. "Are you ready to see it, or would you like to sit a little while first. I have just brewed a pot of coffee and I know how much you like your coffee."

Betty shook her head yes to the invite for coffee, and walked the familiar hallway into the Cooper's warm and inviting kitchen. Nell first handed Betty Mae the tiny, baby girl and then walked to the cupboard, took down two mismatched coffee mugs and poured them full of steaming coffee. Knowing Betty Mae well, Nell added one teaspoon of sugar to her cup.

"What's the story on this little one?" Nell asked, as she once again took the baby girl from Betty Mae. "It never ceases to amaze me at the stories behind each child we take into our home."

Betty Mae shared the information, at least the little bit of information she knew about Rebecca—that the mother was incarcerated for the second time, had been forced to give up her children for adoption, and that she had no idea whatsoever as to the whereabouts of the father, or fathers as it were.

"I just know, Nell," She continued. "That there are four little girls without a family right now. You have Rebecca, and I'm about to place the other three siblings in the Grant home this afternoon."

Nell was shocked that there were four little girls. Betty Mae had mentioned Rebecca's sister to Nell earlier, but Nell and Jim felt like they could not handle more than just the baby, but four children?

"Oh my, I had no idea there were four little girls, Betty Mae. What will become of them all? Do you have any hopeful adoptive parents yet? My, oh my, who could possibly want to take four little girls into their home?"

Two hours after Betty Mae dropped Rebecca off at the home of Jim and Nell Cooper, she and an assistant from Social Services delivered Rebecca's three sisters to the Grant home. Sandra, shedding tears as she walked hand in hand with her two little sisters, Tabbatha and Roseanne, walked slowly into their new home. As a seven-year old, she had no rights to state her opinion on the matter, nor did she know how. She just knew that, even at her young age, she would keep track of where Rebecca was living, and that she would do everything in her power to keep all of her family together. She had no idea the difficult task that laid ahead of her and her sisters...no idea at all.

CHAPTER EIGHTEEN

The Figure in the Shadows

At around 8:00 am, on a Thursday morning, five days after Mandy Sue Donnor's body was found dumped in an open field, and after all of the tests and autopsy were completed, and after no one had come forward to claim her body, this once beautiful woman, one of God's children, but a definite broken soul, was laid to rest in an unmarked grave in a small cemetery in Jefferson County on the west end of Dawson. Detective Olson had called Father Ramsey and asked that he say a few words over Mandy's grave, and the priest did so willingly. No one brought flowers and no one was there to weep for her—she came into this life and then she died, and it seemed that no one cared. The Father, the Detective and two employees from the cemetery were the only four people in attendance at Mandy's final resting place.

However, a little after midnight on the day of her burial, an unknown figure, dressed all in black and carrying a black, mangy cat, laid a single rose on Mandy Sue's grave. He let the black cat roam around the grave for a few minutes, hoping that maybe the cat knew its master was buried there. The stranger picked up the cat, and as the figure turned away and disappeared into the shadows, a single tear fell from the stranger's eye falling onto the back of the black cat. A gloved hand wiped away the moisture, and a voice barely audible whispered, "I'm so sorry Mandy, so very sorry", and looking towards heaven, asked, no begged God to forgive him.

Craig Olson called Missy Baker and asked her to dinner on Friday evening. Missy had told him she would love to, but that she already had a previous engagement. Then, boldly she had asked. "How about lunch instead"? Having been caught a little off guard by her spontaneous request, but wanting to see her again, Craig had said yes.

Missy had wanted to see the detective again too. After their meeting at the Dawson City Morgue, and having had supper with him that same night, she had hoped he might call on her again. She had already made a date with Jeremy for Friday night at the Paradise Bar and Grill in Lakewood Hills, to settle their football bet, but she really wanted to see Craig again, so she had just blurted out that lunch might be a real treat.

So, here they were, at a lovely little Bistro in downtown Dawson having lunch. She was wearing a delightful pink, peasant blouse and billowing long aqua, pink and white skirt, with white flats on her feet. Narrow bands of silver and gold decorated her wrists. The matching loops in her ears clinked when she flipped and flaunted her long blond hair. She seldom wore bracelets, as they at times interfered with her crutch walking, but not today. Today, she wanted to look her best, so she wore the matching bracelets and ear loops. She hadn't dated much in the past few years, not so much by choice, but just because no one in her line of work seemed to be too interested, or perhaps because of her slight disability—she wasn't really sure. What she was sure of was that being with Craig Olson had made her feel safe, and being around him had sent little flutters through her stomach. She liked that feeling, and wanted to feel more of the same.

Now here they were, having lunch, talking together as if they had known each other their entire lives, instead of just five days. They talked about their families, their jobs, their likes and dislikes, and although he hadn't asked, she shared with him how and why she walked with one crutch?

"I wish I could tell you it was a sports accident, or something really tragic or interesting that caused me to be disabled, but I can't, Craig. Truth is, it's a dull story. I was born with one leg shorter than the other. As I grew, my bad leg grew too but not ever enough to catch up with the good leg, so therefore I have a severe limp, sometimes lose my balance, and although I wear a built up shoe and a brace for support, I still need the crutch."

Craig thanked her for sharing, placed his hand across hers on the blue, checkered tablecloth, and told her how pretty she looked.

A little flustered, and blushing now, she pulled her hand away from his, smiled at Craig and continued eating her shrimp salad.

After a three-hour lunch, much longer than originally planned, they made a date to see each other again soon. He promised Missy that he would keep her abreast of the Mandy Sue murder case, and Missy, not thinking about Mandy Sue just then, thought only that this might just be the start of something really good between she and Detective Olson. She wondered what kissing him might be like.

CHAPTER NINETEEN

Just who is Jeremy?

Missy was not the slightest bit hungry when five hours after lunching with Craig Olson, she met Jeremy for dinner at the Paradise Bar and Grill. The Bar was somewhat of a biker bar, but had great food, and a great band on most nights. The tables were lined with paper coverings, and you could, while eating, doodle or draw on the paper with multi-colored pencils. There were also buckets of peanuts on the tables, and shells were just tossed onto the hardwood floors.

Once seated, they each ordered a Coors Lite. After a half hour of talking football and their individual careers, they ordered food and it was then that the subject of the Mandy Sue Donnor murder case came up.

"I'm not involved in the case at all." Jeremy commented. "The Sheriff's Department is not in the loop on this one, but we all keep up on current events regarding police activities in the Dawson area, so I have heard a little about it. I understand Detective Olson is involved in this case. Do you know him Missy?"

She answered, yes, she did know Craig, and yes, she was involved in the case because she had known Mandy Sue when she was alive. The cops had brought her in for questioning and to identify Mandy Sue's body.

Jeremy asked her a few more questions about the case, and Missy thought him to be a little more nervous than usual. Normally, Jeremy would make a pass or two at her, and ask if she was seeing anyone. But tonight, he was much more serious than usual, and although he was somewhat of an artist, he didn't draw funny pictures or cartoons on the paper tablecloths for her like he usually did when they were at the Paradise. He just chatted, and kind of doodled around with the colored pencil at his plate as they ate their food. Jeremy asked her to dance a couple of slow dances after their meal, laughing as their feet crunched through the peanut shells, and Jeremy did ask to see her again, but she said she appreciated his friendship, and she would like to leave their relationship just as it was. Although somewhat disappointed with the turn down, and after another Coors Lite, and noticing the time, they called it a night. As she stood up to leave, Jeremy offered to pay the check even though it was her turn to pay; she noticed his doodling around his place setting. The letters O, B and A, were scribbled over and over the paper coverings at Jeremy's area. OBA? Missy wondered at the meanings of those letters, and promised herself she would ask Jeremy about them when they left the Bar. However, the more she thought about it, the more she decided against asking him. She would ask Craig Olson about the letters instead. As she got into her car, she thought "There was really something off about Jeremy, tonight, something really off.

CHAPTER TWENTY

The Garden Party

On the opposite side of town, and with no knowledge whatsoever about a dead girl, or a private eye or detective, or four little homeless sisters, caterers were busy setting up tables and chairs, under two large, white canopies. Caterers were getting Mrs. Bernard Livingstone ready for her end of the year Fall Garden Party. The Keystone Lawn Service had been by early the previous morning to mow and trim, and prune the flowers and bushes, and the Signature Florist delivery truck had just arrived. The florist was setting up large bouquets of white, bronze and gold mums, yellow daisies and bright yellow roses. The bouquets were accented with green fern, baby's breath and large gold bows. Five of these bouquets were set on tables covered in brown, gold and green silk coverings, which would be filled later in the afternoon with platters of delicious finger foods. A jazz band, "The Better Five" would be setting up soon, and the dance floor was being laid out as Devorah walked throughout her beautifully manicured back yard.

She was more than pleased. Miriam and Betsy had done their appropriate jobs perfectly, and all would be in place in approximately three hours for their many guests—guests of high influence and high society. The guests would be greeted by the Livingstone's darling daughter, Katherine, who would be dressed in the finest children's attire and then the guests would walk through their lavishly furnished home and into the manicured back yard. There, three young women, dressed in starched white blouses and black pleated skirts would offer everyone champagne or sparkling water. White twinkling lights had been strung from the patio area across the back yard, around the swimming pool into the canopies and around the make shift dance floor. The vases of fall flowers were accented by smaller vases of the same fall colored flowers and design, and had been placed in the center of each of the eight tables, also covered in three colors of silk and yellow linen napkins. Everything was all set up for the luxurious sit-down dinner.

Devorah Livingstone stood quietly, gazing at this beautiful setting, and was most pleased. This dinner would most likely make the society pages of the Dawson Review tomorrow or Sunday and once again she would be the envy of her friends. She smiled, and walked assuredly back into her home.

CHAPTER TWENTY-ONE

Can This Case be Solved?

Detective Craig Olson looked at his calendar on Monday morning, noting that it had been over ten days since Mandy Sue's body had been found dumped outside of Arribio, and wondered why there had been no real leads in the case. The tire tracks found at the scene belonged to an Escalade, the small piece of clothing had been a part of the dead woman's clothing, and yes, the blood was definitely hers, but no finger prints of any value had been found on anything or anywhere close to the crime scene. He now waited patiently for the autopsy and final toxicology reports. Perhaps those results would give him more worthwhile information.

"Whoever committed this murder," Craig said to himself. "Did a bang up job of covering up the crime. But, there has to be something I'm missing, and I **will** find the missing link. No murder gets by Craig Olson." He chuckled to himself, but deep down inside he felt that this case might never be solved. This was one of the best cover-up murder scenes he had ever witnessed. There were absolutely no clues or evidence found either at the telephone booth scene or at the actual murder scene. 'This has to have been done by a professional killer, or a hit man, or who knows, maybe even a cop." He said aloud, although no one was around to hear him. "Yes, I wonder if this could have been done by a cop or maybe more than one cop." He hoped not.

The thought of murder by cop made him sick to his stomach, but it wasn't unheard of, especially in bigger cities like New York or Chicago, or even Los Angeles, but Dawson, Colorado? Never. Craig knew that there were dirty cops everywhere, and once and awhile he heard stories of bad cops in Dawson, but no one could ever prove it. For that matter, no one had ever accused a cop of a burglary, or a payoff, or heaven help him, a murder—but he knew it was possible, and if that was true, God help us all.

Craig was especially suspicious of a hit by cop, since Missy Baker had left him a telephone message late last evening, and said that she had found something really strange. She had felt a need to go to Mandy Sue's grave to pay her respects and after stopping in at the cemetery offices and having been given the grave site number, she had been somewhat surprised to find a wilting, single, red rose lying on top of the brown pile of dirt covering Mandy's body. She had called Craig right away, and when he didn't answer, she did what any good PI would do, left him a message, and then picked up the rose with a tissue, and placed it in a large zip lock baggie. She had also been very careful walking around the grave, and seeing no obvious shoe prints in the dirt, had left the area after saying a final prayer for her departed client.

Craig called Missy shortly after 9am the next morning, but he too had to leave a message. "I'm going to the cemetery in a few minutes Missy. If you get this message in time, meet me out there will you, and bring the rose?"

Craig took his time getting out to the Jefferson County Cemetery, and having been to the burial site previously, he parked his car close to the site and walked directly to it. He walked the perimeter, looked around for anything foreign lying in the grassy area, and as he poked respectfully around and through the dirt piled up on the grave site he ran across something **really**, really, strange—cat feces. He wasn't sure at first, but one whiff of the small lump, and he knew—it was cat poop!

As he continued poking through the dirt, and after having placed the surprise in a plastic bag, his telephone rang.

"Hi handsome." Missy said cheerfully. "I just got your message, and since it will take me a good thirty minutes to get to you, do you want me to still meet you there, or meet you back at your office?"

Smiling at the sound of her voice, Craig said, yes, he was finished at the site, and yes, to please meet him at his office. He asked if she had had lunch, and when she said no, he volunteered to pick up a couple of burgers and meet her back at his office. They could chat over lunch.

She agreed, and as she placed her cell phone back in the case attached to her Buick's dashboard, she smiled, and headed for Craig's office.

CHAPTER TWENTY-TWO

The Gray Pick-up Truck

Missy drove gingerly through Dawson taking her time to get to Craig's office. She found herself thinking about him more and more during the last few days. He was an incredible professional, and she enjoyed working with him, but it was more than that—she liked him, liked him a lot. She had been involved romantically a few times over the past ten years, but nothing ever really meant anything, and most men these days just wanted one thing, and she wasn't about to play that roll with any man—at least not until now. She smiled reminiscing about the two times this past week that Craig had kissed her, and she admitted she liked it, and wanted more out of this relationship.

WHAM! As Missy turned onto Broadway Street, slowed down and looked for a parking space in front of the Dawson police building, a gray pick-up truck struck the back of her old Buick, then quickly backed away, drove out and around her and sped away.

"What the heck was that"? She said out loud and somewhat startled. "Why not watch where you are going? JERK!" She barely had enough time to get her senses about her, but took just a quick second to notice the Ford emblem on the back of the truck, and catch an HG1; partial letters and numbers of the license plate as the driver sped away.

Being directly in front of the police department, two officers standing outside of the building, quickly ran up to her vehicle, and as she rolled down the driver's side window. She assured them that she was okay, and would park and then report the incident.

Craig Olson's cell phone rang as he was waiting in line at the Hamburger Joint a block away from the Dawson Police Department.

"Craig Olson." He answered cheerfully. "Missing Persons Division."

"Hi Craig. It's Stan. I have those autopsy and toxicology reports you've been waiting on. The reports on the Donnor case."

Stan Robertson had been the ME for the Dawson Police Department for over 25 years. He was the best there was, and could almost always help Craig solve his murder cases.

"Wow, that was fast, I just spoke with you a few days ago. What bit of good news do you have for me?"

"It did take me longer than usual. "Stan said. I've been swamped." He continued, "Along with a massive amount of cocaine in her system, several stab wounds and severe brain trauma due to a gun shot wound to the head, and other massive injuries of which any of them could have caused her death, the murder victim was a little over two months pregnant."

"Whoa. Are you sure?" Craig asked. "I mean about the pregnancy?"

"Tests don't lie these days Craig." Stan replied. "Wasn't this woman a prostitute? Can't imagine that she would allow herself to get pregnant. But for sure, someone wanted this woman dead, and wanted her death to leave a message for someone."

Craig chatted a few more minutes with the ME, thanked him, and picked up his and Missy's lunches. He couldn't believe that Mandy Sue Donnor had been pregnant. A John? A boyfriend? A lover? Wow, he thought to himself, this puts a whole new outlook on this case. He walked out to his car, a spring in his step, and a renewed hope that this case could and would be solved—soon.

CHAPTER TWENTY-THREE

Hit or Miss

"Pregnant! Mandy Sue was pregnant? Are you sure Craig?"

Missy could not believe what Craig had just told her. She had parked her car, filed a report with the police department, and then met Craig for burgers in his office. First, she handed him the wilted rose that she had placed in a zip lock bag, and as she did so, he told her about the cat feces he had found on his trip to the gravesite.

"Cat poop?" Missy exclaimed, smiling. "Are you kidding me? You found cat poop on Mandy's grave? I don't mean to be disrespectful, Craig, but how can this be of any importance? You know how many geese, and birds, and yes, stray cats and dogs run through cemeteries these days?"

Craig laughed too, at not only the fact that the both of them were discussing cat poop while they ate hamburgers, but how cute Missy was when she laughed.

"I know, I know. It's weird, but you never know what miniscule item is going to help you solve a case. The rose may give us a clue, and so might the poop." Craig was still laughing.

They continued eating their lunches, and talking about the case when Missy asked Craig again if he was sure Mandy had been pregnant?

'Yes, I'm sure about the murdered woman, Missy. Stan Myerson is never wrong. He's one of the best ME's in the business. It seems that someone really wanted her out of the way, and made sure by the violent way she was murdered that others got their message as well. Maybe she was killed because she was pregnant. Who knows at this point? But, I intend to find out, and hopefully, find out soon."

The two drank another cup of coffee, and when Craig got very quiet for a moment, Missy asked him what was on his mind?

Having mentioned to Craig about the hit and run earlier, he asked Missy. "Do you think the truck that hit you, well, that it was just a random incident, Missy? You know, the person or people who killed Mandy most likely knew that you had been working with her. You did mention that earlier. Could be that the bad guys think you know more than you ought to. What do you think?"

Missy quickly responded, that no, she didn't think so, but as soon as she had said no, she sprang from her chair, her crutch falling onto the floor and excitedly said, "Craig, did you know that Mandy Sue had a cat? A black cat! I saw it both times I was at her apartment. Do you know what happened to that cat? Did someone take it? Did it go to the animal shelter? Did anyone find her cat?"

Craig stood up, put his hands on her shoulders and said, "Missy, you should have been a cop, but you are definitely a hot shot private eye. This is the first time I've heard that the victim had a cat, and no, as far as I know, no one ever mentioned a cat, and I know for sure there's no cat mentioned in the police report. Wow! Good job Missy!"

CHAPTER TWENTY-FOUR

The Dawson Post Society Page

Betty Mae Sullivan always looked forward to Sundays. It was the only day away from her social worker position when she could finally relax. She had gotten up by eight o'clock, made and drank two cups of coffee, dressed casually and made it to the nine o'clock church service at the Community Christian Church. Being in church always calmed her nerves, and church was a place she could bring all of her wants and needs of her clients, and lay them at the foot of the cross. Yes, she prayed and asked the Holy Father for her own wants and needs, and thanked Him for His blessings as well. She found solace in church, and always felt refreshed when she left. She was then able to start helping her clients on Monday mornings with a newfound vigor.

Having stopped for breakfast at a diner close to the church, and picking up a few groceries for the week, Betty Mae returned to her modest apartment and sat down to read the Sunday Dawson Review. Having read the business section through and through she then turned to the Society pages, which always made her chuckle. Today's front-page society news was about the Livingstone's—well about Mrs. Deborah Livingstone anyway. "The lovely lady" so claimed the reporter, "dressed in a green silk organza gown for late afternoon wear, was the talk of Dawson when she put on one of her best Fall Garden Parties ever!"

Betty continued reading. "The delightful event was blessed by the prominent Catholic priest, Father Ramsey, and other guests included Bryan and Gerri Jensen, the Chief Medical Director at Dawson General Hospital; Chief of Police, Terrell Olander, and his beautiful wife, Geraldine, the honorable Judge William Bennett and his wife Theresa, the honorable Judge Christianson and his friend Betty Sinclair, Chairman and CEO of the Dawson

Community Center and the Dawson Country Club, as well as many local senators and their wives, and chairmen of the boards of local charities." The article continued by describing the beautiful flower arrangements, the delectable and delightful food and drinks served, the incredible Jazz band that played until way after midnight, and of course a description of the adorable, Katherine, Dr. and Mrs. Livingstone's darling adopted daughter.

Betty loved reading about "those" in high society, and one reason she loved reading about the Livingstone's was because they were adoptive parents. Betty very seldom had the chance to follow through on children in her care, but when she did, there was always a feeling of great satisfaction. She was so thankful that little Katherine had found a wonderful set of parents in a very prominent home.

CHAPTER TWENTY-FIVE

In Too Deep

Bryce Jenkins tossed and turned, finally leaving his sleeping wife and walked quietly down the stairs to their family room. The clock on the wall showed 3:30am. He had gone to bed shortly after 11:00pm, and after an attempt to make love to his wife of almost twenty years, and finally declaring to her that he was just too exhausted from the day's events, she had rolled over and gone to sleep. He, however, could not sleep. He continued to go over and over the previous ten days events—the beating, rape and murder of Mandy Sue Donnor—and his own sexual exploits at the ranch.

Officer Jenkins had been a good cop, having graduated from the Academy with honors and had been hired immediately as a rookie in Dawson's police department. He and his wife had been high school sweethearts, and married shortly after he became a cop. They had been blessed with three beautiful children, had a wonderful relationship both with each other and with their children and the entire family were very active in their church. But things happen—life happens, and Bryce had not seen the changes coming. Their relationship was in trouble. He was never home anymore, and their families' needs were not being met; financially, emotionally or physically. Now he was in the OBA—in so deep that he could never, ever get out—he had helped commit a murder and he was beside himself with grief and guilt.

Shortly after his agreeing to join the OBA, he had been ordered to frequent the "ranch" as an undercover. The OBA needed to find out if rumors of money laundering or sex trafficking and prostitution were actually happening at Olivia Bartlett's ranch. He was placed undercover as a local businessman in desperate need of companionship and love. He had been forced to pay for sex (the OBA paid), and on his third time at Olivia's, he had been placed with Mandy Sue Donnor. She was a sweet young thing; beautiful, with a sexy body, and was not afraid to give him anything he requested. At first the guilt was almost unbearable, but each time the OBA gave him a pay-off, with one half—five hundred—of it going to Olivia, the guilt began to fade away as his new private bank account grew quickly, he found out soon enough that Mandy Sue had been one of Olivia's "girls" since the age of fifteen. A run-a-way, Olivia had taken her in, trained her, brainwashed her and until recently Mandy had been one of her more popular girls.

One slow night, after being with only one john, Mandy walked around the off-limit gardens of Olivia's beautiful ranch house and grounds. Mandy had heard voices, and being an inquisitive young woman, had checked out where the voices were coming from. She had followed the sounds to a hidden, outside, walk-in entrance to the basement of the guesthouse, or so she presumed. One of the cellar doors had been left open and she silently and quietly moved a few flowerpots hiding the entrance and bravely walked, quietly and unseen, down into an underground room or basement. There was a beautiful family-type room, with a large screen television, comfortable looking recliners, several game tables, a wet bar and more. Silently, getting closer to where the voices were coming from. She walked to a partially opened door, a few feet away, behind a large oak cabinet. She watched two men exchanging large sums of money and also saw two or three very young and petrified girls. She wasn't sure exactly what the men were exchanging money for, but she suspected it wasn't good. The three young girls were handcuffed together, and sitting on an overstuffed couch. Each one was scantily dressed, and she could tell, each one had been crying.

Luckily, Mandy had not been seen and she walked swiftly, but quietly out of the guesthouse basement. She had walked a few miles around the ranch property that evening contemplating, what she should do about what she had seen. During her late night walk, she had also seen several vehicles parked on a side road—a road she had never noticed before. Located about a mile from the main road and driveway onto the ranch.

The next morning Mandy asked Olivia too many questions, and wanted more money for satisfying her nightly visitors. Olivia knew that Mandy had always been one of her "sharper" girls, and must have seen or heard more than she should have on the ranch. Olivia knew she would have to take action.

On one of their "trysts" together, Olivia had mentioned to Tyler Morris that she was having trouble with one of her girls, but didn't say what the trouble was. Tyler could not let any of Olivia's girls blow the OBA's undercover operation so he had assured Olivia that she shouldn't worry. Next, he suggested to Bryce Jenkins that he should get much closer to the girls he was spending a lot of time with.

"Find out which of those girls has gotten too nosey for her own good," Tyler had told his undercover agents—including Jeremy Porter.

Mandy had met and had sex with local senators, congressman, judges and other men of prominence, and now she suspected there were those who were involved in drug sales and sex trafficking. All of this was happening in the large basement of the guesthouse. Mandy had been involved at Olivia's long enough—almost 7 years, and although still not real sure of herself or how the outside world operated, she knew that what she had seen and heard was not proper or legal, and she knew that she had heard more than she should have about the goings on at the ranch. There was definitely more to the ranch than just prostitution.

When she had approached Olivia about some of these concerns, Olivia had assured Mandy that she was completely wrong about what she had seen and heard.

"Some of the new girls need to be treated a little more harshly, Mandy." Olivia had said. "Not all of our girls are as sweet and understanding as you've been. They need a little more "instruction" to do their jobs each night. You understand don't you? Now, just keep doing your job and you'll always have a home here." Then, more sternly Olivia had said. "But stay out of the guesthouse basement!"

Mandy had been warned more or less to "keep her mouth closed" or else! Unknown to Olivia, there were already undercover OBA cops frequenting the ranch to get proof of the sex trafficking supposedly going on there. Morris didn't want to hurt any of the "girls", but he needed to get proof that there were illegal dealings and possible sales of young woman going on at the ranch, and that Dawson "higher-ups" could be involved. He had ordered Bryce and three other "unknown OBA members" to teach Mandy a lesson.

When Mandy refused to take the threats seriously, the orders were then given to do away with her. Morris couldn't take a chance on Mandy Sue "blowing" the OBA's chances of exposing a huge sex trafficking ring. If one woman had to be silenced, it would be at little expense if they could stop this huge sex ring. After all, Mandy Sue Donnor was just another prostitute.

On the day of her murder, the four OBA members had staked out her apartment, watched as an unknown woman walking with a crutch had entered Mandy's apartment and then left, and when the coast was clear, the four had followed Mandy to the telephone booth, beat her up, and taken her out of town and killed her. They had shot her up with cocaine, stabbed her, shot her in the head and one of the members had raped her after she was dead. Bryce had never seen anything like this before in his life. He had been educated to help and protect, not to rape and murder. He had run about 100 yards away from the scene and puked up his guts before getting back into the car and driving away. The other members had laughed at him, slapped him on the back, and told him to get over it.

At around 9:00pm the evening of Mandy's kidnapping and murder, a young man had entered Mandy's apartment building, walked directly to her door and ignoring the yellow tape across the front of the door, quickly placed his key in the lock and entered. He walked from room to room, softly calling out for Mandy's cat. After only a few calls, he found Mittens hiding under the bed. He talked softly to the cat, and as Mittens came out from her hiding place, the unknown man picked her up and cradled the cat in his arm.

"You did good Mittens." The stranger said. You hid well. Not even those stupid cops found you. I promise I will take good care of you, and I'm sorry about your mama. She just wouldn't listen. Now she's never coming back to take care of you ever again. But, I'll take care of you, Mittens. I promise.

The stranger came and went quickly, and not one person had noticed him.

CHAPTER TWENTY-SIX

Settling In

One month had gone by since the four young sisters were placed in foster care. Nellie was enjoying the 6-month old Rebecca, and being such a good baby, Nellie was easily able to handle her three foster children. Her husband Jim, was also a wonderful father for the children, but it was Nellie who really gave them the most love and attention. The Grants too were trying their best to settle in with the three older sisters. The two younger girls were very easy to love and take care of, but Sandra, the oldest girl was a bit more of a challenge. Sandra insisted daily that she needed to see her baby sister, and constantly asked, no, almost begged her foster mother to take her to where Rebecca was housed. Finally, Janice Grant, a kind and gentle soul, had contacted social services and Betty Mae had granted Janice approval to go to Nellie and Jim Coopers home for a sister's visit.

When Janice Grant pulled her car into the Cooper's driveway, Sandra jumped out of the car before Janice had brought the car to a complete stop. Nellie Cooper was sitting in her grandmother's rocking chair, on the front porch of their modest home, bottle-feeding Rebecca; gently rocking her as she did so. Her two other foster children played quietly with their toys at her feet. Nellie did not get up out of the chair, but continued to feed Rebecca as Sandra ran up the front steps to where Nellie was sitting.

"Hello." Nell said, smiling. "You must be Sandra. I'm so very glad to have you visit us today. If you give me just a few minutes more, I'll be finished feeding your baby sister, and you can sit here in the rocking chair and hold her. Would you like that?"

Sandra shook her head yes, and sat down cross-legged on the floor with the other two foster children. Janice Grant walked up the stairs and sat down on the top step. She said hello to Nell, thanked her for giving her and Sandra a little of her time, then sat back quietly and watched.

Sandra waited patiently, saying very little, and when Nellie finished feeding, and then burping the infant girl, she stood up. Immediately Sandra also stood up, and traded places with Nell in the old rocking chair. Sandra smiled and spoke to Rebecca and the baby responded back with baby sounds as Sandra spoke gently and sweetly to her baby sister.

After watching the two siblings for a few moments, the two foster mothers made small talk, and then Nell, out of hearing range of Sandra, asked about the two other sisters. Janice assured her that they were doing well, had adjusted fairly well, but that she didn't know how long she and Chet could keep the three girls in their foster care. She admitted that they were good little girls, but she and Chet were not as young as they used to be. Although their family was raised, and they wanted to help out children in need, she wasn't sure if they could keep the girls long term.

"Do you think you and Jim could take the two-year old?" Janice asked. "I think we could handle the two older girls, at least for a little while longer, but three is just way too much for us to handle. We are going to try to take the girls on a trip somewhere, possibly to Disney Land around the holidays—If they're not in a permanent home by then. We have no idea if and when the girls will be adopted, so we thought we would take them somewhere fun. I doubt they have ever been to any place fun, let alone Disneyland."

Nell applauded Janice and her husband efforts regarding their three foster children and said that she would speak with her husband, and also with Betty Mae, and perhaps they could help out with one of the sisters. Nell too, admitted to Janice that she doubted any adoptive family could or would take all four girls together, which she then added, would be devastating to Sandra.

"I pray each day that these little girls will find a good family, Janice." Nell said, sincerely, "But I think Betty Mae will have a hard time finding the right parents for these precious little girls."

CHAPTER TWENTY-SEVEN

Romance is In the Air

Four weeks after Craig and Missy first met, Missy Baker, one of Dawson, Colorado's finest Private Investigators, was working steadily on three new cases. A mother had called Missy pleading with her to find her sixteen-year-old son whom she firmly believed was not a run-a-way, but had been kidnapped. Two days later, a distraught fifty-five year old man had called asking for her assistance in finding his missing grandson who was a straight A student in school, a star athlete, but who could not get along with his step-father. He was certain the stepfather was somehow involved in the disappearance. Then finally, a younger woman had asked for ideas on how to locate a lost or stolen World War II medal of honor that had belonged to her great grand father. It had been stolen out of her bedroom. She was afraid that someone had either broken into or entered her home illegally.

Missy accepted all three cases, because this was her career, and she loved helping others, and probably most importantly, she needed a paycheck. A woman could definitely not live on love alone, although she was beginning to think that "love alone" might just be a possibility with Craig. However, still at the top of her priority list as a PI, was to help Craig find Mandy Sue Donnor's killer.

She and Craig had spent many hours working on the case, and although Missy had only had one incident that may or may not have had something to do with the case—the hit and run in front of the police station, Craig was very concerned that Missy might still be in danger. Craig had interviewed the superintendent at Mandy Sue's apartment building, asking about her black cat. Had he seen anyone at the dead woman's apartment on the night of her disappearance? Could he remember anyone coming to the apartment on the day of Mandy's death? Could he share anything at all about the young woman who had lived in his apartment building for over a year? No, No and No, is all the superintendent had curtly said as he slammed the door in Craig's face.

During the past few weeks, Missy had finally taken the time to call Jeanine at Dawson Human Services. Missy had promised earlier to check in on the four little girls that had recently been placed in foster care, but with the Mandy Sue Donnor case and her own cases solely on her mind, she had almost forgotten her promise. She had spoken with Jeanine, and had been informed that she needed to get approval from Betty Mae, the social worker in charge of the little girls case. Jeanine knew that the girls had been placed but had no idea with whom, or where. Missy promised herself to take a trip to the social service's office where Betty Mae worked as soon as she could get away. Missy also asked herself, why would a private eye need to check on children in the foster care system? The mother was in prison, there was no trace of the father and no other family members were interested, as far as Missy knew. But Jeanine was a good friend; she agreed to get approval to check on the four little girls. Perhaps there was something a PI could do to help the case.

In the mean time, Missy and Craig had become almost inseparable. They of course were working together on the case, but they were also becoming more and more a couple. They enjoyed each other's company at lunch or dinner, and they had even taken in two movies and gone to a play in downtown Dawson at the Buell Theatre. They realized that they had a lot in common, both in their individual careers and in their social and personal lives. After only a month, Missy knew that she was falling in love. She was pretty sure Craig felt the same, although neither one had spoken the actual word—love.

During one of their dinner dates, the conversation on why Missy had become a Private Investigator came up. Missy, dressed in a light blue, silk, long-sleeved blouse, with matching skirt (which seemed to make her blue eyes sparkle even more than usual), had looked directly into Craig's eyes and said. "I wanted to be a detective, like my daddy. I went to two years of law school after college, then registered at the police academy, but due to my disability, I was turned away."

Craig, noticing the sadness in those blue eyes, reached across the table, took her hand in his, and said, "I'm so sorry Missy. But tell me, didn't you have an idea that you would be turned down? I mean because of your disability? You are always so upbeat, so funny, never sad, never upset, at least you never act like your disability bothers you. I hope I'm not out of line making that statement, but please, go on."

"I love people, people of all types, shapes, color and needs I guess." She replied. "When I was turned down at the Academy, I talked a long time with my daddy, and he assured me that I didn't need to be a cop to work for and with people in need. He told me I should either become a lawyer, or if I didn't want to be closed up in an office or a courtroom every day, I should go out to the people and help them out there—out there where I could work one on one with them, help them in their darkest hours, and yes, make fairly good money besides. My problem", she continued, "is that I want to help people so badly that I end up doing so much work without ever charging them. I guess I'm a "softie".

Craig had leaned over the table and kissed her on the cheek. When they had left the restaurant, Missy had invited him into her apartment for coffee. After two more hours of talking and sharing bits and pieces of their lives, they had moved on to the bedroom, and had made love for the first time.

Yes, only six weeks after meeting Detective Craig Olson, and only a few weeks after the devastating murder of Mandy Sue Donnor, Missy knew that Craig Olson was the man she wanted to spend the rest of her life with. The man who only after several weeks—knew her, understood her and loved her. She couldn't wait to call her daddy.

CHAPTER TWENTY-EIGHT

The Fundraiser

None other than Mrs. Devorah Livingstone chaired the fundraising committee supporting the Queen of Heaven Orphanage. Being a woman of prominence, a member of Father Ramsey's church, (even though she had been raised Jewish), and a most beloved member of the community, there was no one else that could possibly be in charge of one of the most popular fundraising affairs in all of Dawson. Devorah knew all the right people, and no one dared say no to any of her many, many requests. She found businesses to donate the food, the door prizes, the decorations, and more, and as she and the doctor were involved in so many organizations, she had no trouble getting donations, a band, people to run the game booths, a master of ceremonies from a local television station—any thing Devorah Livingstone needed or wanted—Devorah Livingstone got. She was one of the most dedicated and loving women in the community—or so everyone thought.

Craig Olson had seen to it that four police officers and/or detectives had the weekend in late September off, so parking and security would not be a problem at the fundraiser. It was a known fact that the Livingstone's also made large donations each year to the Police Orphans Fund, and well, let's just say, that no one said NO when Devorah asked for assistance of any kind.

As planned, Craig invited Missy to the event. She offered to help in the game booths where many children from the orphanage and the community would be participating. After volunteering at the Friday night, and Saturday daytime events, she and Craig would attend the gala held in the large fellowship hall attached to the church. Over 250 people had purchased $200.00 per person tickets to the black tie dinner and dance.

Missy had gone shopping the weekend prior to the event and found a darling black strapless knee length gown trimmed in silver, and since she could not physically manage high-heeled shoes she found cute little silver sandals that matched the dress perfectly. Her older sister promised to curl her beautiful hair in ringlets on top of her head, and she would wear a black orchid flower clip where the ringlets cascaded down the back of her neck. She could not wait for Craig to see her in her new "garb".

After a wonderful spaghetti dinner, entertainment and karaoke on Friday evening, the Saturday event began at 8:00am, with a breakfast, fashion show and tea for the ladies and continual games all day long for young and old alike. Missy had volunteered to man the bowling ball booth, where children were given 3 chances to knock down all ten pins, and win a prize. With three volunteers helping her set up pins, hand out prizes, and control excited children, the hours seem to fly by.

Around 1:00pm, two women with six children in tow between them approached the booth. Missy encouraged the older children to try their luck with the game. Missy couldn't help but notice that one little girl was very slow in her actions, and the mother encouraged her, helped her with loving hands and instructions.

"Amy, you can do this honey." She told the child sweetly. Mama will help you." The other mother with three little girls, all dressed alike in blue jeans, pink tee shirts and pink tennis shoes, also encouraged her daughters to take part in the games. A little shy at first, the little ones seemed to be taking instructions from their bigger sister and as the older girl encouraged them and egged them on, the fun began. Missy applauded the children as they knocked down pins, and wanted to do it again. Please, they would ask, can we do it again? When each child had won at least one prize, Missy complimented the mothers on their beautiful children, and how well behaved they were.

"We're foster mothers." One woman replied. "Our social worker invites us, and all of the foster parents in the community to be a part of this event each year. It gives all of the foster parents a chance to get to know one another better, and to give our foster children a chance to get involved with other children, and for us to get involved in the community."

"We foster parents work hand in hand with the Queen of Heaven Orphanage," replied the older foster mother. "We know that many foster children, when homes are not found for them quickly, are placed at the Orphanage to await adoption. It's a very good home, just very sad that so many children end up there, as no one wants to adopt them."

Janice, the older one of the two women, wiped a tear from her eye, just as the oldest foster daughter asked her if she could stay for awhile with the baby being held by the other foster mother. "Can I just stay with Nellie awhile, please?" She asked. "So I can play with and hold Rebecca?"

Janice and Nell smiled at one another, knowing what was coming.

"Janice, if it's okay with you, please take the girls around to the other games, and I will sit down on one of the chairs by the food table, and Sandra can feed Rebecca. It's okay. Sandra wants to spend time with her sister."

Missy watched all of this, her heart breaking. Here were six precious children, all being cared for by volunteer mothers; all six with no families of their own. Oh my, she thought to herself, six little broken souls, with no one but these wonderful women to care for them. As she continued to watch Nellie with three of the children, she wondered if these little girls were perhaps the children that Jeanine had asked her to check on. She doubted it. That would be an incredible coincidence, but she decided to ask anyway. She asked two of the volunteers to watch the booth for a few minutes, and Missy walked over to where Nellie sat.

"Hi. I'm Missy Baker." Missy said politely. "I wonder if I could ask you a question?"

Nellie introduced herself, then Sandra, and told her the baby's name. She said, of course, Missy could ask her anything at all.

"I have a friend, Jeanine Simpson." Missy began. "She works at Human Services, and she's mentioned to me that she had a case where there were four little girls having to be placed in foster care, and she's asked me to check on them. I know that sounds strange, and to be honest, it seemed strange to me, too. I'm a Private Investigator in Dawson and I'm not sure why Jeanine requested this of me. Anyway, do you mind me asking if you know anything about four sisters who are being cared for in the foster care system?

Smiling now, Nellie said that yes she knew all about those little girls. She looked over at Sandra, and then at the baby, and shared with Missy that yes, she was caring for the youngest sister, Rebecca. Sandra was her older sister, and along with Tabbatha and Roseanne, her friend, Janice, was caring for the three.

Missy was surprised, no shocked, to say the least.

"Goodness!" Missy exclaimed. "What a coincidence that you should stop by my booth. Can you tell me, if I'm not being to bold—are the girls getting ready for adoption? Are you going to adopt any of them? How about Janice? Is she going to adopt any of them?

Missy knew that she was being very brazen, but now her curiosity was aroused and she couldn't stop asking questions.

"I'm afraid," Nellie said. "That the girls have not yet been placed. It's very difficult to find one family that will take all four girls, and Sandra here, wants to make sure all of them stay together. I'm not sure that will happen. Janice and I, and our husbands cannot adopt them, and so far, although it's only been a few months, our social worker has not found an adoptive family." As she spoke, Nellie softly touched Sandra's shoulder, smiled at her and assured her that everything would be fine.

Missy wanted to ask more questions, but she realized that she needed to get back to her booth, and she also did not want to pry anymore. She told Sandra how pretty her baby sister was, and what a good big sister she was to want to take such good care of her. Missy said goodbye, and went back to her booth.

CHAPTER TWENTY-NINE

Elegance at its Finest

The Saturday evening black tie event for the Catholic Charities and Queen of Heaven Orphanage was one of the most successful events Devorah Livingstone had ever chaired. As she inspected the ballroom prior to the $200.00 a plate dinner, she smiled to herself as she noticed those in prominence and power beginning to gather. She had worked diligently to make this one of her best events ever, and it certainly was turning out that way.

There were more than one hundred items donated and in place for the silent auction; paintings by local artists, crystal, bottles of vintage wine, sculptures, autographed sports paraphernalia from local NFL, MBL and NHL teams. The highlight of the evening would be a 10-day all expense paid trip to the Caribbean, auctioned off to the highest bidder.

Craig and Missy left the Saturday afternoon events around 4:00pm, exhausted, but anxious for the evening event. Craig saw to it that four more police officers were in place, so he and Missy could enjoy the Saturday evening festivities and those who had worked Friday night and all day on Saturday could go home to their families. He dropped Missy off at her apartment and promised to be back at 6:30pm to pick her up.

Missy couldn't believe that Craig had purchased two tickets to the event, but he assured her that he owed Father Ramsey so much and he also believed in the Catholic organization and the orphanage. This was Craig's way of paying him back. After all, the money raised would go to a very good cause.

Missy was very anxious to be a part of one of the most popular social events of the season. She took her time getting showered and dressed and her sister had fixed her long hair beautifully. She anxiously awaited Craig's arrival. She couldn't wait to see his reaction when he saw her in the beautiful black dress. It had been a very long time since she had been wined and dined, and she was loving all the attention—true and real attention from a handsome, wonderful man.

When her doorbell rang, Missy grabbed her crutch and walked slowly to the door. She opened the door wide, and there he stood—one of the most handsome men she had ever seen, all decked out in a black tuxedo—holding a bouquet of red roses.

"My gosh Missy!" He exclaimed. "You look gorgeous!"

"Thank you." Missy mumbled, somewhat embarrassed, and then said, "You don't look too bad yourself Detective."

Craig walked into her apartment, kissed her gently at first, then harder, and Missy gently pushed him away, sweetly telling him that they had to be at the fundraiser in less than twenty minutes, but to hold those feelings until later. He chuckled, but agreed.

Craig dropped Missy off at the front door of the Church of Christ Fellowship Hall, and went to park his car. He found a parking place close to the front door, thanks in part to one of his policeman acquaintances that had "saved him a spot".

Craig showed the volunteer at the door his tickets, and they were given their table number. They were also given directions on the silent auction and directions to the cash bar. Craig purchased each of them a glass of Chardonnay, and they walked hand-in-hand to the long line of tables where the silent auction items were displayed.

Missy wrote down a bid for a set of crystal wine glasses, and Craig signed up for a chance at an autographed Dawson Bears Football. They both looked at each other and broke out laughing. Missy was thinking romantic evening, roaring fire, and wine in a beautiful crystal wine glass, while Craig was thinking jeans, tee shirts and a football game. Craig hugged her, kissed her on the forehead, and once again, hand in hand, they looked for, and found their table.

The couple was seated at a table for ten, and one of the other guests included the Mother Superior of the Queen of Heaven Orphanage. Craig introduced himself and Missy to the nun and they sat down to wait for the festivities to begin.

At exactly 7:00pm, Mrs. Devorah Livingstone, dressed in a divine black silk gown, etched in black and silver lace, with matching quarter length sleeved jacket, was escorted to the microphone by the Reverend Father Ramsey. The crowd broke out in a tremendous applause, and then all stood up to also show their appreciation.

Devorah thanked the crowd gathered under multi-colored twinkling lights, and asked that they remain standing for a beautiful rendition of the AVA MARIA to be played by harpist, Jennifer McDonald, a member of the Dawson Symphony, and to please remain standing for the invocation to be given by the Father. The crowd quieted down immediately, and the rendition of the AVA MARIA cast a reverent silence on the entire room of over five hundred partygoers. After another round of thundering applause, Father Ramsey gave the invocation, and asked the guests to be seated.

As Missy began to eat her appetizers of stuffed artichoke and crab cakes, she looked around the room filled with Dawson celebrities, professionals, CEO's, politicians, nuns, priests and more. As her eyes scanned the beautifully decorated room, and the incredibly beautifully dressed men and women, she caught a glimpse of someone who looked very familiar. At first she didn't recognize him, but after a long, second look, she realized that the man with a recent hair cut, dressed in white tuxedo jacket and black pants was non other than Jeremy Porter. A beautiful blond woman, dressed in an all white knee length cocktail dress, with plunging neckline, with emphasis on the "plunging", was clutching on to him as if he might get away. She wondered why in the world Jeremy, a Jefferson County Sherriff's deputy would be invited to an event of this caliber? Where would he get $200.00 for a ticket? And who was the blond bombshell he was with?

"He always had a crush on me." She thought to herself. "Could I be just a little bit jealous? No way. No way."

She turned her eyes away from him, as Craig asked her politely if everything was okay? She said yes, she was fine, but when their meal of dill-crusted salmon with new potatoes, bacon wrapped asparagus and deep fried cinnamon apple wedges were served, she suddenly remembered the evening out with Jeremy. She had never asked Craig if he knew what the initials O.B.A. stood for. She made a mental note to ask Craig about it as soon as they finished their meal.

CHAPTER THIRTY

Hearsay or Truth

Craig and Missy enjoyed their pear torte with whipped cream and black coffee, and when the band began to play, Craig asked Missy if she could, and would, like to dance.

"I'm okay with slow dances", she admitted to Craig, "However, I have a hard time with the fast ones."

Craig said the slow dances were perfect, as that way he could hold her close.

Missy was in love. She had never felt this close to any other man, well, except for her daddy, in her entire life. Craig seemed to not only enjoy her company, but had no problems at all with her disability and although she worried a little bit about his being a detective, she just knew this would be the man she would spend the rest of her life with.

Around 11:30pm, after thanking Mrs. Livingstone for the delightful evening and after making a point to thank the Reverend Father Ramsey for his charitable work with the orphanage, and especially thanking Mother Superior for sharing their table, the two made their way to the door. As they walked from the Hall to their vehicle, Missy once again noticed Jeremy Porter and his blond friend also walking through the parking lot. At first, she wanted to approach him, but on second thought, she decided to leave well enough alone. She had a gut feeling that there was something about Jeremy Porter that she did not know, and honestly didn't want to know. She had watched him a few times throughout the dinner and dancing, and on more than one occasion he had, what seemed to be a serious conversation with a popular court judge; Judge Christianson.

"Very weird." Missy said out loud.

"Did you say something?" Craig asked her, as he opened the door to his vehicle.

"No." She said. "I'm sorry Craig, my mind was somewhere else. I'm really sorry, but I saw an old friend here tonight, and I feel there is something really strange going on with him. Do you mind if I ask you something, or tell you something?"

Missy spent the ride home sharing with Craig all she knew about Jeremy Porter. They had been friends a long time. She was sure he had always had a crush on her. He was a Sheriffs deputy in Jefferson County, Colorado. She had seen him a few weeks back, and she had thought him to be very nervous, or upset that night. She had seen the initials OBA doodled on the tablecloth next to his plate, and did Craig have any idea what those initials might mean?

They sat out front of Missy's apartment building talking not about the wonderful evening they had just shared, but about Jeremy Porter and the OBA. It wasn't exactly how either one of them had wished to finish off the evening, but when a Private Investigator and a detective get together, any topic is possible, and this new piece of information they both agreed, might just be what they both needed to solve the Mandy Sue Donnor case.

"I'll tell you what I know, Missy." Craig had said. "It may or may not be the truth, I just get hearsay a lot at the precinct. Sometimes, we detectives check out the hearsay or gossip, and sometimes we sweep it away, out of our minds. In this case, yes, I have heard about the OBA on a few occasions First of all, you need to know that the OBA stands for Officers for a Better America. As far as I know, it's a group of men, and yes, women, who are unhappy cops, or maybe a better word is, dirty cops. They are men and women, who for whatever reason need more money, hate authority, need more satisfaction from the job, and think the good cops aren't doing enough. There are evidently a number of reasons that the OBA was started. As far as I know, this is a secret organization, set up to clean up our city and help good guys out of bad, maybe sticky situations. Evidently the members feel like the rest of us are not doing our jobs properly. Also, I understand that they, the dirty cops, get those in high society: judges, politicians, doctors, chairman of the board types, "off the hook". For example, if you get a traffic ticket, or worse, a DUI, or get caught with a lady of the night, well, these men pay off a dirty cop to do away with the ticket, the photo, the jail sentence, etc."

Craig continued to tell Missy what he had heard over the past few years, but no one had ever been caught, no one ever had enough proof of dirty cops, and no one knew where the OBA met, or who was in charge. "For all I know, Missy." Craig continued, "It could all be lies."

"I wonder if Jeremy could be involved?" Missy replied, an uncertainty in her voice. "He's always been a good deputy, as far as I know. He's been with the Jefferson County Sheriffs Department over 10 years. I just can't imagine that he would be involved in anything this sinister."

Craig told her that he would do more checking, and as they exited his car, told her kiddingly, "You're the PI, how about doing some digging on your own? But, please, be very, very careful. These men and women are not, as I understand, to be messed with.

As Craig unlocked her apartment door, and started to kiss her goodnight, Missy, stopped mid-kiss, put her hands on Craig's shoulders and blurted out. "Craig, Craig. Remember when I had the fender bender in front of the Country Club, or did I ever tell you about that, oh well, never mind that, did you know that I was positive the silver-haired guy that rear ended me, slipped the cop on the scene a few bills? Did I ever tell you that Craig?" She continued, now bubbling over with excitement. "I knew it, I just knew it. That cop was dirty. He never intended to give that silver-haired fox a ticket. The cop paid him off! He paid him off Craig. I was right there with a dirty cop! I have his name and badge number Craig. Come in, let's find it!"

"So much for a romantic ending to this evening." Craig thought to himself. "This is what I get for falling for a Private Investigator."

CHAPTER THIRTY-ONE

Cop Turned Killer

Jeremy dropped off his "friend" at her apartment, thanked her politely for being his date for the night, and returned to his own place about 8 miles away. He needed a date for the fundraiser, and one of the OBA members, Janice Poltice, had obliged. Jeremy had absolutely no interest in Janice. She was needed for the job at hand. Tyler Morris, head of the OBA somehow, had gotten Jeremy two tickets to the fundraiser and counseled Janice on how to act, what to do, and to remember she was doing this for the cause.

The OBA was very close to breaking into a large sex trafficking group in the Dawson area, and good-ole-judge Christianson was the suspected leader of the group. He was known to be a guest at the fundraiser. It was hard for Jeremy to imagine that a court judge, a man of prominence and one who was loved by all he met and worked with, could be involved in such a horrific trade. Jeremy knew that several OBA members had been "paid off" to keep Judge Christianson on the bench. The judge was under observation at all times by the OBA, and just a few weeks ago, the judge had been on one of his "binges". An OBA cop had pulled him over; mostly to make sure he didn't harm anyone. The good-ole-judge had let the cop/member know that he was coming into a great deal of money, and was the member interested not only in receiving a large sum of money to cover up the judge's sins, but a little "sweet nookie" on the side? The member, having taken an earlier bribe from the judge, had once again kept the judge out of jail, the story out of the newspapers, and the member had gone straight to Tyler Morris with the information.

This is where Jeremy Porter had come on the scene. Tyler Morris knew that Jeremy would make a good undercover. He first placed him at Olivia's, getting close to the "ladies", and keeping his ears and eyes open. He had run into the judge on more than one occasion at the ranch, and on one of those visits, he had watched the judge take care of business, then leave, get in his car, drive around the block, and immediately watched him come back and park a short way down one of the back roads on the ranch. The judge walked back to Olivia's, walked through the gardens in the back yard, and Jeremy watched as the Judge moved a few flower pots and pots of bushes, to a hidden entrance to the basement of the guesthouse where he presumed business was handled. Jeremy could not get close enough to hear any of the goings on, but he waited long enough to watch the judge and two other men exit the basement, get in their individual vehicles and drive away. Jeremy knew immediately that there was more to the ranch than late night sex.

Jeremy had no idea that Bryce Jenkins, the dirty cop also visiting the ranch was an OBA member as well. Tyler Morris had kept Jeremy away from the meetings, away from all the other members, strictly to keep him as an undercover on all things of dire importance to their cause. So, the few times that Bryce and Jeremy had been at the ranch at the same time, they had no idea each were there on request of Tyler Morris.

The problem, and a large problem it had become, was that Jeremy and Bryce were both seeing Mandy Sue Donnor. The larger looming problem began when Jeremy found himself falling in love with Mandy Sue. Yes, their sexual encounters were one of a kind, but after months and months of these encounters, Mandy and Jeremy, both admitted, that they wanted more of their relationship, and Mandy wanted "out of the business". She also shared with Jeremy that she knew there were things going on at the ranch that were not honest, and probably against the law. She had shared with Jeremy what she had seen in the basement at Olivia's guesthouse.

Jeremy was heart broken. He could not tell Mandy that he was undercover. He could not let her go to the cops, and although he cared for her a lot, and wanted her out of the business, his first priority was to let Tyler Morris know what was going on with her. Tyler had told Jeremy to talk to her first, then threaten her, maybe scare her a little, but when neither of those things convinced Mandy to keep her mouth shut, Tyler had ordered Jeremy, and three other members to "take care of her". One of those members was Bryce Jenkins.

"I don't think I can do that, Tyler." Jeremy had said, almost pleading with Tyler Morris "This is a very sweet, yes, maybe confused young woman but kill her? I don't think I can do that."

But, as always, it was for the good of the OBA. The members needed to crack the sex trafficking ring, and if that meant disposing of someone who was getting in the way of doing just that, well, so be it.

Jeremy, always in disguise, had met with Bryce Jenkins, Marvin Grayson and Johnathan Serrvigio. They had found Mandy twice, beat her up both times and dumped her a few blocks from her apartment. When the beatings had done no good, and she continued to threaten to go to the cops, they had staked out her house, watched as a disabled woman came and went, and then followed Mandy to the telephone booth, where they shot her up with drugs, beat her, killed her and dumped her on the outskirts of Dawson.

Jeremy watched as the member, Bryce Jenkins took part in the murder and then watched him puke his guts up. Jeremy had wanted to do the same. First of all, his heart fell into his shoes when he saw Missy Baker at Mandy's apartment. Secondly, killing Mandy was the most horrific thing he had ever done. He had fallen in love with the prostitute and the worst thing he had ever done was to make love to her dead corpse—all to prove to the other members how tough and dedicated to the cause he really was. Jeremy and Mandy had made plans to get her "out" of the business, away from the ranch and now, he had planned her brutal attacks and then murdered her. Jeremy had pulled the trigger. Jeremy had put on the best act of his life—he waited until he got back to his own apartment before he had discarded the disguise, and then vomited until there was nothing left but a gagging reflex in his throat. Then he cried, cried like a baby, and wondered how in the world he had gotten himself into this mess. God, if there really were one, would never, ever forgive him.

Jeremy had placed a rose on Mandy's grave, gone back to her apartment in yet another disguise to pick up Mittens, and then he had drunk himself into a stupor. Complaining of the flu to take off work, he was back to work as a Sheriff's deputy three days later, and back to working with the OBA undercover.

His last OBA assignment had been to put a scare into Missy Baker, and keep an eye on her. "Make sure she doesn't know anything. Make sure and keep an eye on her". The last words he had heard from Tyler Morris before he had Janice Poltice, in her gray pickup truck, rear-end Missy's old Buick in front of the police station.

CHAPTER THIRTY-TWO

Time Goes On

Missy worked diligently over the next three months on several cases. She was a very good Private Investigator, and now that she knew the detective in charge of missing people, she had that extra "edge" in Craig Olson's knowledge and experience as well. She and Craig worked together, when they could, and through it all, their main focus was still to find Mandy Sue Donnor's killer. They had no new leads, had checked and rechecked the leads they did have, and still, nothing. They both hoped and prayed that one day soon, there would be a new lead.

On her own, Missy looked into her friend Jeremy's past, his current status, his family, his friends, and except for a few minor things, she could find no dirt on Jeremy Porter. She hated spying on him and she had even called him one time to "catch up" as she put it, and they talked for a few minutes about the upcoming football season. Not once did she sense anything amiss with her friend.

Missy and Craig tried very hard to get free from private investigative and detective cases as often as possible, and although difficult, when they did have free time, they would spend leisurely time together; going for evening walks (sometimes Missy would use her wheelchair), having quiet dinners at Missy's apartment, taking in a movie, or just spending quality time together talking about their pasts, their families, and lately their futures.

One evening after Missy had spent a very long day with one of her clients—the grandfather with the missing grandson— she and Craig had enjoyed an evening eating Italian cuisine, drinking wine and making love, this time at Craig's apartment. At around 11:00pm, Craig suggested that rather than going back to her apartment, she should stay the night. Missy was surprised. During the past several months, whether they were at his place or hers, they had always gone back to their separate apartments. Missy, still lying in Craig's arms, turned, kissed him gently, and said yes, she would love to. Waking up the next morning, next to the man she loved was one of the best moments of her life and she believed that after all these years, she had found the right man, the one who loved her deeply and accepted her for who she was. It was also the first time that Craig had told her he loved her.

Two weeks later, after introducing Craig to her parents, who accepted him with open arms, especially her detective daddy, Craig and Missy moved into Craig's apartment together. It was to be the beginning of a beautiful relationship.

During this same time period, Dr. and Mrs. Livingstone were meeting with Father Ramsey and the Mother Superior at the Queen of Heaven Orphanage. Although Devorah Livingstone was not in favor of his idea, the good doctor felt that it was time to adopt another child—a brother or sister for Katherine. Bernard Livingstone knew that his wife was not a good mother to their daughter, but was certain that if there was a second child, all of them could possibly become a more loving family. Mother Superior took them around the Orphanage, introduced them to two beautiful little girls, one seven and one nine, but Devorah didn't seem to be interested in either one. Then they returned to the Mother's offices.

"I don't feel really good about adopting another child at this time, I mean." Devorah remarked properly, as she removed her white gloves from her beautifully manicured fingers. "I know Bernard is ready for another child, but I really would like to wait a little longer. I have so many things that I need to take care of you know, Reverend Mother, and I do appreciate all your help and concern. I know the right child will come along soon, and perhaps you could call us when you feel you have the right child for us." She stood up, said goodbye to Father Ramsey and Mother Superior and motioned for her husband to do the same.

Bernard was noticeably irritated with this wife. He loved Katherine. He spent most of his free time with his child, because his high society wife spent NO time with her. He really wanted another child. He also knew who wore the pants in his family, and he did as he was told.

Pleasantries said, the affluent couple left the orphanage, empty handed—exactly the way Devorah had planned it.

In the Cooper and Grant foster homes, four little girls were adjusting to their new environments. The two foster mothers had made sure the girls saw each other at least twice a month, as Sandra, the oldest daughter requested. It made all of the little girls happier when they saw each other. Janice Grant made it very clear to her charges on a daily basis, that there were four sisters, not three, and that she would do everything in her power to keep all four siblings together—always. Nellie Cooper agreed. Although she and Jim had chosen to not take another of the sisters into their home, they did agree to make sure the four girls were kept together, even for short periods of time. The Grants too, had agreed to keep the three sisters until an adoptive family was found. They were getting very attached to Sandra, Tabbatha and Roseanne—something they never thought would happen.

Sad to say, when that adoptive family did immerge, it would be the undoing of four little girls. If there is no love in a family, how can a family thrive?

BOOK
TWO

CHAPTER THIRTY-THREE

The Queen of Heaven Orphanage

It was the week of Christmas. Snow had fallen on Monday and Tuesday, so the city of Dawson, Colorado was covered in a blanket of white. The sounds and sights of Christmas were everywhere—in schools, churches, at the mall, on street corners and especially in private homes. Christmas lights of all colors and shapes decorated the insides and outsides of homes and businesses, and the home of Janice Grant and Nellie Cooper were no different. Both foster parents had made a point to have a Christmas tree, decorations throughout the home, and a few lights on trees and bushes at the front of their individual homes.

The two foster mothers had taken all six foster children to the local Mall one afternoon for photos with Santa. Then the two families had spent an evening together, enjoying hot chocolate with lots of whipped cream, and watching a Christmas movie appropriate for small children. Each child had received one gift on Christmas Eve, and after church services, more singing, laughing and good night hugs and kisses at home, the older children went to bed dreaming of the jolly old man and his flying reindeer with great anticipation. The two foster families did not disappoint the children in their care.

Later on Christmas day, Missy and Craig had called Janice Grant, and asked if they could stop by and bring gifts to the older sisters. Missy still had no idea why she was involved with these precious little girls, but ever since she had seen them at the church fundraiser she had made a point to stop in once or twice to see them. Missy felt like perhaps God was keeping her in touch with these little ones, but for what reason? She did not know. Sandra was always a little standoffish with Missy, but Tabbatha and Roseanne always welcomed her with open arms.

Missy would read the younger girls stories, or play games with them for an hour, and invariably the younger two girls would ask her why she had a funny leg, and was she married, and did she want any babies? Missy would answer as best she could to keep them satisfied and herself from tearing up. She always made a point to give Sandra a hug, but anything more, and Sandra would push her away and show no interest in Missy.

Missy would always leave the foster home asking herself, why? Why would such beautiful little girls have to be in this situation? She wished at times that she was married and in a financial state to adopt these children, but she knew that would never or could never happen.

Three days after Christmas, the Grants, as planned, flew to California taking the four homeless children to Disneyland. The Grants knew that Sandra would be the only one to ever truly remember the trip, as the other three sisters were entirely too young, but they wanted the girls to have one of the best holidays of their young lives—a holiday to remember. It was an exhausting trip for the older foster couple, but very worthwhile. A lot of photos were taken, and memories made. Janice Grant had no way of knowing that an evil adopted mother would destroy all of those photos one day.

Both foster mothers were beginning to have doubts that the four sisters in their individual homes would ever have an adoptive home. Nellie and Janice had both spoken, on more than one occasion with Betty Mae, and Betty Mae assured them that she was trying very hard to find one adoptive home for all four sisters, but it was turning into a very difficult and time consuming endeavor. She was afraid that, within a few weeks, if a family was not found, the four sisters would be placed at the Queen of Heaven Orphanage—she would have no choice.

So, as feared, in January, the social services department (and Betty Mae), made the decision to take the four sisters, Sandra, Tabbatha, Roseanne and baby Rebecca out of foster care and place them all together at the Queen of Heaven Orphanage. Betty

Mae called Father Ramsey, who set up an appointment with the social worker, the foster parents and all four sisters to meet with Mother Superior and her assistants at the Orphanage.

The Queen of Heaven Orphanage was built as a home for lost and homeless children, especially girls, in the early 1900's. Mother Cabrini, a well-known nun in Colorado, first started a retreat and camp for homeless children in the Colorado Mountains. (A monument in her honor still sits high a top a mountain range west of Dawson). Later on Mother Cabrini and her Order bought farmland in Dawson, which included a large farmhouse. The Order turned the farmhouse into wards, large bathrooms, showers and kitchen areas, and took in young girls ages two to fifteen. Within months, Mother Cabrini's orphanage was at capacity, and a few years later a larger four-story facility was built on the same property, which soon housed more than 180 young lives.

Walking into the orphanage, a person would have been amazed at rows and rows of metal beds, covered in stark white bed coverings and embroidered white pillowslips—hand made and donated by members of the Dawson Catholic Church women's groups. Alongside each bed stood a wooden straight back chair and a small two-drawer dresser. Younger children were housed in one ward, while older children were placed in another ward. There were several wards, all watched over by nuns trained to keep the children in perfect order. There was a bell that rang announcing bedtime, another bell rang announcing meals, with stern orders of "no talking" during meal times. The orphanage, although filled with love and tenderness, also was quite strict. No one bathed or showered without a covering, as there was absolutely no nakedness allowed anywhere or at any time. There would be a great price to pay if any young girl touched any part of her body or any other girl's body. Over the time period that the orphanage was in operation, it was estimated that over 20,000 girls passed through the Queen of Heaven Orphanage before it was sold and then torn down so the Colorado Department of Highways could build an interstate highway through Dawson.

The Queen of Heaven Order of Nuns ran the orphanage with the help of charitable donations from the community and the Catholic Charities of Dawson. The Catholic Charities, through donations and volunteerism supported the orphanage, and also fed and housed the homeless of Dawson, provided care for the elderly, provided assistance to victims of crime, and provided safety to children who were less fortunate. As a safety net for the helpless and broken children of Dawson, the Queen of Heaven Orphanage seemed to be the best place to put the four sisters.

For Sandra, there was an elementary school attached to the orphanage that she would definitely attend, and a preschool was available for Tabbatha and Roseanne. At first glance, the inside and outside of the orphanage looked to be a clean, sterile facility—perhaps too sterile—but Mother Cabrini wanted only the best for her young children. It seemed the best decision—Betty Mae, Father Ramsey, Mother Superior, her assistants, and the foster parents all agreed.

So it was, on a cold January day, and with a heavy heart, that the foster parents willingly handed over four small and broken souls to the care of the Queen of Heaven Orphanage. Betty Mae, Father Ramsey and two nuns from the orphanage came to Nellie Coopers home early in the morning. Nellie had packed up Rebecca's few material belongings, warmed a bottle of formula, just in case the baby got hungry or fussy on the trip to the orphanage, and after kissing her goodbye, tears streaming down Nell's face, she handed the tiny soul over to Betty Mae. The same event took place just thirty minutes later, when the same concerned people walked the steps up to the Grant home, knocked on the door, accepted a few material items that the three little girls called their own, and then the three sisters walked hand in hand out of the house to their new, hopefully, only temporary, home. There would be laughter and tears, loneliness and a lot of prayer and quiet time. The nuns would be kind, but there would be very few hugs or kisses showered on four little girls, and there wouldn't be for many, many more years to come.

CHAPTER THIRTY-FOUR

The Case May Just be Solved

At the Dawson Police Department, months after the murder of Mandy Sue Donnor, a frustrated Craig Olson, went over and over his files of the yet, unsolved murder of Mandy Sue. He had never been so frustrated by a cold case. However, a break was about to come his way.

On a cold February morning, an accident involving a gray pickup truck and a Chevrolet sports car was brought to Craig's attention by a rookie police officer. The driver's of both vehicles had only suffered minor injuries, but the license plate number on the pickup, matched three of the numbers on the pickup truck that had rear ended Missy Baker a few months prior. The rookie cop had done his homework.

Sitting back in his office chair, arms stretched over his head, he smiled at the silver-framed photo of Missy Baker on his desk, and said, "Sweetie, I think we just got a break". He immediately picked up his overcoat, threw it over his shoulder and headed down the stairs and out the door to the accident division, just a block away.

Craig was surprised to find out that the driver of the gray pickup was a policewoman—Janice Poltice, a three-year veteran of the department, with an impeccable record. She had been off duty and on her way to the grocery store when a teenager in a sports car had run a red light and broadsided her pickup just a few blocks from her home. Neither she nor the seventeen year old kid in the sports car had been injured, but when the police arrived on the scene, and the officer put the license plates on both cars into the cruiser's computer, the gray pickup truck's license number immediately flagged yellow—the first three letters and or numbers on the pickup truck was on the "watch" list for a previous hit and run accident.

As Janice watched her damaged pickup truck being towed away, and as she got into the back seat of the policeman's vehicle, she thought immediately of the OBA. Tyler Morris had specifically warned all OBA members that if they ever got into trouble of any kind, they were "on their own". There would be no one to assist them. Janice wondered how she would get out of this, and what kind of an excuse she could use for hitting Missy Baker's old green Buick, if and when they figured out she was driving the vehicle in question on the day of the hit and run. She had about a fifteen-minute ride to police headquarters to come up with a plan. Although the temperature outside was 33 degrees, Janice could feel the sweat running down the sides of her forehead. She thought about offering the officer a bribe, but he looked young, probably a new recruit out of the academy, and instantly she scrapped that idea: this rookie cop would bleed true blue, and most certainly would not take a bribe.

Craig checked in at the desk on the main floor of the police station's accident division, showed his badge, signed in and went directly to interrogation where Janice sat, looking so out of place. The cop on duty motioned for Janice to get up and follow him into a cold, dark room, where there was a table and two chairs.

"A detective Olson is here to see you, Poltice". He said, frowning. "You can sit with him over there at the table." Pointing to a metal table, bolted to the cement floor, Janice walked over, and sat down. Craig Olson waked in, introduced himself and sat down at the table across from her.

Janice Poltice was an attractive blond with a beautiful complexion. She was dressed in faded blue jeans, a blue CSU sweatshirt and white tennis shoes. Her hair was pulled back into a ponytail with a white ribbon. Craig could see that she was not uncomfortable, but was probably unaware, or in no way ready, for what lay ahead. He thought to himself. "She's in trouble. I wonder if she realizes it."

"Janice." Craig asked, looking down at a few papers in his hands. "Officer Janice Poltice? I understand you are a policewoman for the department. So sorry you are here, but I have a few questions. You know you have the right to have your police union representative here with you. Do you want your rep here, right now, before I ask you any thing further?"

Janice softly said that no, she had nothing to hide, had done nothing wrong, and he could ask her anything at all without her union representative being there.

Craig asked again if she was sure, and when she, somewhat agitated now said yes, she was sure, he began the questioning. He started by asking her about her career, where had she graduated from, did she have her own police cruiser, did she have a partner, did she walk a beat, anything at all to keep her calm and cooperative.

He then asked her about the day in question. Where was she on the day of the supposed hit and run in front of the station? Did she own the gray pickup truck? Could he see her license and registration? Had she been in any accidents prior to today? He continued. Did she know her pickup was in the police pound and would be completely gone over for any evidence that could prove or disprove that the pickup was involved in any kind of prior accidents? He then shared with Janice that there had been a witness to the hit and run incident, and that three of the license plate numbers on her pickup truck were a perfect match to the first three numbers and letters of her license plates.

Craig watched closely, but Janice showed no signs of nervousness or fear as she repeated once again that she had no idea of any hit and run incident.

After twenty more minutes of interrogation, Janice had answered all of Craig's questions, didn't seem to be afraid or worried at all, until Craig asked her one more question. Had she ever heard of the OBA, the Officers for a Better America organization?

Craig had taken a chance on asking her this question, but he remembered what Missy had said about seeing a woman at the Catholic Charities Fundraiser with her friend Jeremy Porter— the same Jeremy Porter who had been scribbling and dabbling the letters OBA at the Paradise restaurant. It was a long shot, but what did he have to lose? He wanted to solve the Mandy Sue Donnor case, and this woman just could be the missing link they needed to solve the crime. Plus, she fit the description of Jeremy's date to a T.

As soon as Craig mentioned the OBA, Janice began to squirm.

CHAPTER THIRTY-FIVE

Four Broken Souls Begin
Their Journey Into Hell

The nuns on the baby ward at the Queen of Heaven Orphanage were delighted when little Rebecca was delivered to their area. They quickly laid the year and a half old child in a crib next to another baby named Chrissie Jane. It was unusual, the sisters realized, that children under two years of age were taken in at the orphanage, but didn't question it. Sister Johanna brought in diapers, a bar of soap, a small washbasin, towels and washcloths and placed them on top of the small dresser next to the crib. She also placed a white bucket for soiled diapers next to the dresser. She then placed a white sticker with Rebecca's name on the front of one of the dresser drawers. In turn, Sister Beatrice went directly to the clothes closet which held all types of donated baby clothing, and found three or four outfits, shoes and stockings, and a frilly pink bonnet. She immediately brought them back to where Sister Johanna sat rocking a somewhat fussy Rebecca in an old fashioned, white rocker.

Even though Rebecca had only been with Nell Cooper a few months, she missed the only mother she had ever known, and currently was showing her displeasure with the entire change going on in her life. Just who were these women in black and white attire anyway?

Over the next two hours, the two loving nuns bathed their new charge, put her in new clothes, stockings and shoes, fed her a full bottle, and after rocking her to sleep laid her down in her metal, stark white covered crib. Sister Beatrice laid a soft white teddy bear next to the sleeping child, crossed herself with the sign of the cross, and then touched the baby's forehead with the same sign of the cross.

"Sleep well, little one." She said softly. "May Jesus and our Blessed Mother Mary, and all of the Saints bless and keep you."

On the second floor, in a much larger ward, Sister Margaret and Sister Eileen were getting Rebecca's older sisters settled in. Sandra asked more than once about Rebecca, but the nuns assured her that her baby sister was doing fine, and she could see her after the noon meal. Sandra seemed okay with the Sisters' promise.

Each child was given their own bed, dresser, chair, four solid colored dresses befitting little girls, shoes, long stockings, undergarments, a brush, comb, toothbrush and soap, a towel and a washcloth. After each sister had been given a bath and their hair had been washed, they were dressed in the colored dresses, with white pinafores over their dresses. The pinafores were white with large bows tied at the back. They were even given small bows to wear in their hair. Amazingly enough, when the girls were all dressed up in their matching outfits, no one, absolutely no one, would have thought they were homeless little girls, living in an orphanage. They were beautiful. As the two loving nuns looked them over, and took them on a tour of the facility, they also commented to each other that it would not take long for these children to be adopted.

When Father Ramsey returned to Mother Superior's office, the first thing they discussed was a possible adoptive family for the Holmgruff sisters.

"Do you think we have a chance of keeping all four girls together, Mother?" Father Ramsey asked. "It's what the older girl wants. I too believe that it would be in their best interest to keep them all together."

Mother Superior agreed, and as though she had planned it all along, commented that she should make a call immediately to the Livingstone's.

"Dr. and Mrs. Livingstone have been looking at adopting another child." She said smiling. "They were here just before the holidays, but Mrs. Livingstone wasn't interested at that particular time. I do feel that they would be willing to take all four girls. They have a large home, the means to care for the girls, and they are such wonderful people, and work so hard for Catholic Charities, this orphanage and the community. I really feel God needs us to give them a call, and set up a time to meet with them. What do you think, Father?"

Father Ramsey agreed whole-heartedly. He knew the Livingstone's well, and suggested that Mother Superior give them a call while he was still at the orphanage. So, it was done. Mother Superior made the call and shared her idea. Devorah, elated at a call from Mother Superior, agreed to speak with her husband as soon as he returned from the hospital later that evening, and she promised to call Mother Superior in the morning. When Devorah hung up the telephone, she swore under her breath, knowing that this would be exactly what her husband would want. She also realized that taking in an entire family of young children would be the best thing she could ever do to make sure her name would remain high on Dawson's high society pages. She smiled at the thought of the prestige this adoption would bring to her status in the community. She also made a mental note to call around and find another maid or nanny to help out in their home. She did not plan to take care of four more children. Katherine was more than she could handle as it was. Yes, she would give Bernard a large family, but she didn't plan to lift a finger to help.

CHAPTER THIRTY-SIX

One Step at a Time

Craig Olson gave Janice Poltice a break, allowing her to go to the ladies room (with a female officer), and took that time to call Missy. He needed to know a little more about Jeremy Porter, and what she had seen the night of the fundraiser. He called her number and hoped that she would pick up. He smiled when she answered on the second ring.

"Missy, it's Craig." He said chuckling. She would recognize his voice anytime. "'We may have a break in the hit and run incident. It's possible that break may lead to solving the Mandy Sue murder. I need a little more information. Oh, by the way, how's my favorite PI?"

Missy laughed, said she was fine, that she loved him, missed him, and then asked what was happening with the case.

He clued her in to what had happened so far, and then asked her for a description of the woman who had been with Jeremy Porter the night of the fundraiser? Had she ever seen her before? Had she spoken with Jeremy since then? Was there anything else she thought unusual or suspicious on the night of the fundraiser? Anything at all that might help him continue in his interrogation of Janice Poltice?

Missy said that the woman was blond, and chuckling now, said that she had very large bosoms. She then quickly asked Craig what his suspect was wearing. Anything sexy?

"It's freezing outside Missy. It's winter remember? She's in jeans and a heavy sweatshirt." But, smiling now, said, "Yes, she's, well, she might just be a little well endowed. However, I really didn't notice until just now when you reminded me!"

Missy laughed. Craig laughed harder, and then she told him that she thought the woman with Jeremy had been nervous.

She even spilled her drink on a man she was speaking with that night. She had thought nothing of it at the time, but the man she had spilled her drink on was none other than a prominent judge in Dawson.

"Christianson, or Christian. His name was something like that, Craig. He is one of the more popular judges in Dawson, and I wondered, first of all, how and why Jeremy ever got into the fundraiser on his salary, and why he was hob-knobbing with a judge. I don't think he had a serious girlfriend at the time. The woman, I never knew her name, seemed to be hanging all over Jeremy while they both talked with the judge. Might not be anything important, but it was a curiosity for me, since I know Jeremy quite well." She continued. "I guess all of it was, or just seemed out of perspective for me that night. Or, it could have been that I only had eyes for this awesome detective, and I was seeing things, or in this case didn't see enough!"

Once again, the two lovers laughed, and then Missy remembered something else.

"Craig, this may be really silly, but the dress the woman with Jeremy was wearing, was just like a dress I wore last year. Now, don't laugh. Promise me you won't laugh, but I had to have an evening dress for an event my parents invited me to, and well, I don't ever dress up, so I rented the dress." She said again. "Craig don't laugh! I could afford $25.00 for a rental dress, but I couldn't afford $150.00 or more to purchase one. Plus until I met you, I never went anywhere fancy enough to wear a nice evening dress!" So, she continued. "The dress that woman with Jeremy was wearing was a rental. I'll swear to it. I can tell you where she got it, and since this sweet little PI is bored today, I will head right over to Georgia's Rentals on Broadway and see if I can dig up some info for you. Okay?"

Craig thanked her for her information and insight, and said he had to get back to the interrogation. Missy agreed to touch base with him later on that night, and asked him what time he would be home for dinner? They agreed on 7:00pm.

When Detective Olson returned to the interrogation room, the first thing he asked Janice was if she would like some coffee. She said no, that she was fine. He also asked her again if she wanted her Police union representative contacted. This time, not surprising to Craig, she had said yes.

Craig knew right then and there that Officer Janice Poltice had something more to say. Was she hiding something? This interrogation was just beginning.

CHAPTER THIRTY-SEVEN

The Living Hell Begins

After three meetings in three weeks between the Livingstone's, Father Ramsey, Mother Superior and three of the four little girls living at the orphanage, the decision was made after one month, that Dr. and Mrs. Bernard Livingstone would take Sandra, Roseanne, Tabatha and baby Rebecca to live with them. It would all transpire on Valentines Day.

Sandra, the oldest sister was elated that a family would take all four of the girls. She and her beloved sisters would be a family again. Once and for all, Sandra felt that all her pleading and begging had paid off. She had kept her family together, and now a beautiful life was about to begin. The new parents had introduced the four girls to their big sister, Katherine, the new part time nanny, Claudia, as well as Miriam and Betsy, in their beautiful new home. Life could have not been any better.

On the first day in the Livingstone home, the four girls, their big sister, their new parents, and Devorah's parents had a lovely dinner of fried chicken, mashed potatoes and gravy, corn, salad, bread and butter, and ice cream and strawberries. There were large glasses of milk, and Devorah encouraged the girls to eat as much as they wanted, to drink at least two full glasses of milk—to help them all get stronger and to stay strong.

Sitting in the huge dining room, at the large table, with beautiful china, glassware, cloth napkins and excellent food, the girls didn't know how to act or how to show good manners. The only thing they had been taught about good manners was what they had learned at Janice and Chet's home. On more than one occasion, Devorah reminded the girls, especially Sandra, about good manners and how expensive the china was, and that they should be oh so thankful that they were now in a good family, and not living in an orphanage.

The four girls shared one bedroom. Katherine had her own room, and made it very clear early on that no one was allowed in her room unless invited. The good doctor and his wife, although supposedly sleeping in the same bed, also had separate rooms or offices—one for the doctor and a second for Devorah. Both offices also had a bed. The Livingstone's knew they would have to move to a bigger home with more bedrooms soon. It was surprising to some that the orphanage had allowed the doctor and his wife to take on four more children without extra bedrooms, but they were the Livingstone's after all, and no one dared question the courts decision. The girls were placed. Dawson County or Social Services were no longer responsible for these little girls and everyone involved was happy—or so it seemed at the time.

Devorah Livingstone spent a lot of time with baby Rebecca, now being called Becky. Perhaps it was because Becky was just that—a baby. She was cute and cuddly, and Devorah showed her the most attention—at least much more attention than she showed the other three girls. Devorah did not care for Sandra from the very beginning. Perhaps it was because now Katherine had competition for Devorah's affection, which made no sense at all because to be honest, Devorah did not care for Katherine any more than she cared for any other child. She and the other four girls were only in her home so she could please her husband, and keep up her social status in Dawson.

Devorah was upset with three-year-old Tabbatha from day one. When the Livingstone's took the four girls into their home, Tabbatha had a rash or skin infection. Whether it was fear from her rash being infectious, or if it made Devorah feel dirty, (no one ever knew), she just stayed away from Tabbatha. She never showed her any affection of any kind, and was at most times very unkind to the little girl. Doctor Livingstone, you would have thought, could have taken the young girl to a doctor if he could not have diagnosed or treated her skin disorder himself, but that never happened. He more or less ignored the child's illness, and it was a "given" that whatever his wife wanted, his wife got.

Devorah just locked Tabbatha in her room and stayed completely away from her until she was cured of the skin disorder.

The Livingstone family lived in their original home for the next year, and it was during this first year that tragic incidents began, one after another. Devorah Livingstone never missed a community meeting, never turned down the chairmanship request of any large gala or ball and spent numerous hours at the Dawson Country Club dining and dancing with her husband, or attending luncheons with her well-to-do friends. What Devorah Livingstone did NOT do was ever love or care for the four adopted children in her charge. What she did do was torture, demean, belittle and kill—with all of it being ignored or covered up by those in authority—those who at any time could have supported these children or reported their abuse, and at the least helped save four little broken souls from a life of pure hell and in Tabbatha's case—death. But they didn't.

CHAPTER THIRTY-EIGHT

Janice Poltice Goes Under Cover

After only one more hour of interrogation, with the police union representative present, Janice Poltice, began to talk. The talk of OBA had shaken her to the very core. She knew that unless she cooperated with the police, and detective Olson, she was going to lose her job on the force and have a record, if not jail time. She also knew that no one from the OBA would be there to assist her. She also thought of her aging mother and father, and what a hearing, or court trial, or heaven help her, a prison sentence would do to them. What had started out as a friendly date with Jeremy Porter, and an undercover gig to try and get close to a dirty court judge, had now gotten her in deep trouble, and she knew it. The hit and run incident was a minor charge, but being a part of the OBA would put her behind bars for a very long time.

Janice, after sitting alone for a few minutes when the detective had left the room, decided to cooperate. Craig first asked her about the hit and run. Who had ordered the hit? Janice told him that the OBA had just wanted to put a scare into a woman and had Janice follow the woman in the green Buick for a few days. Then they asked Janice to bump her car, flatten a tire, do something minor. If the woman who walked with a crutch filed charges, or worse, kept delving into the Donnor murder, they would put a scare into her again. However, what they were looking for didn't happen. The woman did nothing more, and Janice wouldn't have to scare her again. Evidently, the woman was not a concern any longer because Janice had not been asked to do anything further.

"If she only knew." Craig thought, smiling. "If Officer Poltice only knew Missy Baker!"

Craig Olson was relieved that Officer Poltice was cooperating. It did tell him however, that Missy had been seen the day of Mandy Sue Donnor's murder, and that DID concern him.

Moving forward, Craig informed Janice that her involvement with the OBA was possibly much more than just the hit and run, which was a misdemeanor. She may very well be part of an unsolved murder case in Dawson, Janice realized that there was no way she was going to get out of the hit and run charge. It was possible that she would have to take the wrap for being involved in a murder, or worse of all, being a member of the OBA, unless she cooperated.

"I will tell you anything you want to know, Detective." She said shyly. "I know nothing about a murder, but I do know about the OBA, because I joined their organization a year ago. I only know Jeremy Porter from the night I was asked to be his companion at the Catholic Charities fundraiser, and to try and get close to Judge Christianson. I do not know why or who Judge Christianson is, except that he is a high ranked court judge in Dawson, and the OBA is out to get him. I also do not know what Jeremy Porter does for the OBA; I just know that he is also a member. One thing though, I've never seen Jeremy at an OBA meeting. I do believe the OBA has him dong undercover surveillance only." She continued, her eyes tearing up. "I needed extra money, and the invitation to join the OBA sounded so good to me. They promised that all of us on the police force could help clear the city of dirty politicians, prostitution and more, and be there for those in high places if they needed a lending hand. I really wanted to help in any way I could. You and I both know, detective that our police force cannot keep up with all of the garbage living in our beautiful city. I just wanted to help more, and make some extra money on the side. I'm just so, so sorry."

Craig acknowledged her concerns, but also reminded her that she had promised to "protect and to serve", and she had gone way beyond that promise.

"Janice". He said, now getting into her face across the metal table. "I am going to make you an offer. First of all, I want you to admit that you hit a woman in her car, and then left the scene at the front of the police station on the date aforementioned. I then want you to write out why you hit the woman's car. Tell me who ordered you to hit her car and if you know why you were asked to hit her car, write that down as well. Then, with approval from the head of my department, I want you to continue to be an OBA member, act like nothing ever happened here today, and I want you to go undercover—undercover for the Dawson Police Department, into the OBA. You know you have one choice here don't you?"

Looking at her union rep, she said. "I'm not sure I can do that, Detective." She replied. "I know someone will tell Mr. Morris, head of the OBA, that I've been here all day, and I will be interrogated at the OBA next time too. How am I supposed to handle all of that? I'm not sure I can do it. I'm afraid for my life now. What if the OBA comes after me? My life right now isn't worth anything if they know I squealed on them."

Craig assured her that he would protect her, put her with another cop from the department. Put him or her undercover in the OBA as well, but Janice would have to cooperate to the fullest.

"I think you can help us bring down not only the riff-raff in Dawson, but the OBA itself." Craig said. "I also promise that when this is all over, we can put you in protective custody. Your life, as you now know it, will be over, but you could be a hero too. Think it over, and I'll be back in a few minutes."

With that Craig got up, shook hands with the union representative, and left the interrogation room. As he shut the door, he leaned up against the hallway wall, and let out a sigh of relief. Closing the Donnor case was close to becoming a reality. He couldn't wait to tell Missy. He pulled out a pen and pad, and wrote down the name, Mr. Morris. He wondered if Janice Poltice knew that she had slipped up. Officer Poltice had already given the police department a lead—a lead into the OBA.

CHAPTER THIRTY-NINE

The Killing of the Innocent

A few months after the four children moved in with and were adopted by Bernard and Devorah Livingstone, their small lives began to fall apart. Devorah spent many of her days, (at least part of the days), with the five children she had adopted, while her husband spent all day in his private practice, and staying late most evenings at the Rocky Mountain Regional Hospital. When Devorah had to leave home for her social gatherings, either the secretary or the nanny watched after the girls. When she was home with the children, with the exception of Katherine, whom she seemed to treat with kindness, she at first tolerated the four. As time went by, she could no longer even tolerate them. Her body, mind and soul began to seethe with rage, not even rage, more like hatred—horrific hatred. For no reason at all, she would roughly remove Becky out of her high chair—her meal only half eaten— sit down on a chair, put Becky over her lap and just wail on her little buttocks with her wide open hands. Becky would cry and cry, placing her baby hands on her little bottom, crying ouchie, ouchie. When Sandra would try to calm the baby girl, Devorah would slap Sandra across the face, and scream at her to leave the room. After each and every incident, Devorah, would scream at Sandra asking. "AND WHAT DO YOU WANT TO SAY TO ME?" Sandra would say meekly, "Yes ma'am". The four sisters were instructed to never call Devorah mama or mother, but only "ma'am".

If Bernard Livingstone knew what was happening in his supposedly loving home, he never said a word, or shared his feelings with anyone. In the beginning, he showed a little love and attention to the four girls, but mostly he showed attention to Katherine whom they had adopted as a baby. He never asked his wife "why" she treated the children as she did. He just turned his back on all of the suffering—suffering that would soon end in a death, no a murder, a murder that would be swept under the carpet, as it were, by a dirty cop, a Catholic priest and an organization that "did not want to become involved, unless it meant money in their pockets."

On numerous occasions Sandra would ask her father for help or tell him what Devorah was doing to all four of the sisters, and to please, please help them. His only reply would always be the same. "Your mother is always right. You need to obey your mother."

The day that the Holmgruff sisters were brought into the Livingstone household, Dr. Livingstone stopped living the oath of his profession—the Hippocratic oath—to uphold specific ethical standards (One being: FIRST DO NO HARM!) Because of his lack of upholding this oath, one small child would die, and three small girls lives would be broken—broken souls forever.

CHAPTER FOURTY

A Week in the Life of the OBA

Jeremy Porter received a call on his burner telephone, from Tyler Morris at 9:30am—the morning after Officer Poltice's minor fender bender.

"Jeremy." It's Morris. "I need to let you know that Officer Poltice was brought into the Dawson Police Station. She was involved in a minor vehicle accident. Our mole has informed me that she was brought in because her license plate came up as a "caution" on the police computer, evidently due to the hit and run incident I suggested a few months back. She asked for her union rep and has been charged with a misdemeanor. She was interrogated for over three hours, and is now out on her own. As far as I know, she held up as a true, reliable OBA member, claiming innocence to the hit and run order placed on the handicapped woman, who by the way, turns out to be a Private Investigator in Dawson by the name of Missy Baker."

Morris continued. "I don't think we've seen or heard the end to this interrogation, because, **no one** gets interrogated for three hours for a misdemeanor. We have to use caution here, so, here's my plan. I want you to ask Poltice out on a "real" date soon, and until you get all of the information out of her that we need, to clear her and keep her as a member of the OBA, I want you to wine and dine her. Make her feel like you really care about her, while getting all the information out of her that we need. Poltice could put the OBA into a rather precarious position if she was to confess, Porter, and that can't happen. If she won't cooperate, well, you know what you'll have to do. The OBA Porter. It's all about the OBA."

As the telephone call continued, Morris also reminded Porter that it was time to put some real heat on Olivia's house of prostitution, find out when the good judge would be visiting again, and get more involved with the goings on in the basement of the ranch house.

"We're getting really close to proving that Judge Christianson is the head of the sex trafficking ring supposedly operating from the ranch. Officer Jenkins brought us some more information detrimental to our bringing down that rotten character and when we bring him down, we'll as always, give the Dawson cops and the CBI a heads up, and then the credit, but we're going to do all of the work first. That's who we are, Porter. We don't care how we bring down the garbage, just that we get the job done. The police in Dawson cannot get it done on their own."

Jeremy hung up the telephone after promising Tyler Morris that he was "on it". He thought of Missy in passing. That was all. This was business. She should never have stuck her nose into the OBA's business.

He would go to the ranch tomorrow evening, visit with the sweet, eighteen year old Angie once again, and see if he could get himself invited into the basement. He had been in the basement of the ranch twice now, had not been seen or been caught, and had enough information on his tape recorder and his telephone camera to set in operation a massive take down. He had found out that there were at least seven prostitutes at Olivia's, all eighteen years of age or younger, and that more than thirty young women ages twelve to twenty, brought in from Mexico and South America had been sold to the highest bidders. There were men or organizations throughout the western United States buying and selling these poor girls.

What Jeremy didn't know yet, was who was bringing in the girls, at what times, and who besides the good judge was involved. He hoped to find out soon enough. He did know that Olivia had "purchased" one of the girls for her own use at the ranch, and that bothered Jeremy. Previously, all of Olivia's girls had been true run-away teenagers, and Olivia had given them housing, food, clothing, along with training for providing men pleasure, both at the ranch, and then, when they were older, making a living on their own—out on the streets. Jeremy had seen the new girl briefly while spying on the goings on in the basement, and now he had seen the same young girl entertaining a dark-haired, tall, athletic looking gentleman.

The whole idea of buying a girl for sex, well, it made Jeremy sick to his stomach. Olivia and the Judge, and whoever else was involved in buying and selling young girls needed to be put away for a long, long time.

Bryce Jenkins counted out the twenty, one hundred dollar bills in his pocket, and smiled as he thought of the good week he had enjoyed at someone else's expense. There was a politician he'd gotten out of a DUI by having the ticket "disappear" on the day of court and the chairman of the local hospital who had been excused from a possible rape charge—the charge suddenly dropped when the accuser, amazing as it seemed, had changed her mind. The really high payoff came when he managed to get a sharp and very handsome assistant principal at the local high school off the hook for being intimate with a sweet, sexy, red-headed senior. It was amazing to Bryce how much his "clients" paid him, and how much the OBA got paid for keeping people in high places out of trouble and out of the lime light.

Jenkins wasn't too sure that the last pay-off was going to hold water, however. The sweet, sexy seventeen-year-old senior was just that, a seventeen year old, and Bryce wasn't sure the kid would keep her trap shut. Her parents on the other hand were happy to keep their mouths shut when the OBA (unknown to them), gave them a tidy sum of money to do so. They had assured Jenkins that they would handle their daughter. It was always amazing to Bryce how often money could cover all sins—including his own. "Money really does talk." He thought to himself.

Bryce counted the bills once again, and as he always did, wondered just how long this life style would last. Surely, one of these days, someone would squeal, would spill the beans, or would ask for more money—blackmail money—to keep their mouths shut. Until then, he was enjoying working for the cops and for the OBA, and he was really enjoying watching his bank account grow.

For now, however, the pressure was on him to once and for all get the "goods" on Judge Christianson, and with the help of another OBA member, still in disguise and known to Jenkins only as Shorty, (not Porter), they just might close that deal soon. The OBA was putting the pressure on to do something, and to do it now.

Since the murder of Mandy Sue Donnor, Jenkins enjoyed the sexual encounters with the prostitutes at Olivia's ranch, but he no longer got "involved" with any of the young women like he had with Mandy. He had a job, and a job it was—bring down the garbage that kept infiltrating Dawson. Plus, what he was not getting at home, he was getting at Olivia's. Life as he knew it, was good.

CHAPTER FOURTY-ONE

The Darkness Begins

As the months went by, so did the abuse of four young girls in the Livingstone home. On one occasion, Becky had caught a horrible, congestive cold, and in order to keep it away from everyone living in the Livingstone household, Devorah had put Becky into the dark, cold dreary basement. There was no heat in the unfinished portion of the basement where she literally threw Becky on the couch, with only a pillow and thin blanket to keep her warm and comfortable. While laying on the couch, and although there was a television, Becky looked at the blank television screen and saw what looked to be the devil, coming out from behind the television. She saw horns, a red face, but not knowing what he possibly could or might have to do with her and her siblings in the future. In horror, she just stared at the freakish character, not knowing that this was going to be what her future held—paralyzing fear—before the face disappeared.

The other little girls while watching television in the living room dared not talk to their father about what their "ma'am" was doing and had no idea what their little sister was going through in the basement. Even Devorah's secretary and housekeeper knew to keep their mouths shut if they wanted to keep their jobs.

After hours in the cold, dark basement, Devorah finally allowed Becky to come back to the main floor and Devorah acted like nothing had ever happened.

Devorah had begun to force feed all of the girls, all except Katherine. On most days the girls were fed a small, decent breakfast, but at noon time when Becky would come in for lunch, Devorah would make her eat two to three peanut butter sandwiches—just peanut butter and bread, no butter, no jelly or honey. The other girls were at a different school, where they were served lunch, but Devorah would force-feed them when they returned home from school. She would pour them each one glass of milk AFTER they had eaten the sandwiches. Then she would insist that they drink a second glass or even a third glass of milk, and if they did not eat the sandwiches and drink the milk, she would literally force-feed them. The young girls would choke on the sticky substance, cry, and then get slapped if they didn't follow her every demand. Then, the two older girls were ordered to run up and down the stairs to the basement as well as the second floor of their home. She would continue this ritual until they would cry from fatigue, upset stomachs or headaches, or until they vomited up everything Devorah had forced them to eat. She would call them horrible names and tell them how fortunate they were to have her as their mother, before demeaning or hitting them again.

When Bernard came home from the hospital Devorah would tell them what awful girls they were, that they were "mental" and he should make appointments for all four girls to see a shrink, because they were all crazy, dum-dum, stupid girls. Bernard did nothing. If he had only known—the worse was yet to come.

CHAPTER FOURTY-TWO

The Death of an Angel

It was during the first year with the Livingstone's, in fact it was less than a year after the four sister's adoption had been finalized that a terrible tragedy occurred. Tabbatha, four and a half years old at the time, after being hit several times that day, and because of it, or in spite of the beatings, had wet herself. Devorah ordered her to go into the bathroom, run the bathwater and wash herself. A child as young as Tabbatha had no idea of how to regulate a cold and hot water faucet, and after running the "hot" water only, she took off her clothing, and stepped into the boiling hot bath. As she did, she screamed a most heart-wrenching scream, and then fell onto the edge of the bathtub, severely hitting her head. Hearing the screams, Sandra ran into the bathroom, saw her sister in the tub of scalding hot water, yelled for Devorah, and before Devorah came, Sandra had pulled Tabbatha out of the tub and laid her on the bathroom floor. When Devorah walked into the bathroom she of course accused Sandra of hurting her sister, of causing the accident, and screamed for her to "get out of the way". Devorah took the screaming child into the dining room, sat her down hard onto the same soiled chair, and before calling Bernard, told Tabbatha to sit still and to not move.

It was as if Devorah's mind had completely left her body. Her face was bright red, and shaking her finger directly at Tabbatha, told the child that if she wet the chair and herself again, she would get another beating.

Bernard came home shortly after his wife's hysterical telephone call. He did not call 911. He did not take the child to the emergency room. Instead, he wrapped Tabbatha's burned hips and legs in white gauze, checked the bump on her head, and told her to remain seated, as her mother had requested. During this time Tabbatha wet herself again. Noticing the urine dripping down the side of her Oak dining room chair, Devorah screamed obscenities at the child, and then slapped her hard across the face again. Tabbatha screamed, her little arms and hands stretched out, begging for help from her big sister, Sandra.

The three sisters watched their mother torturing one of their sisters in total silence, knowing, that if they made a move, they would be beaten next. Sandra looked at Bernard, pleading with her eyes for him to take control.

"Get this stupid child out of my sight!" Devorah screamed at her husband.

He gently picked Tabbatha up from the soiled chair and carried her semi-conscious to her bedroom.

Dr. Bernard Livingstone placed the very sick child on the bed. He never checked her vital signs, never checked her burns and did not stay with her to console her or to keep her awake in case of a concussion. A child this young, with severe burns and a possible concussion should have been hospitalized immediately after the incident. She was not shown any medical or personal attention and little Tabbatha died during the night, less than one year after being adopted by supposedly loving and caring parents. All alone, this four and a half year old broken soul died—yes, all alone.

Devorah, who would have won an OSCAR for her performance after Tabbatha's death, was supposedly beside herself. She sobbed and sobbed over Tabbaths's little burned and broken body. Bernard called Devorah's parents the social worker and then called Father Ramsey. The father came over immediately to give the child last rites, and console the Livingstone's. While Bernard was trying very hard to control his wife's sobbing and seeming heart break, Sandra walked quietly up to Father Ramsey, telling him through tears, that Tabbatha should not have died, that Mrs. Livingstone hurt her, that Mrs. Livingstone hurt all of the sisters all of the time, and please,

please, would he help them. Father Ramsey told Sandra that there was absolutely "no way" that Devorah would ever, ever hurt any of her children, and Sandra had better ask God to forgive her for telling such horrible lies.

"I will pray for you, you sinful child." He said to the grief stricken sister. "Now, go to your room, get on your knees and pray to the Blessed Virgin Mary and to God the Almighty for forgiveness!"

But, deep down inside, Father Ramsey knew that something was not right in the Livingstone home. He was not the only one, Devorah's parents, and later the social worker all suspected that Tabbatha's death was not an accident. But, once again, no one spoke up.

After Dr. Livingstone had calmed Devorah down, given her a mild sedative and spoken with Father Ramsey, he finally called 911. Having a direct, (not sure it was legal), line in his patrol car hooked into the Dawson 911 dispatcher, Bryce Jenkins and his partner, (also OBA), heard and accepted the call to go to the Livingstone's address. Upon arrival, Bernard invited the officers to come in, and showed them the little girl's body, and then walked them through the bathroom where the accident had taken place. Bernard told then everything he knew; the accidental hot water faucet being turned on by his daughter, that she had probably fallen and may have hit her head in the fall, and that "no" his wife, Devorah, was not able to speak with them at this time.

Officer Jenkins assured the prominent doctor that he would write up the report, and after the Coroner arrived, would speak with the Coroner and they would all agree that his daughter's death was "accidental". He assured Bernard that the Coroner would go along with the findings as well. There would be, upon Bernard's request, no autopsy. Jenkins would see to it.

After Tabbatha's little body, covered in an ugly green, medical cloth, was taken out on a long stretcher to the Coroner's black car, Bryce called the police dispatcher. He made it very clear that he and his partner were on their way back to the station and made sure that no other police officers went to the scene.

"We have everything under control." He assured the dispatcher. "I'll sign all of the proper paper work needed for this accident." The dispatcher agreed.

Two hours later, on the way out to their police cruiser, Bryce Jenkins counted out five, crisp, five hundred dollar bills, that Dr. Livingstone had given him. Bryce, smiling, gave his partner two of the bills, and placed the three remaining bills in his pants pocket. Upon entering his cruiser, he smiled, but after placing his key into the ignition, the smile turned to a frown—that poor, poor little girl, he thought. She should have never died. I'm positive that Dr. Livingstone knows more than he's telling.

With that thought still on his mind, he drove out into the cold night, thinking it was not his problem.

CHAPTER FORTY-THREE

The Dress

It had been a very long day, and Craig Olson was never more relieved than when he entered the apartment he and Missy shared. He kicked off his shoes and slumped down into his big blue, lazy-boy chair. It was 6:30pm. He had been at the office since 5:30 am.

From the kitchen, Missy heard him come in. After wiping her hands on a white, flowered dishtowel, she poured two glasses of Chardonnay, walked into their living room and handed Craig one of the goblets. She sat down on the coffee table in front of his chair.

"Bad day, huh sweetie?" She said sweetly.

"Good and bad day, Missy." Craig said, sitting up straighter now, and taking her hand in his. "But, I'm fine now, here, with you. Do you know how much I love you, Missy Baker?"

Missy leaned over, kissed him softly, then harder, and said. "I'm sorry, Craig. I know this Donnor case has got you buffaloed, and I'm so, so sorry, but it sounds to me like you have a good lead in the Poltice woman, and together, you and I, well, we're going to close this case once and for all." She continued. "I'll finish preparing dinner—It's your favorite—grilled avocado salmon, and then let's talk. I went to Georgia's Rental today, and I got some good information too. You rest, drink your wine, and I'll call you when dinner is ready."

Missy watched Craig, the love of her life, as she walked back into the kitchen. Within two minutes, Craig had taken two or three sips of his Chardonnay, set the goblet down on the coffee table, and had fallen fast asleep. Dinner would have to wait.

Missy had driven to the dress rental shop right after Craig had called her about Officer Poltice. The proprietor, Jackie

LaVon, at the dress shop had been very cooperative. She had pulled out her receipts from the day in question and found one signed by Janice Poltice. Missy had been right on. The sleek, white evening dress, the same exact one Missy had rented a few months earlier, had been rented for one night, had been returned with a large stain on it, most likely from liquor. Ms Poltice had paid the extra fee to have the dress dry-cleaned but the stain had not been completely removed. She now had it on the "for sale" rack. Missy had asked to see the dress. After checking her back racks of clothing, the proprietor had found the dress and brought it to the front desk.

Looking over the dress, Missy had asked Ms. LaVon more about Ms. Poltice. What did she look like, had she said why she needed the dress? Did she mention the event she was going to? Was there a man with her?

"The customer came in at the last minute." Ms. LaVon remembered. "I remember her because she was in uniform, and I asked her was she a police officer? I asked her, as I sometimes do, as to what was the occasion she needed the dress for. You know, just small talk. The customer said, excitedly, that she was going to a fundraiser and chuckling had said she couldn't look like a cop at the event."

Missy asked Ms. LaVon if she could put the dress away for a day, and not put it back on the for sale rack, because it might be needed as evidence in a case. She would check with the detective in charge and get back to her immediately. Ms. LaVon agreed, and Missy thanked her for her time, and left the store—grinning.

"I think there is more to Officer Poltice than just being a Dawson cop." Missy thought aloud. She couldn't wait to tell Craig.

Just as Missy was waking Craig up from his pre-dinner nap, her cell phone rang.

'Hello." Missy said sweetly.

"Missy. Hi, it's Betty Mae from Social Services. I hope I'm not interrupting anything."

Missy assured her that the timing was fine, that she was just preparing the evening meal. Missy asked her politely what was on her mind?

"I hate to be the bearer of bad news, Missy." She said, her voice breaking. "But one of the Livingstone's adopted children died. Little Tabbatha. I wanted you to know about it. I knew, from speaking with Nell and Janice that you had been to see the sisters on several occasions. I am so sorry to have to tell you this."

Missy, visibly shaken, asked a few more questions about Tabbatha. What was the cause of her death? When did she die? Missy also asked Betty Mae if there was anything she could do?

Betty Mae said she had very little information. There was a funeral service scheduled, and she gave Missy the time and place. Betty Mae then thanked Missy for her concern for the little girls and for showing them attention, when she really hadn't needed to.

"I really don't know just exactly why I got involved with the girls." Missy told Betty Mae in a soft-spoken voice. "Jeanine at Human Services asked me to check on them, and honestly, I'm not sure why Jeanine asked me to get involved. Perhaps I will know some day, but for now, I just want to know if there is anything I can do to help. Is there anything at all I can do?" She asked Betty Mae again.

There was really nothing anyone could do. Missy thought about it only for one second before telling herself that she would go to the services, and being a PI might check into the little girl's death. Here again, no one asked Missy, Private Investigator, to get involved. She wanted to check into the little girl's death further for her own curiosity sake.

Missy woke Craig up for dinner and told him about Betty Mae's telephone call. Now it seemed, the story on the little white dress and the information she had collected from the dress rental company had little bearing at tonight's dinner table conversation. The tragedy of little Tabbatha Holmgruff Livingstone was all she could think about. Craig understood completely.

CHAPTER FORTY-FOUR

A Child is laid to Rest

There was absolutely no parking space available in the Church of Christ of the Ressurection's large parking area on the day of little Tabbatha's funeral. Missy, after hearing the news from Betty Mae, and also from Janice Grant, had thumbed through the last two days of the Dawson news as this type of tragedy traveled fast through the Dawson community, especially through the community of high society groups to which Devorah and Bernard Livingstone were a great part of. But, surprising, the child's death had not made the newspapers, except for in the obituaries.

Missy drove two or three blocks around the church before she finally found an empty parking space on Grape Street. She locked up her car, and walked hurriedly to the church on her one crutch.

As Missy entered the church, she looked for a seat and found one close to the front of the sanctuary. There were approximately thirty large bouquets of flowers surrounding the small, white casket containing the body of little Tabbatha Livingstone. The casket was open, and Tabbatha had been dressed in a pretty yellow and white dress, trimmed with yellow daisies. Her little hands were crossed at her chest, and in one hand she held a small silver cross. She looked like an angel.

In the front pews of the beautiful, historic church, Tabbatha's parents, Devorah and Bernard, daughter Katherine, Devorah's parents, John and Elisa Dawkins, several of Devorah's cousins, aunts and uncles and several close friends sat together, all trying to comfort one another. Behind them, in the third and fourth rows from the front, sat Tabbatha's three sisters. Missy did not recognize the two women who were sitting with the three little girls, but there were several nuns, as well as Nell and Jim Cooper, and the Grants sitting with them. How strange, Missy thought to herself, that the three sisters were not sitting with their adoptive parents and adoptive sister. Missy also thought that the three little sisters looked so sad and lonely.

As the service began, Father Ramsey and two assistant priests walked solemnly down the isle together towards the altar where the small child lay—under the beautiful, and massive sculpture of the Blessed Virgin Mary. There were four altar boys, singers, the harpist from Devorah's gala dinner party and two men who read the scriptures. Father Ramsey read more scripture, there was a befitting homily, and throughout the entire service, Devorah sobbed, sometimes screamed out as though she were in severe pain. On more than one occasion, Devorah called out little Tabbatha's name. It was all such a farce. Those seated or in the "standing room only" service sobbed along with Devorah. How awful, they all were thinking, for a mother to lose her child.

There were doctors and nurses, presumably from the Rocky Mountain Hospital where Dr. Livingstone had one of his offices. Also in attendance, were several nuns and staff workers from the Queen of Heaven Orphanage, and employees from Human Services and Social Services. Also in attendance were numerous members of the Dawson Country Club, and other charitable organizations that benefited from Devorah's lavish and profitable galas and fundraisers. There were, Missy noticed, also a few police officers in attendance.

'Strange." She thought. "As the officers in charge of the funeral procession going to the cemetery later on would not have been inside the church for the service. They would have waited outside in their cruisers or by their motorcycles."

"Perhaps." She thought. "They are friends of the family. Or," she thought, and then scolded herself for even thinking it. "Possibly these were officers who had helped out with the supposed "accidental death" of little Tabbatha."

"Oh stop it", Missy told herself. "That is ridiculous. Dr. Livingstone is a rock in this community, or so I understand, and so is his wife." She couldn't quite rid her mind, however, of the thought of "bad cops", "pay offs," "Mandy's murder", "a child's death" and more illegal activities supposedly going on in the city of Dawson.

"Whoa, Missy." She said to herself. "You're mind's not where it should be right now. Get it together. Remember, why you're here."

After a very long funeral mass, the service ended. The small white casket's lid was gently closed. Holy water was sprinkled around the casket, and the pallbearers, with the three priests walking beside it, rolled it out of the sanctuary, out the double doors, and into the black hearse.

Missy stood and watched as the three little sisters—their hearts breaking—Sandra holding Father Ramsey's hand—as they got into a separate car away from their adoptive parents and adopted sister Katherine, and headed to the cemetery. Missy wanted so badly to go up to each little girl and give her each a hug—but she knew this was neither the time nor the place. She promised herself, however, that she would check on the girls and soon. She would also check the guest list. Just who were the police officers at the funeral service and why were they there? As a Private Investigator, she would have no problem getting answers to her curiosities.

CHAPTER FORTY-FIVE

Officer Poltice goes Under Cover

Janice Poltice had no choice but to do as the Dawson Police detectives, including Craig Olson, had requested, no demanded of her. She would either be brought up on vehicular hit and run and leaving the scene charges, be on probation, or, and worst of all, lose her police woman status. So, she admitted to the crime and agreed to the terms.

For over six hours, sitting at the stone cold metal table, she told the detectives all about the OBA and willingly, agreed to become an undercover cop.

"Was being undercover, legally, better than being an illegal "bad cop", she asked herself? At this point in her life, she wasn't quite sure, however, she knew she had no choice. She had to think of her daughter, her parents, and most of all herself—the choice was not that difficult.

She was ordered to continue being a member of the OBA and act like nothing had happened. Detective Olson made sure that anyone with the OBA "breaking into" the Dawson police computers would see that Officer Poltice had indeed been in a hit and run, but was now on probation and doing community service. Her slate would most likely be wiped clean. At least that's what Detective Craig Olson hoped the OBA would believe.

Craig was confident that they were doing the right thing, putting Officer Poltice undercover. The detectives may have gotten a real break in the Mandy Sue Donnor murder case. All agreed that the OBA had somehow been involved. Janice Poltice would now lead them to the OBA, dirty cops, sex trafficking and prostitution rings in the area and most importantly, to Mandy Sue's killer. It was turning out to be a good day.

After being released, Janice Poltice returned to her home after picking up her handicapped daughter from daycare. She hugged the four-year-old tighter than she had ever hugged her before. As soon as she entered her front door her cell phone began to vibrate. She assisted her daughter to the couch in front of the television, pushed the "on" button on the remote, and answered her telephone.

"Hello, this is Janice." She said happily.

"Janice? It's Jeremy Porter. Have you got a minute to speak with me?"

Janice, somewhat surprised at the sound of his voice, assured him that she did have a few minutes. She grabbed a Coors Lite out of the refrigerator before sitting down on the couch, next to her daughter and began a conversation.

"How've you been?" Jeremy asked her.

She replied that she had been doing fine, had been busy, and did he know that she had been picked up by the cops on the hit and run, but had gotten out of the charges?

"I did hear that, Janice." He said softly, "How did you manage that?"

Janice, confidently, gave him a bogus story, and interestingly enough, Jeremy bought it. Luckily for Janice, the police reports, which Jeremy had access to, would verify her story.

"Would you like to go out to dinner some night, Janice?" Jeremy asked her. "Maybe dinner and a movie, say on Friday night?"

Janice, stalled him a little, told him she would have to first find a sitter, and that she wasn't sure two cops should be dating.

"We're in two separate Counties, Janice." Jeremy assured her. "Dating would not be a problem."

"I'm not sure, Jeremy." She continued. "I had a nice time with you at the fundraiser, but I'm not ready for a relationship, if that's what you have in mind."

Janice was doing exactly as Detective Olson had told her— play them, anyone in the OBA. Play them and don't seem to eager.

After another five minutes of asking, no almost begging her to go out with him, Janice gave in and said yes.

They agreed, that if she could get a sitter she would at least have dinner with him, but no movie, not this time. Jeremy seemed to be happy with her decision.

Janice wondered which detective had found out that Jeremy was an OBA member. She had never seen him at OBA meetings, at least not at the bar on Colorado Boulevard. She had only been fixed up with him to attend the Catholic Charities fundraiser—Tyler Morris' idea. There was something unbelievable about Judge Christianson, and she and Jeremy had been invited to the fundraiser to get close to the Judge and they had done just that. She had managed to get him to spill his drink all over her rented dress. In the process she had managed to keep his drink glass, by offering to get him a new drink. Finger prints on the glass would hopefully match the judge's finger prints found elsewhere—perhaps at the "ranch"—to prove he was involved in the basement sex trafficking investigation.

Jeremy Porter's plan was to get Janice Poltice to spill the beans, as it were. He had no idea that Officer Poltice was out to get him to do the same.

CHAPTER FOURTY-SIX

The Nightmare Continues

The funeral procession was more than forty cars deep on the way to the Mt. Olivet Catholic Cemetery. Beautifully manicured trees and bushes lined the roadway to Tabbatha's final resting place, and those driving the same roadways, pulled over in reverence as the entourage passed by. The motorcycle policemen blocked each major street on the way to the cemetery so that all forty cars could remain together in the procession. The entourage entered the golden gates of the beautiful cemetery located on the western side of Dawson in Jefferson County, and parked on both sides of the black paved roadway.

As the mourners gathered around the open grave, Father Ramsey read the proper scriptures for the Rites of Burial, and within a few minutes, the burial service for Tabbatha Livingstone was completed. Mourners returned to their vehicles. Bernard and Devorah stayed only a few minutes longer, each plucking a yellow rose from the large bouquet laying on top of the casket and along with Katherine walked to the long, black family vehicle. Roseanne, Sandra and Rebecca were already in another vehicle with their grandparents. The three little girls did not get a chance to pick a rose from their sister's casket.

Those interested and close to the family had been invited back to the Livingstone's beautiful home, where caterers would serve a light luncheon, and more condolences could be shared.

It was approximately 7:00pm when the final mourner left the Livingstone's home. Dr. Livingstone suggested that they order in pizza for their immediate family, as the four children had eaten very little of the catered luncheon. Devorah agreed.

Most of Devorah's crying and hysterical screaming had stopped once she returned to her home and to her prominent friends. However, once the pizza was delivered and the family sat at the kitchen table, Devorah's hysteria began once again. Sandra had made a small comment about her sister, Tabbatha, (how much she would miss her), and Devorah went ballistic!

"Do not mention that dum-dum, stupid girl's name in my house!" She said screaming at Sandra and slapping her across the face.

As Bernard immediately stood up to leave the table, suggesting to Katherine that she follow him, Devorah took a slice of pizza and literally stuffed it into poor Sandra's mouth, jamming it down her throat with her fingers.

Roseanne began crying, and even Becky, as young as she was, knew this was definitely wrong and began to wail.

"Shut up! All of you! Shut up!" She screamed at the sisters, as Sandra choked, coughed, and then threw up all over the kitchen table.

Devorah grabbed Sandra by her long, brown hair, dragged her from the kitchen chair, and slammed her head into a kitchen wall. Then as Sandra screamed for her to please stop, Devorah slammed her head against the wall again! Devorah let go of the poor, innocent, frightened child and Sandra fell to the floor, dazed, but still conscious.

Tabbatha was gone. Why Devorah had hated the child so adamantly was anyone's guess. Devorah, screaming now at anyone who might listen, said that she had always hated little Tabbatha, and again how glad she was that she was dead.

'I'm glad she's dead!" She screamed at Roseanne, at Becky, at Sandra, at the walls, at the floor, at the ceiling and turning around, her arms flailing in the air, even screamed at Bernard, as he re-entered the kitchen.

For Sandra Holmgruff Livingstone, with Tabbatha gone to Heaven, her hell on earth, her nightmare, was just beginning. Thankfully, Tabbatha's nightmare was over.

CHAPTER FOURTY-SEVEN

Tailing a Bad Cop

Missy had planned on joining Tabbatha's funeral procession to Mt. Olivet Catholic Cemetery. However, as she drove her old Buick around the block, and back to the front of the church to join the procession, she noticed that the police officers that had attended Tabbatha's funeral were not working the funeral procession, nor were they joining in on the procession. Missy watched one officer's cruiser as it turned left onto 44th Avenue going back into Dawson, and the other as it headed right, going the opposite direction. Missy pulled out of the procession line and onto 44th Avenue to follow the officer heading back, she presumed, to the Precinct.

Unknown, but luckily for Missy, Bryce Jenkins, one of the police officers in question, and one who had seen the "women with the crutch" previously at Mandy Sue Donnor's apartment, had not seen Missy at the funeral. If so, he would have wondered why this Private Investigator was at this small child's funeral. Did the woman know Dr. and Mrs. Livingstone? Did she realize that the good doctor was not always "so good"? Did she know about the OBA? And worse—did she know him?

Luckily for both Missy Baker and Bryce Jenkins, Bryce had not seen her at the service. He had gone to the service because he knew Dr. Livingstone, had gotten him out of several scrapes, and plus Bryce still had a conscience and wanted to express his sympathies to the Livingstone family on the death of their child.

Missy, driving steadily three car lengths behind Bryce Jenkins, presumed that he would head back to the Dawson Police Station, check in, get his new instructions, and then head out again into the city. That was evidently not in Bryce Jenkins' plans. He had headed west and entered the ramp onto Interstate

70, taking him to the exit at Sheridan Boulevard. He drove another fifteen blocks or so on Sheridan turned right onto 25th Avenue, and pulled into the driveway of a white, historic, brick home. He got out of the cruiser and disappeared into the front door of the home. Not fifteen minutes later, the officer exited the home, in street clothes, got into a black Ford Taurus parked on the street, and headed back towards the Interstate.

Missy had parked on 25th Avenue, several houses down from the home in question and watched. She then followed the black Ford. The officer drove west again, onto I-70, and exited at Colorado Boulevard where he turned right, drove three more miles and turned into the parking lot of a run-down, seemingly not to classy, bar and grill. She watched as Officer Jenkins parked the black Ford and walked gingerly up to the back door of the bar, knocked twice and was let in.

The driver of a blue, VW Beatle, directly behind Missy, honked incessantly at her as she slowed down to watch the officer turn into the parking lot of the bar. Really irritated now, the VW driver laid on the horn once more before Missy put on her turn signal and drove off the busy boulevard into a Sinclair gas station directly across the street from the bar.

She parked to the far left side of the green and yellow gas pumps, thought over what she should do first, and like any good female Private Investigator, got out of her car, walked into the station and asked for the key to the ladies room. There she sat down on the "john" to format a plan.

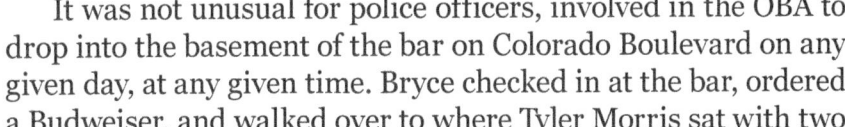

It was not unusual for police officers, involved in the OBA to drop into the basement of the bar on Colorado Boulevard on any given day, at any given time. Bryce checked in at the bar, ordered a Budweiser, and walked over to where Tyler Morris sat with two or three other OBA members.

"Hey Bryce." Tyler said, motioning the man to have a seat. "We need to talk. Thanks for coming so soon after my telephone call. How was the funeral? Too bad about the Livingstone kid."

Tyler Morris began to tell the three men sitting with him, beers in hand, that the time had come to take action on the "ranch" and break up the sex trafficking and prostitution ring.

"I have an OBA member, unknown to any of you, making the final tactical arrangements to raid the ranch, and soon. He has been undercover for several months, and has all the proof he needs to crack down on this abomination, once and for all."

Tyler Morris continued. "Bryce, you need to pick it up a little—you need to visit Olivia's at least three times a week over the next few weeks." Smiling, no smirking, Tyler said. "I'm sure you can handle that, can't you Bryce?"

Bryce squirmed a little in his seat and started to object to what Morris had asked. Having sex with a prostitute three times a week was a little much, even for him. He started to speak but then changed his mind. He knew that what Tyler Morris asked for, Tyler Morris always got.

"I know that the new prostitute, Angie, has been telling our undercover that she's willing to work with us, Bryce, and, get more information on Olivia, the Judge and the entire group abusing and selling those poor girls. Angie tells us that the Judge has been at the ranch at least twice a week lately, always at night. She has also seen him coming up the back road, later in the wee hours of the mornings, at least three consecutive times just this past week alone. That kid is really helping us out here. She wants out from under Olivia, and we've promised her we will do just that—after she's helped us."

Tyler continued. "Bryce, I need you to ask for Angie every time you call Olivia. If you don't want the sex, you'll have to pay Angie for your time spent with her, act like you're "doing the deed" and that will give you the time to talk with her. Angie found the hidden camera in her room, and she and our undercover figured a way to stop it filming for fifteen minutes at a time without Olivia suspecting it's not live feed. This will give you time to get the information we need—when does the money change hands, when are the big boys there, what are the times that the girls are being brought in, money exchanged and the girls sold and taken back out. I know this is a big request of you, Bryce, but you know you will be rewarded. You also know when this is over you're not to ever go back to the ranch again. Understood? We'll give the Dawson cops a heads up, help as far as we can, then we will all disappear." Morris asked again. "Understood?"

Bryce agreed to everything Tyler had requested of him. He had no choice. He left the bar, got into his Ford Taurus and immediately called Olivia for an appointment with Angie.

CHAPTER FOURTY-EIGHT

Suspicions

Missy sat in the restroom at the Sinclair station for a few more minutes. She walked back into the station, handed the manager the key, purchased a diet Pepsi, and walked back to her car. She looked across the street, noticed that the officer's cruiser was still parked in the lot, got into her vehicle, popped the tab on her Pepsi, took a sip, and called Craig.

"Missing Persons, Detective Olson." Craig answered.

"Hi." Missy said in her sexiest, baby voice. "I'm looking for a missing detective, sir, can you help me, please?"

Craig laughed, said hi sweetheart, and asked her what trouble she was in this time?

She shared with him how she had been to one of the saddest funerals she had ever been to in her life, and how she had seen and followed a police officer to a skuzzy looking bar in South Dawson, and what she thought of the entire situation.

"Craig, I think you should see what goes on in this bar. Figure out a way to get someone in there, ask questions. I have a gut feeling that there might be OBA activities going on there. My old crutch and I are too suspicious looking for me to walk into a bar without an escort."

She continued to tell him her suspicions of the cop she had followed, wondering why he had been at the funeral. She told Craig where he lived, about changing cars, and so on.

"I'm going to continue to follow him if and when he ever leaves the bar, Craig. I just wanted you to know where I was, and what I'm up to."

Craig said he would look into it immediately, that with Janice Poltice undercover now, he would check to see if the bar Missy spoke of was the meeting place for the OBA. Janice would know and could get in, ask the questions, and get back to him with no suspicions. He was on it. He told Missy to be careful, and to call him if she got back to their apartment before he did. Was she fixing dinner, or should he pick up Sushi?

She said Sushi sounded awesome.

After two hours of sitting in her old green Buick, drinking Pepsi and visiting the Sinclair gas station's restroom once again, Bryce Jenkins finally emerged from the back door of the bar. He looked around before entering his car as if he suspected something might me amiss. Thinking all was okay; he drove out of the lot and onto Colorado Boulevard. Missy followed him.

In the basement of the bar and grill, Tyler Morris picked up his cell phone and dialed Jeremy Porter's burner telephone number.

"We may have a problem with Jenkins." Morris said sharply. "Meet me tonight, after your visit to the "ranch". Same time, same place. See you there."

CHAPTER FOURTY-NINE

A Cop is about to Fall

Bryce Jenkins drove slowly down Colorado Boulevard towards downtown Dawson and the police station. His mind was in turmoil. He lived with so much guilt these days that he could barely eat or sleep. He could barely do his real job at all. He wondered if he should take a few weeks sick leave. His marriage was on the rocks. His children barely spoke to him. He was having sex with prostitutes. He had turned from being a loving husband and father and one who "protected and served" to one who, well, he didn't actually know anymore—what did he do? Who was he? He had no idea. He was in too deep with the OBA to get out, he had been involved in a murder, he was getting pay offs from doctors, lawyers, judges and others, to keep their records clear, his bank account was growing by leaps and bounds, but for what? He was miserable. Miserable. Bryce Jenkins was breaking. How long would it be before he was just another broken soul? How long?

He had to make a choice. Keep this up and crack, or worse. He had thought more than once about killing himself, but he couldn't do that to his family—or could he? Would they be better off without him? His mind turned over and over like a raging river. He was drowning in his own thoughts and fear.

Perhaps after he saw Angie tonight, he could think better. She helped him go to a better place. Yes, tonight, he would see Angie again, have beautiful, erotic sex, and then he would feel better. Much better.

He turned off Colorado Boulevard onto Interstate 25, and headed downtown to the precinct, a smile on his face but with a troubled heart.

Missy, making sure to stay at least a quarter of a mile behind Officer Jenkins' vehicle, wondered where he was headed this time. Rush hour traffic was picking up, and she had to focus on his Ford. She didn't want to lose him now. Jenkins took the Broadway exit off of I-25, pulled into a Sonic Drive Through restaurant and parked his car. Missy pulled in across the street. Jenkins spent 30 minutes at the drive through, left and once again headed down Broadway to the police station. Missy, listening to her stomach grumble from lack of food, smiled, thinking it had been a long time since breakfast. She realized that tailing Jenkins was about to end, but she had received good, usable information from her investigative work today. She turned off Broadway as Jenkins turned into the Dawson Police Station's parking lot. She was ready for Sushi.

CHAPTER FIFTY

Raspberry Zingers and Peanut Butter Sandwiches

Across town Dr. and Mrs. Livingstone were contemplating moving. Their elegant but smaller home was not large enough for a family of six and they put the house on the market. Even with Tabbatha gone, Katherine still insisted on having her own room, although on occasion, she would allow three-year-old Becky to stay in her room and play with her dolls. This still meant that there was only one bedroom for the three sisters, one for the Doctor and Devorah, and an extra room for Devorah when she needed "time away" from her husband.

The family looked for only one week and found a larger five-bedroom home in another lovely, prominent, neighborhood. There was a large family room with a fireplace, a large kitchen and dining room, and a huge yard for all the children to play in. Why they needed a huge yard was anyone's guess. Two children were allowed out of doors, but not Sandra. She especially, was never allowed to go outside. Never! She was told to stay by Devorah's side at all times. Sandra would sit by her mother. Devorah would tell the young girl all about her own problems and Sandra would watch her sew or stay by her side in the kitchen to watch her cook. While in the kitchen, Devorah would make Sandra eat semi sweet chocolate bars, telling her they were cookies. Sandra, even though she complied with everything her adopted mother told her to do, Devorah would strike her—without warning—hitting her hard across the face, call her stupid, dum-dum (her favorite description). Then she would pat Sandra on the head and tell her that she was a "poor mentally ill child". Sandra's only free time, away from Devorah, was when she attended elementary school. There was no help from Sandra's teachers who noticed Sandra's bruises, because she by now was programmed to "not tell". Neither her teacher nor school personnel ever questioned the Livingstone's. Not one.

On most days, the three sisters were grabbed, pushed down onto the floor, or slapped for no reason at all. When Devorah was really upset, she would grab each girl, especially Sandra, and dig her long, polished, fingernails into the underside of her arms, sometimes puncturing the skin and drawing blood, which always caused bruising. There was never a day that Sandra did not end up with welts and bumps on her legs and arms. Even worse was the drastic weight gain. Devorah would force feed the two older girls on a constant basis, then call them "fatty" or "fat little pigs" or "piggy's". At times, seeing all of this abuse, Katherine would, thinking it normal, attack her sisters as well. It was sickening. Katherine was also programmed, just in a different way.

At least once a week, sometimes more, Devorah would tell Becky to get a treat from the freezer in the kitchen—Zinger treats—always raspberry flavored Zingers and always frozen solid. As Becky sat in her little rocking chair, Devorah would make Becky eat one, then a second, until the box was empty. The Zingers never had time to thaw out. Becky was always told to eat the treats frozen. Then, after eating way more than a small child should eat, Devorah would call Becky fatty or piggy, and even fat-ass!

"I remember the times when I was made to eat an entire box of Zingers at one sitting, because that's what Devorah had me programmed to do. As I got older, I was gaining so much weight that I would get stuck in the little rocking chair. Yet, Devorah continued to make me eat massive amounts of food. I never complained. I just did as I was told."

The girls no longer knew how to say no. The worst being, "I forgot", "I don't know" and of course, "yes or no ma'am".

After years of programming, all of the sisters knew that when Devorah said do something, they did it. They did not argue or disagree they just did it. The three girls no longer had minds of their own, and the programming had only taken a few years! A few years, and no one noticed or cared—not Father Ramsey, not Social Services, not schoolteachers, not friends—everyone turned their eyes the other way. After all, no one thought that as prominent citizens, Dr. and Mrs. Livingstone's would NEVER mistreat a child—would they?

No one knew what was going on behind closed doors at the Livingstone home—no one except for Devorah, Katherine, Roseanne, Sandra, Becky and the secretary and maid and yes, Dr. Bernard Livingstone, loving husband, loving father. No one told. No one dared to tell. Dr. Livingstone stayed away for hours and hours at a time. When he did come home in the late evening hours, Devorah would slap and demean him as well. Why he never had the guts to stand up to his wife, or save his adopted children from the severe abuse is beyond anyone's imagination. How could a man with almost "genius" IQ possibly allow a woman to abuse him and his children, and let her get away with it? Dr. Bernard Livingstone did just that—he let her get away with it.

CHAPTER FIFTY-ONE

Jeremy and Janice

A week after Jeremy's invitation for dinner, Janice Poltice brought her handicapped daughter to her parents' home for a few hours, and met Jeremy at the Mexican/American Café close to her home. She felt much more comfortable driving her own vehicle. That way she could leave when she wanted or needed to.

The two officers of the law sipped on Marguerites, ate a delicious meal of fish tacos and salad, and topped it off with black coffee and Sopaphias. Janice was actually enjoying Jeremy's company. He never asked her anything about her interrogation, the hit and run, how she felt about the OBA—nothing. She was very surprised and agreed to go out with him again four days later.

On their second date, Jeremy picked her up at her home, and took Janice to a basketball game at the local high school. His best friends 17-year-old son was playing in a district rivalry game and although it came as a surprise to her, she actually enjoyed the game and Jeremy's company. She warned herself, however, to be very, very careful.

As the game came to an end (his friend's high school team winning by 3 points), he asked her out for coffee and dessert. She agreed. As the evening progressed, Jeremy began to ask her questions about the hit and run incident, her latest traffic accident, and then asked if she had spent much time at the police station being interrogated? How did it make her feel? Janice was ready for his questioning.

Being prepared, Janice said that yes she had been slightly embarrassed, as she had never been placed in an interrogation room before. She made it very clear to Jeremy that she never wanted that to happen to her ever again. She made light of the conversation, even chuckling as she spoke.

"I know it was stupid of me to hit that woman's car." Janice told Jeremy. "But when Tyler Morris speaks, we listen right? When I was told to put a scare in the woman, I was never told why she needed to have the "fear of God" put into her. I did what I was told. I do kind of regret it. Did you know about the hit and run, Jeremy? Did you know I was asked to do that job?"

When Jeremy didn't answer, Janice continued, trying to get a feel for where Jeremy was coming from and to keep him from being suspicious of her.

"I very seldom see you at the OBA meetings Jeremy. Are you deeply involved, or are you like me, taking crap kind of job orders from Morris? I understand some cops like me are getting paid big bucks for doing jobs for the OBA. So far, I've made about $500.00, not what I'd call "real" money, but I've only been asked to cover up one traffic ticket for some congressman, and of course, the hit and run." She added. "I guess $500.00 isn't bad for a few hours work."

Chuckling again, Janice waited for some kind of response from her date. Then she added, "Jeremy, can you get me some bigger jobs? Do you get bigger jobs from Morris?

Playing with his napkin and showing a slight bit of nervousness, Jeremy told her that he was sorry she wasn't real happy in the OBA, but that she needed to be patient. After all, she was a newbie. She laughed again. "A newbie, huh? That's me?" She asked Jeremy how long he had been involved with the OBA. He tried to skirt the question, but knowing what a smart cop, Janice was, he told her just a little over four years.

"Four years ago, I was approached while on a stakeout in Golden. I didn't think much about it at the time. I was asked if I wanted to make a few bucks. All I had to do was to close my eyes, keep my mouth shut, do the job with a partner, and I did it. Now, I'm hooked. I'm not doing anything wrong, just straightening out the world for the regular cops who are too busy saving their side of the world. I just happen to be making some major money besides."

Before he realized what all he was saying, he told Janice that he was working on a big job right now, and that no one knew who he was or what he was doing. He was undercover. "No one will ever know it's me." He continued. "I'm covering my tracks, and Morris is covering my tracks too. No worries. I'll never get caught." Then continuing, he said. "Janice, you're a smart cop. If you do things right, you'll never get caught either. Just do like you did this time, after your fendor bender, stay strong, keep your mouth shut, and you'll be fine. Once Morris sees the kind of work you are capable of, he'll get you more jobs. Wait on it. Be patient."

Realizing he was saying way too much, he quickly asked Janice if she wanted more coffee and when she said, no, he asked would she like to come to his place for a little while?

Being very cautious, Janice thanked him for the offer, but said sweetly that she needed to relieve her parents and get home to her handicapped daughter. She said, however, that she would like to see him again. Jeremy dropped her off at her front door, kissed her slightly on the cheek and left.

Janice wasn't sure if she liked Jeremy or not, but, it didn't matter. This was just a job. She had a job to do—help the Dawson police department take down a huge sex trafficking ring, perhaps help solve a cold case murder, and get proof that Jeremy was involved. She could not get involved with Jeremy Porter. Never.

When he asked her out again for the following week, she had said yes. Yes, because her career was on the line here. Yes, because she wanted a safe environment for her daughter, and most of all, she had said yes, because she did not want to go to prison or have a record.

Bryce Jenkins pulled into the Ranch's parking lot, checked himself in the rearview mirror, sprayed some mouthwash into his dry mouth, and exited his car. He was dressed in a new pair of khaki pants, a blue and tan plaid shirt and newly polished brown loafers. He did not look like an undercover cop. He looked like a man looking for love.

He knocked on the front door; tap, tap, tap, and a sweet looking, but very young girl opened the door and invited him in. He did, as he always did. He sat down in one of the overstuffed, comfortable, dark brown chairs in the beautifully polished oak wood living room, where Olivia greeted him with a Scotch and water – his favorite drink. She leaned over him showing off her incredible deep cleavage as she was handing him his drink and napkin. She assured him that Angie would be down shortly, and made small talk while he waited.

He tried very hard to not look nervous, but he was. He hoped that Olivia would not notice.

CHAPTER FIFTY-TWO

Missy has a Vision

Craig, Missy and Janice met on a Friday afternoon as the sun shone brightly through the one and only window in Craig's small office. They discussed what Missy had found out on her tailing of the yet, unknown, police officer, and Janice shared what she had found out on her two dates with Jeremy Porter.

"I can tell you what I know about the bar and grill but I have only been to one meeting." She said. "I met the man in charge, Tyler Morris, but I never saw Jeremy Porter at that meeting."

She continued to tell them what information Jeremy had shared with her, and that she felt very strongly that Jeremy was a "special" OBA member, and that Tyler Morris had him doing things no other members knew about.

"I think that Jeremy is Morris' favorite boy. I also think he may know more about this prostitute, Mandy Sue, that you were telling me about, Craig. Jeremy got very nervous when I started asking questions."

Missy had been quiet through most of the conversation: just listening. All of a sudden, she stood up, grabbed her crutch and walked over to the window. She looked out, thought for a moment, then turned and first with a finger in the air, (pointed at no one or nothing in particular), and then touching her mouth with that finger, (she said she was using it to help her think), she hollered, "Craig! You know your friend, Sam or Shawn, or whatever is name is, the Medical Examiner. What was his name?"

"Stan." Craig said to her, with a questioning look. "His name is Stan."

"Well, okay, Stan." Missy said, smiling now and leaning on his desk, looking directly at him. "When he did the examination, the autopsy, everything he needed to do on Mandy Sue, well, do you know if he took a vaginal swab, or DNA from the fetus, or the uterus, or whatever he does in these cases? We know that Mandy Sue was pregnant. Do you think Stan could tell us who the father or male donor of the baby was? Yes, the father! Can he tell us who the father of her baby was with those tests? He saves them all, right?"

Missy kept on talking, excitedly now, until Craig stood up, put his hands on her shoulders and asked her nicely to sit down.

"Okay, Missy." Craig said. "What is it that you're getting at?"

Missy, sitting down now, quietly and sincerely shared with Janice and Craig that something had just come to her, hit her like a silver bullet, or maybe it was a vision.

"Janice said she thought Jeremy might be involved in Mandy's murder. Now I know this is far out. Please, you guys, listen. I've known Jeremy for a very long time, and this makes me sick, yes, really sick, when I think about it, but do you think that since Mandy was a prostitute, and she saw lots of men, well, do you think that Jeremy could have been one of her "johns"? Maybe he fell for her. Could he possibly be the father of her baby?"

Then, continuing, and once again standing up, Missy turned towards Craig and said. "Will Stan have that report, Craig, the one that has the baby's or the fetus' DNA, and could we still have it tested for DNA, the male part of the DNA, or the blood work, or however that works? The one that could prove that Jeremy is the father?" Missy took a deep breath and sat down.

Then, as Craig started to speak, Missy, even more excited now than before, said. "Janice, have you ever seen a black cat at Jeremy's place?"

"What? No, I've never been to Jeremy's house, Missy. He asked me over one night, but I said no. What are you getting at?"

Missy continued the conversation by saying. "Okay. If we imagine or believe that Jeremy had been seeing Mandy out at the Ranch, and Mandy got to close to the "goings on" at the Ranch. She needed to be done away with. If Jeremy had already fallen in love with her, got her pregnant, and then had to kill her, because the OBA ordered him to." Missy took a breath. "Then, a guy in a hoody goes to her grave, leaves a red rose, and Craig finds cat poop on the grave. It all makes sense. Mandy's cat was never found. What if Jeremy was the guy that brought a rose to Mandy's grave, and what if Jeremy has Mittens, Mandy's cat? Maybe the sicko took the cat with him to her grave, you know, to see her mama one more time?"

Missy took another deep breath and sat down again.

Craig looked at his Private Investigator girlfriend and shaking his head said. "Missy Baker, I think you have completely lost your mind and you are also a complete genius!"

More calmly now, Missy said to Craig. "Think about it Craig. It all makes sense. I know that I know Jeremy, maybe a little better than you two, but I'm telling you, the night I had dinner with him, the scribbling on the table cloth with the OBA initials, and now all of what I just said, it makes sense, Craig. Perfect sense! I really think that Jeremy Porter could be our killer."

The three continued hashing over what Missy had suggested. Craig asked Janice to make a point of being invited over to Jeremy's house on one of the upcoming dates, and soon. He also suggested that she make a point of getting another "job" with the OBA and being invited back to the bar and grill for a meeting. Missy would continue doing what she did best—being the best gimpy, Private Investigator the city of Dawson had ever seen.

"She just might be onto something here." Craig thought to himself, smiling. "What a girl! What a girlfriend I have. Yes, she might be on to something."

Chapter Fifty-Three

More Injury and Heartache

On a beautiful Sunday afternoon, shortly after Mass at the Church of Christ of the Resurrection, the Livingstone family went to Devorah' parents, the Dawkins, for a traditional and lovely, Sunday dinner. It as the event of the week for the sisters, and Katherine looked forward to it too.

On most Sundays, Devorah would help her daughters dress for Sunday service, mostly in colorful dresses that she had sewn for all of them. Then, after service, the entire family would spend a quiet afternoon with the grandparents—the only time there was quiet and calm in an entire week. They would play board games, talk and laugh with one another, just like a normal family.

Sandra enjoyed mass, and began to understand the Catholic faith and what participating in the mass and the sacraments meant. What she could NOT understand was why the Priest talked about Jesus loving and caring for all the little children, like herself, and that He cared about little children, but she asked herself, "Why could Jesus not see what Devorah was doing to her and her sisters" Did Jesus not love them?"

When Sandra tried asking Grandma Dawkins this same question, Grandma would always tell her to "shush" and to not talk about that right now.

Grandma Dawkins would always make the best chicken dinner, with all the trimmings. Best of all, Devorah would never scream or slap or demean her husband or the sisters when they were at grandma and grandpa's home. It was the only day in the week when there was calm. Sandra dreaded the time when the visit would end, because she knew what would happen the moment they walked into their own home.

As time went on, Sandra had even asked grandma why Devorah was mean to her and to her sisters and why was she never mean to Katherine? Unlike Katherine who was blond and blue-eyed, like Devorah, the other girls had darker hair and eyes, like Bernard. Grandma Dawkins also knew that her daughter favored Katherine. She suspected that because the sisters' mother was in prison, Devorah also despised the other girls. Most of all, Devorah despised the little girls because Bernard had insisted that they be adopted. Devorah hated her husband for making that decision for the both of them.

Grandma Dawkins suspected that her daughter was abusing her grandchildren, but she too, never admitted it to anyone—especially not to Sandra. Mrs. Dawkins chose early on to stay out of her daughter and her husbands business.

Approximately a year and a half after the sisters had been adopted, and Tabbatha had died, the entire family was at the grandparents once again for Sunday dinner. Grandma had made the mistake of asking her daughter why Sandra had so many bruises on her arms and legs?

"Did Sandra fall?" Grandma asked her daughter, Devorah. "Do you know anything about this child's bruises?"

Devorah did not answer. Instead, she began screaming hysterically at her mother, calling her horrible and heart-wrenching names. As Bernard began to gather up the children and take them from the room Devorah walked up to him, slapped him across the face, and stormed out of the front door. Still screaming, as she stomped down the front walkway, she opened the car door, yelled at her husband to "get the f...k out here and take me home!"

Neither Devorah, her husband, or her children were ever allowed to set foot in the Dawkins' home again—Devorah's orders. Once again, Bernard or Devorah's parents did nothing about the "orders' or the abuse. The one and only place the three sisters had ever found peace and love was now gone. They never saw their grandparents again.

Shortly after this disastrous afternoon, Sandra, once again took the horrible brunt of Devorah's rage. Devorah and Sandra were in the kitchen; Roseanne was in the living room watching television, while Becky and Katherine played outside in their big back yard.

Devorah was in the kitchen, once again force-feeding Sandra. When Sandra put her arm up over her mouth to try and stop the force-feeding, Devorah grabbed and turned her arm into a horrible angle. Roseanne heard the severe "crack" of Sandra's bone, and listened to Sandra's horrific screams. Devorah seeing Roseanne enter the kitchen, grabbed her and Sandra and pushed them outside to where Becky and Katherine—who by this time was oblivious to her mother's actions—were in the carport playing—and told the girls that Sandra had fallen off of the fence and her arm had been broken. "Girls!" Devorah screamed as she ran out into the back yard. "Sandra has fallen off of the fence and hurt herself. We need to take her to see daddy!"

"I remember that it was at this particular time in my life when I realized that my remaining sisters and I were being raised by a monster. I remember that Sandra was never allowed to play in the back yard, and that Devorah lied. Devorah had broken Sandra's arm while inside the house."

"I know now that when the monster mommy broke Sandra's arm, my life changed forever. I no longer felt anything. The correct term I've been told is "disassociation". It occurs when something tragic happens over and over again that your mental being can no longer cope. It's a survival technique that I used over and over in my ten years living in hell with the "Livingstone's". I lived in this mode until I started drinking to "forget", at the age of thirteen."

Dr. Livingstone, on duty at the Rocky Mountain Hospital in Dawson, set Sandra's arm, signed the medical reports as an "accident" on the appropriate medical forms, and sent Sandra, her sisters and his wife home. There were no questions asked, and Sandra made no comments as to her injury to any other staff members at the hospital. By this time, Sandra was so used to the abuse that she no longer tried to get anyone to help her, especially, her father. Four weeks after the accident, Devorah took Sandra to her husband's office due to Sandra's cast being way too tight. Due to the force-feedings, and weight gain, the child's hand was beginning to turn blue. At least this time, Devorah had a little bit of kindness in her heart.

Sandra too, was now fully programmed and the life of abuse was normal for she and her sisters. They would always feel the physical pain afflicted upon them, but they would mentally, no longer feel anything. They learned to cope, and go "into" themselves to handle the abuse. One day, Sandra would "crumble" and there would be no turning back. Sandra would go insane.

Tabbatha had been the lucky one, if you really think about it. She was frail, fragile as it were, and in no way able to fight the woman who was abusing her. God must have been looking down on little Tabbatha, and realizing her frailty allowed her abuse to end. The other girls would not fair as well. Their abuse would continue for years and years, until their only choice would be to "run". Even then, they would be returned to the only family they had ever known—the abusive one. Then they would run again.

CHAPTER FIFTY-FOUR

It's Definitely Love

Craig and Missy finally agreed to take a few days off from work. They had spent all of their waking hours working on the Mandy Sue Donnor murder case, looking into the prostitution and sex trafficking ring and the OBA. Missy also continued to pick up new clients and was steadily making a name for herself in Dawson. She admitted, however, that she loved working with Craig more.

They admitted that they were very close to solving their cases, but that it was taking a toll on them and their relationship. They needed some R and R. After talking about places to go for a few days—places that were fairly close too Dawson, they decided to head into the Rocky Mountains.

On Friday evening having left the police station by 5:00 pm, they threw a few things in an overnight bag and set out to spend the weekend in beautiful Glenwood Springs, Colorado. Glenwood Springs was noted for it's incredible hot mineral springs and spa's—just what they both needed. After making a few calls, they scored a reservation, even on a weekend, at a hotel on the outskirts of town.

It was a two hundred mile long trip to Glenwood Springs, and after stopping in the ski town of Vail for a sandwich, they arrived at their hotel around Midnight. Exhausted from weeks of tireless days and nights working on their specific cases, they checked into their hotel and fell immediately into bed. Even though they had looked forward to a romantic and relaxing weekend, here they were in a beautiful hotel room, and were sound asleep in a few minutes. So much for a romantic evening.

The two spent the entire weekend sleeping late, enjoying room service, making love and swimming in the hot springs pool. They also spent one afternoon at the incredible hot springs SPA. The views from both their hotel room and from the pool were breathtaking, and the weekend turned out to be exactly what they had hoped for.

On Saturday evening, the couple walked a few blocks from their hotel to an Italian restaurant where they enjoyed delicious shrimp pasta, garlic bread and red wine. After dinner they drove to the pool for a late night swim.

It was a marvelous, Colorado evening. There were millions of twinkling stars scattered throughout the blackest sky Craig and Missy had ever seen. Craig squeezed Missy's hand as they walked slowly down the steps into the pool.

While enjoying the soothing, warm water, and with Craig standing behind her, his arms and hands around her waist, they walked back and forth through the shallow end of the pool. The therapeutic water felt fabulous and Missy, who needed no crutch for balance in the water, could feel herself relaxing more and more.

Later, the couple exited the pool, and sat on the edge, their feet dangling in the warm water. Craig took Missy's hand in his, and looking directly into her bright blue eyes, said, "Missy, have you thought about us getting married, and having a child together? I know we aren't spring chickens anymore, but, if not our own child, would you be willing to adopt a child?"

Missy was caught a little off guard. She and Craig had spoken a little about marriage and a family, but with their busy schedules and their careers, which they both enjoyed, plus their ages, she really hadn't thought of children—marriage, yes. She had given marriage to Craig serious thought.

Missy kissed him, and said that yes, she had thought about both. "I love you Craig, and if you asked me to marry you, I might just say yes. MIGHT SAY YES!" She said kidding him. They both chuckled.

In just a matter of seconds, Craig took her face in both of his hands, kissed her gently and asked. "Missy Baker, will you marry me?"

Although not surprised at the proposal, Missy was somewhat surprised at Craig's timing. She had known for many months that she loved Craig and she knew that he loved her, but still she was surprised.

"Wow, Detective Olson!" She exclaimed. "You really know how to show a girl a memorable weekend." She then kissed him gently, and Craig laughed and kissed her back.

"I love you so much, Missy." Craig continued. "I'm not sure how this will work—a hotshot detective and a hot blooded Private Investigator getting hitched? How about it Ms. Baker, will you marry me? I haven't picked out a ring, but I thought perhaps you would like to pick out your own ring, and if you say yes, we will pick out a ring. So." He asked again. "Will you be my wife, Missy?"

Missy started to cry, jumped back into the hot water, turned to Craig, and as she pulled him into the water, she said, yes, yes, yes. They kissed more deeply this time, and Craig couldn't tell if it was Missy's warm tears or the hot water of the hot springs pool that touched his face.

On Monday morning, after a night of champagne and love making, then breakfast in bed, the couple checked out of their hotel and drove to a jewelry store on the main street of Glenwood Springs. After trying on a few engagement rings, Missy chose a very simple, but beautiful ring by Ritani. It was a .75-carat solitaire with matching wedding band. Missy loved it. It fit her finger perfectly!

Craig took the ring from off her finger, stating that this would be the ONLY time the ring would ever leave her finger. He wrote out a check for the amount owed and handed it, along with his identification, to the sales clerk.

Right there in the Monarch Jewelry Store, Craig got down on one knee, asked Missy to marry him again, and slipped the white gold engagement ring onto her finger—much to the delight of the owner and the other clients in the jewelry store.

CHAPTER FIFTY-FIVE

A Life Ends

On a side road on the outskirts of Arribio, two miles from the Ranch, two men sat in an unmarked car. They were dressed in dark clothing and each held a rifle. They waited patiently. The vehicle's lights were off, but the motor was running.

They were waiting to silence Bryce Jenkins.

Earlier in the week, Tyler Morris had met with Jeremy Porter for fifteen minutes in a local church sanctuary. They had knelt at the rail, acting like normal parishioners, faking prayers and talking softly—no, Tyler talked. Jeremy listened.

Tyler had informed Jeremy that the time had come to "take care of" Jenkins. "He's putting the OBA at terrible risk." Tyler had said.

"He was a good pick when he first joined the OBA, Jeremy." Tyler had said. "I really thought we could trust him to handle the big jobs, but he's panicking. He's turning down job requests and only asking for jobs out at the Ranch. I think he's become a detriment to our organization. I believe Bryce was only in it for the money. He needs to be taken care of."

"Can't we warn him, threaten him, any thing but kill him?" Jeremy asked. "He doesn't know me, because I've been in disguise each time we've been working at the Ranch. I've seen him in action several times at the Ranch, and I think he's steering us in the right direction. He's given us good leads. I think he needs another chance." Then Jeremy added. "For God's sake, Tyler, he's got three kids!"

As the two continued their discussion, Tyler agreed with Jeremy on some of Bryce's good points, but not on the point of "trust". "Bryce Jenkins can no longer be trusted," Tyler said. "I know for a fact that he's asking too many questions. He's hanging out with the same prostitute night after night. He's a big problem. It's time to eliminate him. It's the best thing for the OBA. You need to check out his latest girl too. I think her name is Angie. She may also know way too much. We can't have another girl screw up our chances of bringing down the Judge and his counterparts. We're too close—way to close to have someone screw this up."

Bryce Jenkins was just leaving the Ranch. He and Angie had not had sex, instead, she had given him more information on the sex trafficking ring; when and how often the young girls were brought in and out of the basement, and the names of all the prostitutes working the Ranch. Angie had given him a description of Judge Christianson as well as a description of two other men she had seen.

Each time, after being with a "john", Angie had hidden in the bushes outside the walk-in basement and watched the men coming out of the basement. She watched them walk to their vehicles, and drive out the back road off of the ranch. One night, around midnight, she had even walked down the back road for almost a mile. She saw the men meet up with two more men, each in separate cars. She had written down all of the license plate numbers.

Angie was amazed that Olivia had not caught her. Olivia trusted her, more than her other girls. Angie had gotten by with the secretive, late night walk.

After two hours in Angie's bedroom, Bryce had turned the video/camera off for just a few seconds. He replaced the tape with an old tape showing the two of them in bed together. He put the tape back on live feed every fifteen minutes. Afterward, Bryce had paid Angie for their time together and left by the front door. Olivia had followed him to the door, thanked him for coming again, and kissed him on the cheek. She watched him get in his car and leave.

As Bryce entered his car, his cell phone beeped. He read a text message from an unknown OBA member stating that Bryce was needed at midnight on the back road of the Ranch. He had been given explicit directions. Bryce had driven towards that location. As he slowed his vehicle down, he turned a corner onto the back road. The last thing Bryce Jenkins saw in this life was a black or dark blue Dodge with two men leaning up against the front of the vehicle. Each man pointed a rifle directly at Bryce's windshield.

Two bullets ripped through his windshield, and hit him directly in the forehead. Bryce Jenkins died instantly. His last thoughts were of his three children.

CHAPTER FIFTY-SIX

A Life Lost

Bryce Jenkin's body was found early the next morning, slumped over the steering wheel of his car. Blood had dried on his forehead and face, and traces of blood had run down onto his blue and tan plaid shirt. A ranch hand that worked just a few miles from the Bartlett Ranch had found the body and he had immediately called the police.

The CBI was on the case immediately. The back road was roped off and closed to the public while all pieces of evidence were collected, bagged and taken to the lab. A small piece of paper found in Officer Jenkins' pants pocket was of special interest to the investigators and it was carefully placed into a separate plastic bag and marked "urgent".

The Dawson Police department personnel were devastated at the news of a fellow officers' passing and flags throughout Dawson were lowered to fly at half-mast. The word was that Mrs. Jenkins and her family were taking the news fairly well, and since Officer Jenkins was a tenured officer with an immaculate record, his wife would receive full police officer death benefits. She had asked the police department to assist with her husband's funeral service.

Although Craig did not know Officer Jenkins personally, Craig sympathized with the department and the officer's family. It was never easy losing an officer of the law, and never easy losing a husband or a father. He had been asked to participate in the investigation due to the possibility of Officer Jenkins being involved in someway at the Ranch, and with the OBA.

Craig's mind was running on maximum overload— thinking, thinking... Was Jenkins involved in the OBA? Did he know too much about the Ranch so he was killed? Could he have been the cop that Missy followed to the bar that day? Question after question, and Craig tried to sift them all out. Now, what he needed was answers—proof and answers.

Craig was saddened at the officer's early demise, especially while in the line of duty, but in this case, Craig wondered if Bryce Jenkins had been on duty. Had he been working as an under cover at the Ranch? Was he on duty at the time of the murder? Was he about to break the sex trafficking ring wide open? Did he know Jeremy Porter? Was he working for the OBA or for the Dawson Police Department? So many unanswered questions.

Craig was sad, but also excited. Bryce Jenkins' murder was adding fuel to the flame of the already out of control fire burning in Craig's gut. The Jenkins murder might be just what he was looking for, the final clue in solving the Mandy Sue Donnor murder case. He couldn't wait to talk to his man, Stan, the Medical Examiner.

Janice and Jeremy set a time for another date just a week after Janice, Craig and Missy had talked strategies in Craig's office. It was also only two days after Jeremy and another OBA member had taken out Bryce Jenkins. For Jeremy, it was just another job for the OBA. He felt no remorse. Yes, Jenkins had been a fellow police officer, but it no longer mattered to Jeremy Porter. He followed his god and mentor Tyler Morris, the man who would change the city of Dawson—the man who would change the world; an evil man who was slowly rotting Jeremy Porter's mind and breaking his soul.

Janice had begun to worry when after a week Jeremy hadn't called her to ask her out. She had seriously considered calling him and inviting him over to her place, when he finally called.

"Janice?" He asked when she answered the telephone.

"Hi Jeremy." She had said softly. "Nice to hear from you."

"I didn't recognize your voice." Jeremy had said. "Are you okay? It didn't sound like you when you first answered."

Janice told him that she had been sick with a cold—a lie—but it had worked—he had wondered or showed concern for her.

They chatted for a few minutes about the shooting of Officer Bryce Jenkins, the senselessness of it all, and then Jeremy had asked her out to dinner. When she had said yes, she suggested that instead of gong out, why didn't she fix them dinner instead.

"Do you want to come to my place, or I could fix dinner at your place, Jeremy? You asked me to come over earlier, and I was so sorry to have had to say no." She reminded him, feeding his ego.

"I felt badly about that, but I have to always consider my daughter first. You understand, don't you Jeremy?" She asked sweetly.

Before he had time to reply, she asked him jokingly, if he had cooking utensils, or was he a typical bachelor with nothing but paper plates and plastic silverware in his kitchen?

Jeremy laughed at her. He thought, "I really like this woman, and yes, maybe if she comes to my place, we could do more than just have dinner." He visualized her naked body lying next to him on his black satin sheets—yes, he could plan a very romantic evening—not that Janice was a woman he could ever get serious about or marry but a man had needs, after all.

There had only been one woman he had wanted to marry and she was dead—his fault. Plus, he remembered Tyler Morris telling him that dating Officer Janice Poltice was his latest job assignment, and only that—a job. Heck, he could do this job and enjoy it too. Just like his connection with Mandy Sue Donnor had started out—a job.

He shook off thoughts of Mandy Sue—no sense hashing that over anymore. He had loved her, really loved her, but what was done was done.

He told Janice, that yes, he would love for the two of them to cook dinner together at his place.

She asked what foods he liked, and they decided that she would purchase the ingredients to make lasagna, green salad and garlic bread. He would get the wine.

He assured her that he had utensils to cook with, and yes, he would purchase a couple of nice bottles of red wine.

As they were about to hang up the telephone, Jeremy surprised her by asking. "Janice, by the way, I have a cat, you're not allergic to cats are you?"

"Bingo!" Janice thought to herself. "Bingo!"

CHAPTER FIFTY-SEVEN

The Telephone Call

Missy had been in seventh heaven, as it were, for the entire week after she and Craig had gotten engaged. She had immediately called her parents, and, as she knew they would, had set a time for her and Craig to come to the house for dinner. Missy, knowing her mother well, suspected that there would be more than just the immediate family for dinner. It would be a celebration of their daughter "finally" catching her man. Missy chuckled at the thought. She had called close friends to share her news, but most of all and much more importantly, she and Craig had spent every night that week, at home, talking about their futures.

Missy knew her mother would want a big church wedding, and Missy and Craig agreed that they would too. They both had large families and lots of friends, and they didn't want to leave anyone out. They agreed, however, to have a spring wedding. The main reason being that solving the Mandy Sue murder case was a priority. Until it was solved, there would be no time to plan a wedding.

During this same week of joy and celebration, Missy received the telephone call sharing the sad news that little Tabbatha Livingstone had died. Missy said, that, "yes, she knew."

"I had no idea if you knew." Nellie Cooper said, sadly. "I usually don't keep this close of track on my previous foster children, but, those four little girls were so precious to Jim and I, and well, I know that you loved them too Missy, so I wanted to let you know. I'm sorry it took me so long to call you, but I'm glad you already knew."

"I was at her funeral. I saw you and the Grants sitting close to the front of the church, but I guess you didn't see me." Missy then asked Nellie. "Do you know anything more about her death?"

Nellie told her what she knew, which was very little, that Tabbatha had died at home, from some type of accident. Nellie, Jim, and the Grants had attended the funeral, which was so very sad, but Nellie knew very little else.

"I didn't have a chance to speak with the other sisters at Tabbatha's services." She continued. "I just know they looked so sad and confused. I just hope they are happy in their new home."

Missy asked Nellie if she knew where the Livingstone's lived, or if she had a telephone number, but Nellie said, no, she didn't have that information. She assured Missy, however, that the Livingstone's were a very prominent family in Dawson, and that Dr. Livingstone had his own medical practice, so Missy could probably get the information easily.

After speaking a few more minutes with Nellie, they said their goodbyes and hung up. Missy, again, couldn't believe that Tabbatha, such a sweet and precious little girl was dead. Her private investigative mind began turning and she wondered what might have happened. It really wasn't her concern, or her business, but she had really loved those four little girls, and had felt so sorry for them and their situation. She thought she just might look into their where abouts and soon.

CHAPTER FIFTY-EIGHT

Surprise at the Cemetery

Five days after Bryce Jenkins' murder, and on the day of the funeral, Stan had called Craig with the results of the autopsy. He had died of two bullet wounds to the head and had died instantly. He had been dead approximately 5 hours when he had been found in his car.

"I have been in touch with the laboratory technician, Craig." Stan continued. "I guess the cops have some really good clues. There were no rifle casings, and there is so much traffic on that dirt road that they could not get any really good tire tracks. Whomever shot Bryce evidently never bothered to check him out or his vehicle after the shooting. They must have killed him, freaked out, got spooked, who knows, and left the scene immediately."

Stan continued by telling Craig that Bryce Jenkins' plaid shirt had shown traces of Scotch—perhaps from a spilled drink, traces of a perfume called "Blessed Virgin", (for which Stan and Craig both laughed), and the "tech" had found strands of long, dark, possibly brunette hair on the dead officer's shirt and pants.

"But the best of all, Craig." Stan said. "There was a slip of paper in Bryce Jenkin's pants pocket, with—can you believe this—license plate numbers or at least they presume they are all license plate numbers. And, even better than that, two of the license plate numbers have already been identified as belonging to city employees or are city official's vehicles! I don't have names, because that's really not part of my job as an ME, but it looks like there may be big troubles coming down for some big boys in Dawson."

Craig was almost beside himself with excitement. He felt hot, started to sweat, and as he stood up from his office chair, walked around his office, and asked Stan for any other bit of information he could share, he took a huge swig of his bottled water.

"I'll send you the final reports, Craig." Stan replied. "I should have all my reports in another day or two, and I'll see to it that you get all the lab reports too, as soon as I get them. Also, Craig, I guess there has been a lot of activity over at the Bartlett Ranch the last few days. You know that large ranch over by Arribio. The body was found just east of that ranch, I think maybe, the body was found on or close to the ranch property. Anyway, word is that the police think there may be irregular activity of some kind at that ranch, you know, not just horses and cows! Perhaps Officer Jenkins had been there the night of his murder. Just for your information, you know." Stan continued. "The ME just sits back here in his steel and cold department. I don't get all of the low down, but this seems to be a really big deal—well, you know, when a cop dies, it's always a big deal!"

Craig thanked his good friend, and as he was about to say goodbye, remembered Mandy Sue's pregnancy.

"Stan." Craig said. "I know you're a busy guy, but I have another favor to ask of you. Remember the prostitute who died several months ago, the one that was a few months pregnant? Well." Craig continued. "The DNA. Can you dig out all the findings for me on the DNA of the uterus or fetus? I'm not sure what reports you have on the two month old fetus, or what samples you guys take, but here's the thing. I need to see if there is any way you can match up the baby's or fetus' DNA for me, because I just may have a suspect. I will need to figure out a way to get the guy's DNA too, but when I do, and with your help, I just may be able to find that poor girl's killer."

Almost begging now, Craig told Stan how important it would be if Stan could help him out with the cold case, which he told Stan, was not really cold. Stan assured him that they had stored enough DNA from the fetus to get some "goodies", as Stan called them, on the male donor. He would call Craig as soon as he had the information.

Across town, at the Dawson Community Church of the Master, the funeral for Officer Bryce Jenkins was just ending. The church, of course had been packed. Police Departments from around the state had sent one or more representatives to pay honor to Officer Jenkins, and of course, there were many, many officers in attendance from the Dawson Police Departments.

Missy had attended the service representing both she and Craig. She was there in a capacity of both a concerned Dawson citizen and as a Private Investigator—the latter, sadly, being the most important. The church was at standing room only when she had entered, and she stood at the back of the beautiful sanctuary with several other latecomers. She looked around for anyone she might possibly know, and surprising, well, maybe not to surprising the way the Mandy Sue Donnor case was going, she noticed Jeremy Porter sitting a few pews in front of her. He would be there, of course, as he was a cop too...but?

She did not recognize the man sitting next to him.

Missy was mesmerized by the beautiful and caring messages of love and promises of the hereafter, the wonderful and appropriate musical renditions, and she thought to herself how much she missed going to worship. She had always been a fairly faithful, churchgoer, but since she had met Craig and he was so very busy 24/7 and couldn't attend church with her, she had stopped going regularly too. She knew she had to make a change, and an effort to attend church more often.

"Life is too short". She reminded herself, noticing Bryce's sobbing children sitting towards the front of the church. "Life is to short."

Missy left the church, got into her Buick and fell into line with others in the long funeral procession to the Mt. Olivet Cemetery. She had no need to see this officer placed in the ground—it was the investigative side of her that was driving to the cemetery. After more prayers and scripture readings and the final Police Department salute to Officer Jenkins', he was laid to rest. His wife, clutching the American flag, and her children, said their final goodbyes. The children each plucked a red or yellow rose from the spray of flowers covering his casket. His, presumably oldest daughter sobbed uncontrollably, and was assisted to the family car by the minister.

Before leaving the beautifully manicured cemetery, Missy walked around the gravesites, reading several of the writings on the stones. There were those stating, "in loving memory" or "a beloved wife or husband" or, just the name, date of birth and death. As she walked towards the street and her car, she noticed a fairly new grave. The grass had begun to grow back, covering the black earth, but there were still areas of just earth—no grass. She stopped to read the writings on the large grey stone. Beautifully carved, with an angel, wings outstretched, to the left side of the stone, it read, "Our loving daughter". That in it self was not unusual, but what was unusual and a shock to Missy was the name—Tabbatha Livingstone.

Missy walked carefully over the uneven grassy area, making certain to not step on the grave, laid her crutch down next to the gravesite, and sat down, legs crossed, close to little Tabbatha. Tears began to fall down Missy's face, as she thought of the few times she had seen her. This quiet, beautiful child, her sisters and the horrible fate they had seemingly been handed.

"Such a waste." Missy thought. "Such a waste. God, what were you thinking?"

CHAPTER FIFTY-NINE

Jeremy Porter, You're Going Down

Janice Poltice was nervous when she knocked on Jeremy's front door, two bags of groceries in hand.

He answered quickly, invited her in, and lightly kissed her on the cheek as she entered.

Janice, dressed in dark gray slacks, an ivy-league, buttoned down collared shirt, in matching gray and black stripes and in matching black spiked heels, she was stunning. Jeremy immediately remarked at her beauty and style as he took the bags of groceries from her and set them down on the counter. He turned, took her in his arms and kissed her gently, then harder. Janice pushed him away, gently, reminding him that she had a delicious dinner planned for the two of them.

"First things first, Jeremy." She said smiling.

Jeremy asked if she would like a glass of wine, and when she said yes, a large, black and seemingly friendly cat, brushed her leg.

A little alarmed, but prepared to meet a "suspicious" cat on this date, Janice, bent down and stroked Jeremy's pet cat.

"She is beautiful, Jeremy." Janice exclaimed. "What's her name? It is a "her" right?"

Smiling, Jeremy picked up the cat, told Janice that yes, it was a female, and that her name was Mittens.

"Mittens." Janice said, nervously petting the feline. "Cute name, Jeremy. Is it because of her white feet?"

Janice had never felt more like running in her entire police career, but she was ready to run now. She thought. "The cat. This cat is most likely Mandy's cat. The cat that did its "duty" on the grave of Mandy Sue Donnor. The man she was fixing a meal for might just be Mandy's killer." Janice took a huge swig of her wine, and then drank the rest of it. Jeremy noticing, asked her if she was okay and would she like a refill? Janice said yes—definitely yes.

After two glasses of red wine, and realizing that she was on police business, and this night she might just do her part in putting a potential murderer away and clear her record, she settled in to making dinner. She and Jeremy cut salad greens and vegetables together, and every now and again Jeremy would lean over kiss her on the lips and tell her how happy he was to have her in his home.

The dinner was delicious, and later on sitting on Jeremy's' brown leather couch, sipping coffee with Kaluha and cream, Janice began to gently ask Jeremy questions—questions about Jefferson County Sheriff's Office. Did he like his job? How long had he been a Sheriff's Deputy? Non-suspicious questions. She also shared her life with him. Why she was divorced, how it was to take care of a handicapped child and how she went to the Academy and become a police officer.

The evening was going just as Janice hoped it would, when around 10:00pm, the telephone rang. Janice heard the ringing but realized that the telephone on the coffee table was not the one that was ringing. Jeremy jumped up off the couch, and walked swiftly into the bedroom where Janice heard him say "Porter, 124". Wanting to listen more, but needing to take this opportunity to gather evidence, she walked into the kitchen, took Jeremy's soiled napkin and wine goblet off the kitchen counter and placed them into her oversized bag. She was just coming back into the living room when Jeremy returned.

"I'm sorry about that." Jeremy said, taking her hand in his. "I had to take that call." Stumbling over his words right now, and remaining standing, he told Janice that he had a separate telephone for the Sheriff's calls and that he was so sorry, but he had to go.

"There's been an incident, Janice." He said, nervously. "I have to leave. I'm sorry. I hate to end this wonderful evening, but you know work? I have to leave."

Janice was somewhat relieved that she could leave early. She said no apology was necessary, that it was late, and that she had enjoyed a wonderful evening. She offered to clean up their "mess" in the kitchen, but he said not to worry, he would clean up later. She was again relieved that she had taken the time to get into the kitchen and collect evidence—maybe evidence that would put this potential killer away, without Jeremy knowing.

Janice got into her car and watched as Jeremy backed his vehicle out of his garage, and sped down the street. She stayed over a block in back of Jeremy, not wanting him to see her following him. She wasn't certain she could pull this off. She felt she had enough evidence to take Jeremy Porter down, but she wanted more evidence; something big that would seal his fate forever.

Janice followed him at a safe distance for more than two miles. Finally, he pulled into the driveway of a large brick, two-story home on the outskirts of Golden. The house set back off the driveway a few hundred yards, and was secured by an eight-foot tall fence. As she passed, Janice memorized the address, (printed in red letters on a large white mailbox), at the entrance of the home. She slowly drove past the house, and parked a block away.

As she waited, pondering what to do next, she pulled a latex glove from her purse. She put it on and carefully plucked several black cat hairs off her gray pants. She placed them in a bag, and silently said to herself. "I got you, Jeremy Porter, you lying, SOB. I got you!"

CHAPTER SIXTY

The Insanity Begins

Sandra Livingstone continued to be the target of Devorah's rage, and although Sandra tried her hardest to protect her remaining sisters from their monster mother, she could not.

Devorah would first scream at her daughter to lie down on the floor, and at one time, she sat down hard on Sharon's outstretched legs until the child lost all sensation in her legs and feet. Sometimes, when Sandra would come from a psychiatric or detention facility, Devorah would make Sandra go into a corner of the den, squat down underneath the book shelves, and sit with her legs underneath her, with her butt pressing down on her ankles and feet, until her legs went numb and her feet tingled.

Becky would walk through the living room, past the den, and hear Sandra talking. Becky peeked in, and noticing that the television was not on, wondered whom Sandra was talking to. Becky would say "hi" to her older sister, and wondered if Sandra had lost her mind, since there was no one else in the room.

"I knew that day, then and there, that my sister was crazy, that Sandra had completely lost her mind. My big sister was going insane. I also felt guilty because when Sandra and Roseanne were at home and monster mommy was hurting them, I would get a reprieve—monster mommy would not hurt me when she was hurting Sandra and Roseanne."

Becky knew however, that her time was coming. She knew that if and when both her older sisters were gone, it would be her turn for the abuse, and hers alone. Becky was primed, watching Sandra and Roseanne's horrible abuse, and it taught Becky survivor skills. She thought about ways to "cope" and what her "strategies" would be with Devorah, when the time came. A small child planning a strategy to survive—how absolutely horrible—a little girl who should have been playing with dolls, swinging on swings or making life long friends—was planning, instead, on how to survive her childhood.

CHAPTER SIXTY-ONE

The Beginning of the End

Jeremy walked up the marble stairs to a massive oak door, inserted with a beautiful stained glass Columbine, the Colorado state flower.

He rang the bell, and waited only a few moments before the door opened and a man of massive physical stature, in his late fifties, stood in the doorway.

"Come on in. Glad you could come so quickly. Hope I didn't pull you away from anything important."

Jeremy walked in and shook the hand of one of Colorado's finest District Court Judges—Donald Christianson.

The Judge invited Jeremy to follow him into the massive library, asked him to take a seat, and asked if he wanted a drink?

Jeremy declined the drink offer, and took a seat in a dark blue Bradford recliner as the Judge poured himself a Scotch. The Judge then sat down in his black swivel chair behind a luxurious Oak desk.

"We've got trouble, Porter." Christianson said, somewhat irritated, sipping his Scotch. "You and I previously agreed to never meet in my home, but we have a serious problem, and I needed to see you immediately. You weren't followed, were you?

Jeremy assured him that he had not been followed. He had left his home, checked his rear view mirror often, and had circled around the Judge's impressive neighborhood twice before pulling into the Judge's driveway. No, they were safe to talk here.

"The word is that the cops got a warrant to check out the Ranch. They're out there now, checking out the house and surrounding buildings. Evidently, Bryce Jenkins' body was found on the Bartlett property. Not good. Evidently, he had been doing more than screwing the girls at Olivia's place, he had one of his "girls" doing surveillance for him, and on the night of his sudden and unexpected demise..." Donald, stopped, took a breath and showing more and more agitation now, continued. "The cops found a couple of license plate numbers on a scrap of paper in Jenkins' pants pocket. Thank God, my license plate number was not one of them. However, two of the team, Joseph Garcia-Gomez and Jack Faraguay's plate numbers were! We're screwed, Jeremy!"

Standing up now, the Judge's face got redder, as his voice got louder and louder.

"You are an idiot, Porter. I thought you were a good partner to bring in on our little moneymaker at the Ranch, but it seems I may have been wrong. I thought you were keeping an eye on things at the Ranch. How did you let this happen? How could you not know Jenkins was sticking his nose into our business? He was a cop, too, you know! One of your own! You were there, supposedly to keep a close eye on things for me! Keeping an eye on things for the both of us! I took you in as a partner because you promised to keep the "ring" a secret, to keep Olivia quiet, for a cut—and now we've got to change our plans, move our business, get off the Ranch and quickly!" The Judge was literally screaming, waiving his finger in his face, and screaming at Jeremy!

Jeremy, unafraid of the Judge's size and stature, slapped the Judge's hand away from in front of his face, stood up, and said. "You Son-of-a-bitch! I've done everything you asked me to do! I visited the Ranch often! I kept you and your buyers from being found out. I screwed every young girl that Olivia set me up with. I kept our operation going smoothly! I promised you I would be a good partner and could get the "girls" in and out of Dawson with no problems. I've done my job, Judge. It was not my fault that Jenkins got killed on the Ranch. Someone else has got to be involved here, Judge. Someone else—not me—is screwing you!"

The Judge poured himself a refill and sat back down. Jeremy walked around to the front of the Judge's desk, leaned on the desk, looked him straight in the eye and said. "I need to get to the storage lockers now! We need to get those girls out of those lockers, move them somewhere else, and you need to contact your buyers and tell them everything is on hold for the time being." Jeremy continued. "You need to calm down Judge. Get your act together. Think. Think. Think about the million bucks you're getting on the next truckload of girls. You don't want to lose that money do you Judge? I know I don't want to lose my share, that's for damn sure!"

The two men talked for a few more minutes, and Jeremy headed out the door, with final instructions to "move" the merchandise to the "other" location.

Jeremy sat down in his car, took a deep breath, and grabbed a black duffle bag from the back seat. He took out a blond wig and blond mustache, a black shirt and pants, a plaid brown and black sport coat, and black shoes. He added a large opal ring, a Rolex, and two gold chains around his neck. He had quickly changed into his "disguise".

Before pulling out of the Judge's driveway, Jeremy thought just for a moment that he might have crossed the line this time. First of all, when he decided to get involved he was sure he could handle leading a "double" or even a "triple" life. First as a partner in the Judge's prostitution and sex trafficking ring, second as an undercover for the OBA to "take out" the Judge, and on top of it all, he was supposedly, a clean-cut, working Sheriff's Deputy for Jefferson County. Now, he wasn't sure who he was. One thing he did know. He was in deep shit.

Jeremy Porter's plan had been to join in on the sex trafficking ring, make a few bucks, turn the Judge and his counterparts over to the authorities, take his share of the money and get away free and clear. That was all! Then, because he turned into a money hungry mongrel he had become a bad cop. He took money from the OBA to turn in the Judge and his buddies, took money from the Judge and his buddies for covering up the sex trafficking ring, was an undercover **good** cop at Olivia's and worst of all he had committed murder—twice!

"My God!" He cried out loud. How did I get in so deep? I am screwed!"

A half block away, Janice Poltice watched Jeremy back out of the long driveway, or at least she thought it was Jeremy. It was Jeremy's car, but as the car passed by she noticed the guy driving was a blond. "Where was Jeremy?"

CHAPTER SIXTY-TWO

Show Me the Warrant

At 4:30am Craig Olson's cell phone rang. Rousted from a sound sleep, his arm around Missy, Craig, turned over, reached for the lamp on the bedside table, and after four rings, answered.

"Craig, it's Janice." She said excitedly. "Sorry to call so early, but you need to hear me out. I'm at a warehouse on the east side of Dawson, uh, around Peoria and Interstate 70. The sign on the warehouse says, uh, Westerman's Detail Shop. I followed Jeremy Porter out here about four hours ago. I didn't know it was him at first, well, long story. I'll tell you all the details later. Anyway, I'm parked across the street, in sight of the side door, and I think something big is going down. There have been two large vans parked outside the door for about half an hour. So far, fifteen or more young Mexican or Latino girls have come out, all blind folded, with two mean looking guys, and I mean really mean looking guys, and the girls were all placed in one of the vans." Janice continued. "I think that there might be girls in the other van too. I can make out two numbers on one of the license plates—Texas plates, a number, maybe a six and a number four, but that's it. I'm too far away."

As Janice continued talking, Craig got up, grabbed a pen and paper, and wrote down the partial license plate number. He told Janice to sit tight, to stay in her vehicle, out of sight, and that he was coming to her as soon as he could throw on some clothes.

"I'll be there in less than thirty minutes, Janice." He said excitedly. I'm calling for backup. If Jeremy and his buddies are moving those girls we have to catch them in the act. Let me know if the situation changes. I'm on my way. Oh, by the way. Good job Poltice!"

Craig woke up Missy, told her what was happening, and asked her to call the police again. "Tell them Detective Olson called earlier, and latest instructions are to come in with no sirens, no flashing lights, and to stand down and stay out of sight until I get there. Remind them that the suspects are probably armed, but that there are several hostages!"

"We need to catch Jeremy and his buddies in the act of transporting young girls—if indeed that's what is actually going down." Craig thought to himself. "God, help those innocent young girls."

Janice had followed the vehicle she thought was Jeremy's to a warehouse on the east side of Dawson.

She hadn't been certain that it was Jeremy—the driver was blond instead of dark-haired—until she had watched him exit his vehicle. His swagger had given him away—she knew that walk anywhere. Strutting, cocky, SOB—yes it was Officer Jeremy Porter.

Jeremy had knocked on the warehouse door, walked in, and a few minutes later, three other men had driven on site, and joined him inside. Janice wasn't sure what was going down, but she knew it was something important or, better yet, something illegal—who did anything legal at this time of the morning anyway? She watched. She waited. She had called Craig. She was confident that whatever was happening inside that warehouse was BIG. When she saw young women being taken in blindfolds from the building, she knew it was BIG and illegal.

Several miles away at the Ranch, as Jeremy Porter was trying desperately to cover his tracks and get fifteen or more young girls hurriedly out of town, five CBI officers and four Arribio police officers had broken down the front door of the ranch house. They had rousted Olivia and seven surprised and scared sleeping young women out of bed. Two men, presumably Olivia's "watchdogs" tried running, but were captured, handcuffed and placed in one of the police cruisers.

Olivia, dressed in a "little or nothing" nightie, was shown the warrant, told to sit down and shut up. She watched officers tearing through every room, every dresser drawer, every closet, and every cabinet in her house. They confiscated the computers, went through every room upstairs, on the main floor and in the basement, looking for clues to illegal activities. Olivia sat helplessly, watching, as officers carried bag after bag of evidence from her home.

After interviewing all of the under age young women found in the ranch house, Angie, the seventeen year old who had been working with Officer Bryce Jenkins, told the officers everything she knew.

"I am so sad," the young woman told them through tears and broken English, "that Officer Jenkins is dead. He was my friend. He was going to help me leave Olivia and this place. He was going to take me away."

Angie told the CBI officer interrogating her everything she knew about the Ranch and about Bryce Jenkins. She told them about the cameras in all of the rooms, the men who came to her room often—men of "importance", as Olivia had told her, men she had to make happy. She said she and one other girl came in a large truck, many months ago. They traveled for many days, were hot and thirsty, and very hungry when they arrived. They stayed at a dirty shop with old cars and trucks inside. Then they were moved to this place where Olivia treated them nicely. Olivia gave them a nice bath, good food, and pretty clothes and they had nice bedrooms. Then, Olivia showed the girls how to make men like them, to let the men kiss them, and have sex with them, and to allow the men to do "other" things to them.

Angie began to cry. "Some girls, my friends, left Olivia after only a few days. I never see them again."

Carrying flashlights now, Angie took the investigators out into the gardens, through groves of trees, lilac and rose bushes, and finally to the entry way to the well-hidden basement.

She showed them where she had hidden on several late nights, both outside the entryway, and inside the basement. She had seen young girls, like herself, tied up, blind folded and given to one or two men who had a lot of money. After other men took the money they took the girls outside, and walked together down a road to where cars were waiting. The girls were pushed into the backseats of the cars and the men got into the cars too. Then, she had run back to the Ranch and quietly went to her room. That's all she knew.

The investigator offered Angie his handkerchief. She wiped her tears, and then she asked the investigator. "Where did the men take the other girls? What did they do with those girls? Why did those girls not stay here with Olivia, like me? What happens to me now?"

The investigator wished he could answer all of the young girls questions, but he couldn't. All he could do was promise Angie that she would be okay.

CHAPTER SIXTY-THREE

The Letter

Samantha Lynn Jenkins, her long black hair pulled back from her face in a ponytail, walked down the steps of her dormitory to the student mailroom a block away. Even though Dawson University was only a few miles from her home, she had chosen to live on campus, and go home on every other weekend. She needed to be away from her overly protective mother.

The Jenkins family had been a very close-knit family, just a few years earlier. Then, after her first year in college, her family had begun to fall apart, and she could never understand why. Her mother and dad, always so much in love, had drifted apart. Her dad was never home. He no longer played ball with her brothers, or sat with Samantha and her mom on the weekends, watching old movies—something the three of them had always loved to do.

It was only a week ago that she had watched her father's body being lowered into the ground at Mt. Olivet Cemetery. She had been devastated at her father's passing and had stayed at home for three days after her dad's funeral. Then, her mother had insisted that she try to continue her studies. Go back to class— that's what her dad would have wanted her to do. So, she did as she always did, obey her mother.

Now it had been almost a week since Bryce's death, no his murder—Samantha hated that word and wondered, "how could anyone murder my father? He was the most gentle, kindest man she had ever known—even for a cop. I loved him so much. How could someone have murdered my father?"

On her way down the block, Samantha stopped to speak to a classmate she knew, bent down to pick up a smashed soda can, which she then placed in a re-cycle dispenser. She took her mailbox key out of her backpack and opened the door to the large mailroom. There, hundreds of numbered mailboxes were stacked one on top of the other. She easily opened her box, #222, and took out a stack of mail. It was unusual for Samantha to have this much mail, but she assured herself that most of the mail would be sympathy cards or letters, a few bills and advertisements. Most she would toss into the recycle bin.

Her dad had always paid her college tuition; given her money for living expenses, and had always put plenty of money into her bank account. Her dad had taken care of all her needs, even assisting her in balancing her checkbook. The only bills she paid on her own were her credit card bills. Most of this mail too, she presumed, would be unimportant.

Samantha quickly sifted through the stack of mail, recognizing familiar return addresses from family and friends, a letter from the student union, a few advertisements for part time employment and a free pizza deal. One letter, however, immediately caught her attention—the return address was her late grandfather's. He had been dead for over five years!

"What the heck?" She thought to herself. "Why am I getting a letter from my dead grandpa's address?"

Samantha left the mailroom, walked out the door and sat down on a bench on the grass outside the Student Union building. She placed the cards and letters next to her on the bench, and immediately opened the letter with her dead grandpa's return address.

The letter was printed on yellow, double-spaced writing paper, similar to a pad Samantha had in her backpack. It was dated one day before her father's death, in his own handwriting:

Dear Sam,

"If you are reading this letter, I'm sure that you have already been to my funeral. Knowing you as well as I do, I know that the return address on the envelope has surprised you. I had to do this for security reasons—I think someone will be going through our mail at home, Sam. Our old friend, Jackson Dodd, grandpa Jenkins' neighbor, has mailed this letter to you, per my request. I saw him just a few months ago and asked that in case of my untimely death, he would mail this letter to you. He's a good ole guy, and was a great friend to your grandpa and to me. Please try and see him sometime soon. Thank him again for me for keeping and then mailing this letter.

First of all, I am so sorry that you and your brothers, and your mother have had to go through all of this, my death, most likely a suspicious death, my funeral and life now without me. I am just so sorry, Sam. Please forgive me.

I got myself into a lot of trouble the past two years, and I realized that the only way to clear my name and my family's name was to do what I did the last months of my life. So, here is what I need for you to do, Sam. I know that I can trust you more than anyone. I love your mother very much, but she would never handle what I am about to tell you. After you have read this letter, and have done what I am asking you to do, then you can sit down with her and tell her everything. Once again, my precious, Samantha, I am so sorry. You were always my angel, my beautiful, angel. I will love you always."

Sam continued to read her father's letter, tears streaming down her face. At one time a young man walked up to the bench, asked her if she was okay, and when Samantha said, yes, he had quietly walked away.

"In the bottom of my old, green army trunk
in the garage, under a bunch of tools, you will
find two envelopes. One is addressed to you
and your brothers, and the other is addressed
to Detective Craig Olson. His telephone number
is written on the envelope, and as soon as you
finish reading this letter, I want you to call
him. Ask him to meet you at the house, as soon
as you can get away, and to open the trunk
with you there. I want him to be a witness.
The envelope has photos—lots of photos, notes,
receipts, and more evidence on the case I was
working on, and the case I know Detective Olson
is working on. Please, Sam, it's very important
that you call him first, and then together, you
open the trunk and give him the envelope.
The second envelope has my insurance policy.
This policy will insure you and your brothers'
welfare for the rest of your lives. The money
will cover all of your college costs, and will see
that you, my darling Samantha, will get into
law school. There is also enough to pay both of
your brother's college costs. I have left you the
name of my lawyer who will inform you of all
the details. Once you turn twenty-one Sam, I
have left you in charge of my estate and you and
your brother's welfare. Until then, my lawyer,
Jerry Gibson, will see to all your needs."

Knowing his daughter well, he knew that this point in the
letter, Samantha would be concerned about her mother, and he
continued to write:

"Your mother will be fine, too, financially.
She will get all of my police benefits. No
worries Sam, she will be fine. She will be able
to continue in the lifestyle she as become
accustomed to."

Samantha chuckled. Her mother was a real "piece of work". She knew it. Her father knew it. Her mother was an awesome, but sometimes irritating, aggressive, woman who enjoyed the finer things of life. Samantha continued reading:

"Sam, you may hear things about me that aren't true. There may be some things you hear about me that are true. I hope you will listen to the good things said about me, and even though I did some really bad things, most of what you hear will be untrue. Just know that I was a good police officer. I protected the city and all of its citizens for almost twenty years. I did, however, get involved with some really "bad" people, and with all of the evidence I am having you give to Detective Olson, those people should be sent to prison and my name should be cleared."

"Samantha Elaine Jenkins, I've loved you since the day you were conceived. I hope you can forgive me, and forgive the men who did this to me. Don't live your life in anger or hate. Forgive, go forward and become a FAMOUS lawyer someday. I will be watching over you."

Love, Dad

Samantha folded the letter, placed it back in the envelope, and chuckled as she again looked at the return address. "Dad really planned this one." She thought. "Even when he knew he was going to die, he had a plan to take down the bad guys, and to keep his family safe and well taken care of."

Looking up towards the heavens, Samantha smiled, pressed her fingers to her lips, and threw kisses upward. "I love you dad."

CHAPTER SIXTY-FOUR

I will not go Crazy

Becky Livingstone was sitting on the toilet where monster mommy had told her to sit. Becky and her sisters were told "when" to go to the bathroom, not when they "needed" to use the bathroom and Becky, now almost eight years old, had been told that she "needed" to go, now!

Becky and her sisters were told when to use the bathroom, when to eat—and how much to eat, when to sleep, even when to think. Force-feeding, name-calling, any type of humiliation was Devorah Livingstone's form of controlling her adopted daughters—except for Katherine. Beautiful, blond-haired Katherine was never abused, not physically anyway. Her abuse was mental. She learned her mother's evil ways—screaming, hollering and hitting her sisters. In her own way, Devorah was controlling Katherine too. It was just a different form of abuse.

"My mother controlled my every thought. I had no choices, no decisions to make, because I was not allowed to think for myself. On top of that, each sister started to squeal on each other; it was the only chance of survival".

Sandra and Roseanne, due to their monster mommy's accusations knew that if they remained in the Livingstone home, they might die. They didn't want to leave their baby sister alone in the torture chamber they called home, but they had no choice. Each sister was now on their own.

The little girl who had worked so hard to keep her little family together was losing her mind.

The Livingstone's called psychiatrist after psychiatrist and finally the supervisor at the Bethesda Mental Health Center in Dawson accepted Sandra as a patient. Devorah convinced the authorities that their daughter was a very troubled child—a child that hated her mother. Sandra would spend the day in the psychiatry ward at the hospital, return home in the evenings, where the abuse would continue, then back to the hospital again the next morning. Sandra would try her hardest to convince her therapists that her mother was abusive, that she was the one who needed help. Once again, no one listened. Finally, after coming back home for the holidays, the Livingstone's had Sandra committed to the Sacred Heart Home in Pueblo. This was the last time Becky saw her sister, Sandra, until Becky turned fourteen and would run to California to find her older sister.

Meanwhile, Roseanne was now undergoing psychiatric evaluations at Bethesda and Ft. Logan Mental Institutions, due to Devorah's insistence—and the good doctor agreed.

It was during this time when Roseanne would come home for weekend visits, although separated from the rest of the family, by being placed in the basement, that Roseanne was severely injured and Becky almost drowned.

Katherine, Becky and Roseanne were at a local swimming park. While Katherine was sitting on the edge of the pool, with her legs in the water, and Becky was treading water in the deep end of the swimming pool, Becky backed into the wall right underneath where Katherine was sitting. Katherine placed her legs tightly around Becky's neck, and pushed her head down with her hands, and kept her underneath the water, until Becky could barely get any air. Becky could have died, and her first thought was that Devorah had put Katherine up to it. Becky knew that Devorah had tried so many times before to kill her, that she could have easily talked her favorite daughter into killing Becky.

"Katherine continued to hold my head under water until I could no longer hold my breath. I was sure I was going to die. Katherine, so much like her mother now, wanted to kill me too. Luckily, I survived. I never told anyone. What good would it have done, anyway?"

During this same outing, Roseanne, while running in the park, hit her knee hard on the corner of a cement bench, severely cutting her right knee, splitting her knee wide open, blood pouring down her leg, as she fell to the ground. Katherine and Becky watched it horror. Becky helped Rosanne hop home, while Katherine skipped the two blocks home, as if nothing had happened. When they got home, Katherine told her parents that Rosanne had run into a bench at the park and was bleeding.

When the other girls entered the home, Dr. Livingstone immediately went to get his doctor's black bag, while Devorah ran for paper towels and told Rosanne to sit on the ottoman, and to NOT get blood on the furniture or carpet! Without giving Roseanne any anesthetic, he stitched up her leg. Roseanne, in horrible pain was unable to scream, because Devorah had her hands over the poor child's mouth, which muffled her screams. The doctor still gave her nothing for the pain. Katherine and Becky sat in the living room listening to their sister screaming, in silence. Later on, after Roseanne was also gone from the Livingstone's, her leg would become horribly infected and with no further medical attention, a blood clot formed on her knee.

Dr. Livingstone did not take her to a pediatrician or a specialist. As always he did nothing. Even after they sent Roseanne to the Sacred Heart Orphanage, and before the Livingstone's gave Roseanne and Sandra back to the state of Colorado, the Orphanage personnel called the Livingstone's telling them that their daughter was crawling, because she could put no weight on her injured knee and leg. The personnel asked that they come and get their daughter and take her to the emergency room or to a doctor. Devorah responded that "No, absolutely not. That girl just wants attention!"

No one ever took Roseanne to see a doctor. Roseanne lived with severe pain for over fifteen years from the blood clot, finally having to have her leg amputated. The abuse was never ending.

When Devorah could no longer tolerate Roseanne, and having her hospitalized in mental institutions did no good, she had both committed to the Sacred Heart Home, an Orphanage in Pueblo, Colorado.

Sandra, after years of abuse, and having spent time in Bethesda and Ft. Logan mental hospitals in Dawson, was now in the Sacred Heart Home, in Pueblo, Colorado; a mental hospital for troubled youth. Roseanne however was the runner. She would be placed in Ft. Logan during the week, and be allowed to come home on the weekends. Each time she came home, she ran. Finally, Roseanne too, was placed at Sacred Heart Home. Devorah Livingstone thought the two girls were entirely to "mental" to live with her any longer. Once again, everyone involved believed what Devorah told them was the truth.

The Sacred Heart Cathedral and Orphanage was built in 1903. It served one hundred and fifty boys and girls at a time. The two older sisters actually felt safe there. But, the damage was done. The girls wanted their freedom, and they would get it, one way or another.

The Livingstone's gave up their adoption rights to the two older girls. Sandra and Roseanne were right back where they had started, in an orphanage. Roseanne managed to get out and live in an Independent Living Center for a few months, but shortly after that move, she, again, ran away. Sandra had already run off when she was fourteen—to California, and Roseanne followed her there. Becky was eight years old and totally alone. There was no one, absolutely no one to protect her from the monster mommy! She would not see her biological sisters again for eight years.

On one of the days when the abuse was so intense that Becky thought that she would surely be killed. Devorah grabbed Becky by the arm, and told her harshly to sit on the floor in the sitting room, She told her to stay sitting and began to take photo albums out of the closet. What happened next was deplorable. Devorah, sat on the floor next to Becky, took each photo of Becky's sisters and, one by one, tore them to shreds in front of Becky.

"This is to prove to you." Devorah. said, a smirk on her evil face. "That you are just like your sisters, no wonder your real mother never wanted or loved any of you!' Again she said, "You are just like your sisters, you were adopted because your real mother never wanted or loved you! Do you hear me? Your mother would have been better off if you all had died! I would be better off if you had all died!"

Screaming louder now, while still shredding the photos, Devorah stood up, and said. "You all came straight from the devil, himself!" Devorah threw the trash can at Becky, and told her to clean up the mess!

Becky knew now, after almost eight years, and for the first time, that Devorah Livingstone was NOT her real mother and that she was adopted. Becky was so programmed by now, and had always believed that Devorah was her real mother, and she couldn't understand why Devorah kept saying "why do you hate me so", when all along it was "Devorah who hated all of us."

"I was glad she had finally told me that I was adopted. That I really did have a mother, a mother who I was sure, had really loved my sisters and me. I knew for sure that our real mother would never have hated us or tried to kill us like monster mommy. No real mother would despise their kids like Devorah despised us."

Becky, even at her young age, wondered why Devorah and her husband had adopted her.

"If she didn't like us, why did she adopt us?"
"This is a question for all eternity. I don't think I will ever have an answer, at least not in this lifetime."

The young girl did as she was told. Down on her knees, tears falling down her cheeks, she cleaned up the shredded photos, piece by piece and placed them in the trashcan. Later in life, Patricia, a dear friend of Becky's was looking at photo albums, when she came across photos of the sisters with their foster mother and surprisingly said, while pointing a finger directly at the photo of Becky, "that's MY Becky".

Patricia and Becky had been good friends and racquetball partners for many years. It just so happened that Patricia's husband had lived next to Nell Cooper, and had babysat Becky quite often. Becky's name was written on the backside of the photo. What a small world!

"I knew then and there that there truly was a God. This could not have been a coincidence and I still have that photo today."

Becky did not ever feel that she would go crazy or insane, but she feared that she might die at the hands of Devorah. She told herself then and there, on the floor of her monster mommy's sitting room that she would close her mind to everything that happened to her from that day on.

Becky hated summers. She knew that she would have to clean a six-bedroom, 3-bathroom house, keeping it spotless, every day. She continued to be force-fed, and made to sit by Devorah's side while she watched her soap operas, or Devorah would have Becky sent to the basement. "I can't stand the sight of you", Devorah would shout at Becky. "Get out of my sight!" Having gained another twenty pounds, Devorah, also cut off all of Becky's hair, just as she had done to Sandra. On the first day of school that year, Becky's hair was so short, and she was so fat, that even her schoolmates did not recognize her.

CHAPTER SIXTY-FIVE

Caught in the Act

Judge Donald Christianson tried not to show how nervous he was when he walked into the Dawson County Courthouse for his 1:00pm appointment. He walked up to security, showed his identification, emptied his pockets into the blue plastic bin and walked through the metal detector. He walked in the back door of courtroom number eight, and into his chamber. He had bid his secretary a good morning and poured himself a cup of coffee. He sat down at his desk, looked at his Citizen watch—a gift from his oldest daughter—one more time, and contemplated his future—again.

He had not heard from Jeremy Porter in the past twelve hours, so he presumed, no, he prayed that Jeremy had moved the girls from the warehouse. He was confident the vans were on their way to the new location in Lone Tree, the backup location. Lone Tree was a long way from the Ranch for the final sale and transfer of the girls, but Donald assured himself that his "people" would take care of it. He also admitted to himself that this would be the last sale. The authorities were getting to close.

Judge Christianson looked at his watch again, stood up and took his black robe from the closet, put it on and opened the door to his courtroom. He scanned the room. There were only ten to fifteen visitors sitting on the hard, courtroom benches. In the front seat a young man, maybe fifteen years of age, sat with two very worried looking parents. The judge walked towards the bench, as the security guard called for "all to stand" and announced that court was now in session.

Donald had not been seated more than two minutes and had not had time to look over the paperwork laying in front of him, when the double doors to the courtroom opened and two CBI agents walked in. One agent walked down the isle and up the three steps to where the judge sat. He asked him to stand and to put his hands behind his back. The second agent stood in front of the bench and began to read the judge his rights.

"Judge Donald Christianson?" The agent barked. "You are under arrest. You have the right to remain silent. Anything you say, may be held against you in a court of law....." The judge looked around pleading with his dark brown eyes for the Court Reporter or Security Guard to do something! There was nothing anyone could have done.

Six hours prior to the Judge taking the bench in courtroom number eight, seven people at the warehouse where young girls were being held, had been captured, read their rights, handcuffed and placed in the back of five Dawson police cruisers. There had been four detectives, three CBI agents, and five Dawson cops involved in the raid and capture. One of those detectives had been Craig Olson.

Jeremy Porter, still in disguise, had been one of those captured and he too, had been read his rights. However, as the morning sun had begun to rise, Jeremy had taken off the wig and mustache and had walked with the detective to his vehicle where he had shown the detective his credentials. Jeremy had tried his best to prove that he was an undercover officer on sight, and was in no way involved in the sex trafficking ring.

Detective Olson had not believed a word that came out of Jeremy Porters' mouth.

Craig had ordered Officer Janice Poltice to leave the crime scene as soon as he, the CBI and everyone else involved were on sight. Craig had told her to go directly to the crime laboratory with the evidence she had collected from Jeremy Porters' house the previous evening. Craig promised Janice that he would make the call to the ME and have him get to the lab first thing. Craig wanted the evidence in Stan's hands the minute the lab opened its doors at 7:00am. Janice was to wait until he got there and personally hand him the items in question.

Those captured, along with Officer Porter, included one congressman, one Dawson politician and an employee of the District Attorney's office. With a promise that the DA would go easy on them if they cooperated, the men of importance in Dawson had spilled their guts, giving the name of everyone involved, including the BOSS, Judge Donald Christianson. Jeremy Porter had refused to cooperate. It wasn't until Craig Olson got a telephone call later in the day from Stan, his man, the Medical Examiner, that Craig knew Jeremy was a guilty party. Now, Craig had to prove it.

Craig Olson had been at the crime scene for more than eight hours. He had first called Missy to assure her that he was okay and then picked up his messages, the most important one, he hoped, would be the one from Stan. Craig had been right. Stan's message stated that he had proof that the male donor, the father of Mandy Sue's baby, was indeed, Jeremy Porter. The news was just what Craig had hoped for. It didn't prove that Jeremy had been involved in her murder, but it did prove that he knew her. Craig smiled as he listened to the rest of his messages. The message from Samantha Jenkins especially peaked his interest.

CHAPTER SIXTY-SIX

Case Closed

Craig Olson took a fifteen-minute break and stopped at a Starbucks where he enjoyed an almond flavored latte and an apple turnover. He had called Samantha Jenkins on his way from the warehouse. She informed him that she had class until 4:00pm, but she could meet with him later in the day. She wanted to make sure her mother and brothers were out of the house when the detective arrived. Craig had told the other detectives that he would meet up with them later to fill out what he knew would be pages of police reports.

His part of the "take-down" at the warehouse was over except for getting Jeremy Porter to sign a confession, which he was refusing to do.

Reports coming in from the Ranch were as good or better. Agents were still at the scene securing evidence and dusting for fingerprints throughout both the ranch house and the hidden basement. The seven young women, supposed prostitutes, were "talking" and were being driven to a woman's shelter close by. Early reports were that Olivia Bartlett was also being very cooperative.

The thirty-minute drive across Dawson to the Jenkins' home was a pleasant one. It was early enough in the day that traffic was minimal and Craig enjoyed the "down time". It had been a rough twelve hours.

As he looked down the street for Bryce Jenkins' address, he wondered how Officer Jenkins had managed to live in such an upscale neighborhood. Most of the brick homes were two-story, with massive white pillars, and two or three-car garages. The lawns were beautifully landscaped, with bushes and flowers of all shapes and colors in full bloom. Locating the address, he parked in front of the Jenkins' home, and as he did so, a tall, slender, quite attractive young woman came out of the front door.

"Hi." She said sweetly, but with a tone of sadness. "Detective Olson? I'm Samantha Jenkins. Please, follow me, and we'll go to the garage."

Craig realized that this was going to be a very difficult situation for Officer Jenkins' young daughter. He promised her he would make it as easy on her as possible. Upon entering the garage, Samantha first gave him the letter she had received, and Craig took a few minutes to read it. He told her that he might need the letter and envelope as evidence, and she said she understood.

The two-car garage was very neat, with everything in its proper place—unlike his own. Samantha had evidently been in the garage prior to his arrival, as an old green army trunk was pulled out into the middle of the garage floor. Craig kneeled down next to the trunk, and Samantha did the same. He asked her if she was ready to handle whatever they found inside, and she said yes. He also advised her that he would have to confiscate the trunk but he promised to get it back to her.

"Have you opened the trunk or looked inside the trunk since you got the letter Ms. Jenkins?" He asked politely. She said no.

Craig put on a pair of latex gloves and laid a plastic bag on the garage floor. He easily lifted the trunk lid and took out a variety of pliers, screwdrivers, bolt cutters and other types of tools, laying them gently onto the plastic. The tools were lying in a cardboard drawer, which, when emptied, he also lifted out and placed on the plastic. He first turned the drawer upside down, checking for any other possible evidence. In the bottom of the trunk there were three large manila envelopes. One was marked to Samantha and her brothers. The other two envelopes were addressed to Detective Craig Olson. Craig looked into Samantha's tear filled eyes and asked her if she wanted to look into the envelope addressed to her immediately or did she want to do that on her own time? She took the envelope from Craig's hands, held it close to her chest and said she would look at its contents later. She knew what was in the envelope.

Craig felt that he needed to allow Samantha to remain in the garage when he opened the two envelopes addressed to him. He wasn't sure if it was proper "police protocol", but he knew the moment Samantha Jenkins had left him the telephone message that Officer Jenkins daughter could handle anything found in the old trunk. She knew more about her father, he was sure, than she was ready to admit.

Craig went from a kneeling position to sitting cross-legged on the floor. Samantha did the same, still clutching her envelope. He opened the first envelope, gently and with great anticipation. Could there be enough proof here to put Jeremy Porter away for life? Did Jeremy Porter murder Mandy Sue? Did Jeremy Porter murder Samantha's father? His mind was swirling.

CHAPTER SIXTY-SEVEN

When Will the Abuse End?

On a sunny afternoon, that same summer, when most children were riding bicycles or hanging out at the city swimming pool, Becky, adopted daughter of Bernard and Devorah Livingstone was once again going through hell on earth. Devorah continued to force-feed her, a form of severe abuse, and she would lie and twist situations around making it look as if the young girl was always wrong, and Devorah was always right. This was Devorah's reasoning, each and every time. This at times made Becky question her own sanity. Becky was completely brainwashed by this time. Becky was so confused when Devorah would scream, "why do you hate me so much"? Becky didn't understand. **"I didn't hate her! She hated me!"**

Becky continued to be force-fed and continually gained weight. Her school uniforms constantly changed in size, not because of her age, but because of the force-feedings. She was now also receiving severe abuse from her monster mommy, as severe as her sisters, Sandra, and Roseanne had received. The only difference was, that now Sandra had Roseanne and Roseanne had Sandra, and Becky, as she always feared was alone. Becky had no one!

Becky was not treated well at school by her schoolmates, thinking she was weird and strange; what child wouldn't be, if before school even began, she was made to eat six to eight pancakes with huge amounts of sugar and butter, along with three glasses of milk before she ever left the house. After that meal, Devorah stood at the table with a trashcan, tearing up her schoolbooks. Then at noon, Becky came home for lunch, which consisted of three peanut butter sandwiches, and three glasses of milk. Becky learned, how to sneak one sandwich in her underwear, and then after she left home, throw it over the neighbor's fence.

School was an escape for Becky. First of all, she could get away from monster mommy. Second, she loved books and writing. Becky remembered earlier in her life, writing a story about a puppy that was drowned in the bathtub. Of course, her teacher called Devorah and told her about the horrific story Becky had written. The teacher asked why a young girl would be writing these kinds of stories at such a young age. Devorah answered by stating that her daughter was mentally ill. Devorah never mentioned however, the fact that she tried to drown Becky in the bathtub, after which she wrote that story. Becky looked forward to gym class and playing basketball every day after school.

Katherine, a year older than Becky also played basketball, and Dr. and Mrs. Livingstone would come to Katherine's Little League games, cheer her on from the bleachers, making sure everyone else saw that they were "involved" parents. They could not refuse to let Becky play basketball, because that would look suspicious to their prominent friends.

On a Tuesday afternoon, Becky's gym teacher called Devorah to tell her how talented her two girls were in basketball, especially Becky,

"Becky is very good, especially being left-handed." The teacher had said. "She can shoot from either side of the floor, make lay-ups on the run. She's just very good, and I wanted you to let you know."

Because Becky was the talented one in sports, and not her precious Katherine, Devorah developed a plan in that conniving mind of hers to destroy Becky's chances of being a member of the team.

Her after school duties consisted of emptying the trash and picking up the dog feces in the back yard. Becky did as she was told, every time. On one particular day Devorah told her, after her duties were completed, to wait in the basement until Devorah told her she could leave.

"I should have known Devorah was up to something. I knew that every minute of every day could be miserable for me, and I

should have known. Sure enough, she called me from the basement, dragged me outside and asked why I hadn't picked up the dog poop? I told her I had picked it up. Devorah had taken the poop out of the trashcan and re-dumped it onto the back yard. I thought maybe I hadn't picked it up—maybe I had done it the day before, and she was right? When I said I must have forgot, she called me horrible names, asinine, mentally retarded, stupid, fat-ass, and more. Devorah's favorite saying, as she patted me hard on the head, was, "you poor, mentally ill child".

Becky never played basketball at school again, or in Little League. She could only play in the alley behind her home, only if Katherine would play with her. Devorah made certain that Becky missed school and practice that day, and told the teacher that Becky really didn't want to play the game anymore. Once again, Devorah had taken away the one thing that Becky loved. Devorah's style of torture and abuse had won out again.

"I remember later on in life, long after the Livingstone days, I still loved the game so much that I enrolled in junior college in Santa Anna, California to take journalism classes but it was a cover up just to play basketball. After only a month in school, I was so drunk when I showed up for practice one day, that I was immediately kicked off the team, and out of school."

CHAPTER SIXTY-EIGHT

The Manila Envelope

Craig watched Samantha's face as he pulled out several white business size envelopes from the first manila envelope. He carefully opened the white envelope, took out the neatly folded letter and began to read the first letter addressed to him. He told Samantha that it was much better if he kept the information confidential, for now, but he promised to let her know all of the detailed information, when he could.

Bryce Jenkins gave up his heart and soul in the letters. He shared with Craig how much he loved being a police officer, why and how he had come to join the OBA, what the OBA was all about, who was in charge, where they got their funding and where they had their meetings—the bar on Colorado Boulevard. He gave names; Tyler Morris, Jeremy Porter (alias Jerry Boston/ Shorty), Sam Graves, Jackson Styles, and many more. Craig recognized many of the names, but not all of them. He had wondered what name Jeremy Porter used on all of his "disguised outings". Now he knew.

Bryce continued with the entire story of Mandy Sue Donnor, her years with Olivia, her beatings and who had hurt her, and then, finally her murder. Bryce admitted that he, along with two other OBA members (the names did not ring a bell for Craig), had beaten her. Then, the confession Craig was looking for: Bryce, Jerry, two guys named John Davidson and Tory Spiegel, non-cops, had kidnapped and killed her.

Bryce went into the horrid, gory details of the murder. The place, the time of day, the vehicle they moved the body in. Every detail. Jerry Boston had actually shot Mandy then had sex with her dead, warm body; something that had made Bryce sick to his stomach. He had moved a few yards away from the horrific scene, puked up his guts, and been razzed by the other men for being a "chicken", before helping load and then dump the girl's body.

Craig, stopped reading, took a deep breath and after touching Samantha on the shoulder, continued to read. Samantha had not moved from her spot on the garage floor. She was like a stone, watching Craig with her bright brown eyes—eyes like her father's.

The next letter told of Olivia Bartlett and the Ranch. Bryce's role as an older, executive type, needing love and attention, had been his cover. He was there not as a cop, but as an OBA member. The OBA had planned to get all of the facts on corrupt city officials involved in the sex trafficking ring, those visiting the prostitutes and Olivia Bartlett. When the time was right, the OBA would give the police department a heads-up for a takedown. Bryce admitted that the Dawson police department could not now, or could they ever, handle all of the corruption, murder, burglaries, kidnappings, etc, in the city, unless there could be more hiring's. The OBA was doing what they thought was "good" for the city and its citizens.

He mentioned the name of the "other" prostitute that the OBA had murdered, and that her body had been dumped in the river—just to keep her from identifying members of the OBA. He named ranch hands, limousine companies and their drivers, the dates and times of finding the entrance to the basement, and what he saw there, and the roads leading in and out of the Ranch. He reminded Craig that he had photos of everything written in these letters. He had a number code on each paragraph, which Craig presumed would match a number code on photos—presumably in the other manila envelope.

Bryce went on to tell how many times he had covered up for a high-ranking official in Dawson. He admitted that he had been paid big bucks for making DUI or traffic fines disappear, for court witnesses changing their stories, for setting up judges and congressmen with ladies of the night, and for changing dates and times on police reports and more.

Craig was exhausted from reading. He stood up, asked Samantha if he could have a glass of water, and held out his hand to assist her to a standing position as well.

"It's bad, isn't it Detective Olson." She said, continuing to hold his hand. "My dad was a really good man, a great police officer. I just can't believe he did something so awful that he had to be killed. Did he do things that were really that bad, Detective?"

Craig put his arm around her, and said yes, that he had been involved in some really bad stuff, but with all of this information, Craig was certain he could help clear her father's name.

Craig waited in the garage until Samantha returned with a bottle of water. She handed it to him and immediately sat back down onto the garage floor. Craig did the same. He took two huge swigs of the water, replaced the bottle cap and opened the second envelope. He had read enough. He would re-read all of the letters when he returned to the office. For now, he was ready to see the real proof—the photos.

CHAPTER SIXTY-NINE

Broken

Becky's final memory of her sisters was first of all when Devorah took the one and only material thing Sandra owned and loved—her pink ballerina jewelry box. It had been a gift from her grandparents, the Dawkins, and the only gift she received that Christmas. Devorah said she would take the gift upstairs and place it on a shelf in their room. The next thing, everyone heard was Devorah smashing the beautiful, twirling pink ballerina into a million pieces. Devorah came back downstairs to where the family was celebrating Christmas, and acted as if nothing had ever happened.

This was the last Christmas that Becky ever saw her older sister. Later on, when Rosanne was also placed at the Sacred Heart Home, she remembers Sandra twirling down the hallways in her fantasy world, steadily losing her mind. Roseanne, also knew then, that her sister had lost her mind.

The little girl who had worked so hard to keep her little family together was steadily losing her mind and going insane.

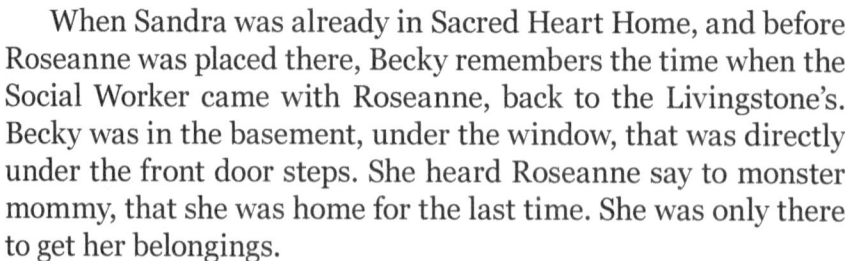

When Sandra was already in Sacred Heart Home, and before Roseanne was placed there, Becky remembers the time when the Social Worker came with Roseanne, back to the Livingstone's. Becky was in the basement, under the window, that was directly under the front door steps. She heard Roseanne say to monster mommy, that she was home for the last time. She was only there to get her belongings.

"I saw a social worker come up to my house. I remember looking out of the basement window and seeing Roseanne with the social

worker. I had already heard Roseanne tell monster mommy that she was home to get her stuff and she was leaving. I felt hopeless, a feeling I had never felt before. For the first time I was alone. Sandra and Roseanne were gone, and I would be the only one left to get the abuse. Sandra and Roseanne were together again at the orphanage in Pueblo. At least they had each other. I had no one. I told myself that day: 'Little Beck, don't throw up, don't cry, no matter what happens, don't let her kill you—survive'. I would not feel the beatings or torture any longer. I couldn't feel anything at all. I would survive. I promised myself—I would survive."

CHAPTER SEVENTY

The Snake

Missy looked at the kitchen clock, poured herself a glass of iced tea and wondered where her fiancé might be. Craig had called her twice; first to let her know about Janice Poltice locating the warehouse, and next on his way to the Jenkins' home. He had promised her that he would be home in time to take her to dinner, their weekly 'night out', and for her not to worry.

"Don't worry? Sure, Detective Olson, I won't worry." She thought chuckling. "Why did men always say that to their women? Don't worry."

Missy had spent a lazy day cleaning up their apartment, making a batch of Craig's favorite chocolate-oatmeal cookies, and looking through the telephone book for the name, Bernard Livingstone. It had been several months since she had seen the little sisters, and now that Tabatha was gone, she hoped the three remaining girls were in a loving home. She really wanted to see them again. She wasn't sure that was possible, but she hoped so. Placing children with adoptive parents was usually private, and all court documents sealed, but yet, she wanted to try and find them. She had found one B. Livingstone, but as it turned out it was not the name she was looking for. She wouldn't give up. She would find out where those little girls were living.

Missy also took time to look through page after page of several bridal magazines, dreaming of walking down the isle with the love of her life. She and Craig had not set a wedding date, but she wanted to start making plans. She had no idea what type or style of gown she wanted, but how fun it was to look.

Just as Missy poured herself a second glass of iced tea, her cell phone rang. A sobbing, young woman asked if she was Missy Baker? Missy said yes, and could she be of help? Missy waited a few seconds, then asked the distraught woman again, what she could do to help her? Settling down a little, the young woman said her name was Jolene, and her car had just been stolen.

"Did you call the police?" Missy asked.

"No, I haven't called them. They won't help me, I know."

Missy asked her again. "Why didn't you call the police? Are you in danger? Are you in a safe place? Where was your car stolen from?"

Jolene, if that was her name explained that her car was stolen from 7th and Dawson Parkway. She just went into a convenience store, leaving her car unlocked, because she would only be gone for a second—and someone took it.

"I have to get it back!" The woman said, panicking now. "I have to get it back. Domino is in the backseat."

Missy, more alarmed now that there might be a child involved, told Jolene to hang up, call the police, and if she still needed Missy's help, she would be happy to help her. "This isn't just a theft, it's a kidnapping. The local police need to get involved, not a Private Investigator!"

The woman began to cry again, and pleading with Missy said. "Domino has to get to a doctor. He swallowed a toy truck, and it's stuck in his throat! We have to find my car! I don't want him to die!"

"Oh my gosh." Missy thought. "Why has this woman not called the police? This child has a medical emergency. What was wrong with this woman anyway?"

Once again, she told the woman, a little more sharply now, that she absolutely needed to hang up and call 911 and to do it immediately.

The woman refused. Once again she repeated that the cops would not help her. "Domino has to get to a veterinarian. The cops won't help me find my car, because there is a bull snake in the backseat. Sissy cops. They're sissy pants cops. They won't help me find my Domino!"

Missy sat down in a chair. Let out a breath and then laughed. Laughed until she almost fell off the chair.

"Lady!" She yelled. "Why did you call me? I'm a Private Investigator, and I look for lost people, or troubled teenagers, or people having elicited affairs, or...WHY AM I TELLING YOU THIS!! Hang up and call the police or animal control or anybody else, but I CAN'T HELP YOU!" Missy hung up the telephone.

Missy sat for a second, and then burst into laughter again. She laughed so hard that tears began to run down her cheeks and onto her white Dawson Nuggets Tee Shirt. It was just what she needed. She had not had a good laugh in so many weeks that she couldn't remember. She couldn't wait to tell Craig. A snake. A snake for God's sake!! Maybe she should have taken the job. She had never looked for a lost snake before. She'd known a few human "snakes" in her life. A snake! She snorted from all the laughing.

CHAPTER SEVENTY-ONE

The Photos

Craig opened the second manila envelope with apprehension. He had no idea what to expect. He asked Samantha if she wanted to continue sitting on the cement garage floor with him, and she said yes.

"I have no idea what your father was into, Ms. Jenkins." He said softly. "I can't show you the photos, but I will share anything I can with you, later. I promise. Just don't get excited if I say something, or show emotion that might concern you. Do we agree?"

Samantha said yes, that she agreed. Craig wished that he had never invited her to stay in the garage. He should have taken the trunk to the department and gone through it there. He turned, looked into this poor girl's face and pulled out the first photos.

There was another letter, rubber-banded around the first batch of photos. The letter said that Officer Jenkins had begun to question the OBA, and what they supposedly stood for. He was also questioning his own judgment. He had purchased a small camera and had installed it onto the side and top of his glasses frame. He also had a lapel pin that was a camera, and although he did not wear that camera each time, it had given him some good photos. He had also purchased a camera that he had used at night outside of the ranch house.

The first batch of photos were of young girls, many of them scantily dressed, dirty, some in tears, matted hair and looking very afraid. There were photos of the two large vans at the warehouse, and of the men who drove those vans. Bryce had gotten close-up photos of Jeremy Porter (alias Jerry Boston) in his blond wig and mustache, two OBA members (Bryce had written their names on the bottom of the photo), and had an incredible close up of the judge.

Craig paused for just a moment and thought. "My gosh! Jenkins should have been a photographic journalist. He missed his calling." He continued looking at the photos.

There were photos of the girls at the Ranch with names added to the bottom of the photos. He had even put their birthplace and date on the photos. Bryce had done his homework. There were photos of Olivia, a man he presumed to be the head of the OBA, Tyler Morris, three or four other political figures in Dawson and several photos of the gardens. He had photos of the basement entrance, and of the actual selling and exchange of money for those poor young girls. Craig felt like a kid at Christmas. He had hit a police department jackpot.

The final batches of photographs were the ones Craig longed to see, the beatings and murder of Mandy Sue Donnor. Bryce had not let him down. There were photos of the three men beating up the young woman, photos of her bloodied body, photos of her apartment house, the telephone booth, and the worst of all—a photo of Jeremy Porter or Jerry Boston, or whatever the hell he was called, shooting Mandy in the head.

Craig began sweating profusely and quickly took a swig of water from the water bottle. If he hadn't, he might have tossed his cookies right there, in Bryce Jenkins' garage, in front of Jenkins' very brave daughter.

Craig continued flipping through the photos. There it was, right in front of him—Bryce had taken a photo of Jeremy violating the dead woman's corpse. Craig stood up quickly, making sure to not drop any of the photos, and headed out the garage door for some air. Samantha quickly followed.

"Are you alright detective?" She asked concern with in her voice. Did you see something terrible? Was it my dad? Please tell me."

Craig, more composed now, told her that no, it was nothing about her father What her father had done was to take photos that would put some very bad guys away for years to come. He assured her once again that her father, due to his police work, would most likely be declared a hero.

Once again, her tears began to fall.

CHAPTER SEVENTY-TWO

Interrogation and Admittance

There were so many men and women taken into custody after the raids on the warehouse and the Ranch, that there were not enough interrogation rooms to hold them all. The detectives were taking turns interrogating them, getting their fingerprints, and taking police photos. The scene was unbelievable! Never. Never in the history of the Dawson Police Force had there been this big of a takedown.

Judge Christianson had been taken quietly out of his Court Chambers and had cooperated fully with authorities. It was amazing how many young girls had been sold and how much money the judge had pocketed over the past few years. What a scumbag. The detectives wanted nothing more than to see him put away for life. Even Olivia Bartlett talked, non-stop, until the detectives had all of the information they needed to convict her and everyone else working on the Ranch.

Their arraignment dates would be set for later on in the week.

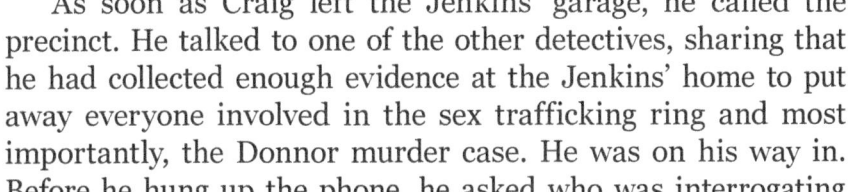

As soon as Craig left the Jenkins' garage, he called the precinct. He talked to one of the other detectives, sharing that he had collected enough evidence at the Jenkins' home to put away everyone involved in the sex trafficking ring and most importantly, the Donnor murder case. He was on his way in. Before he hung up the phone, he asked who was interrogating Jeremy Porter?

"I want to be involved in his interrogation." Craig said boldly. "Keep him in interrogation until I get there, and don't let Porter out of your sight! I want a piece of that dirt-bag!"

Missy looked at the clock on her bedside table. It was almost 6:00pm. She had laid down for a quick nap—two hours ago! She hurriedly got off the bed, straightened out the blue and yellow quilt, and headed to the bathroom to freshen up. As she did so, her cell telephone rang. She was not surprised when it was Craig's voice on the other end.

"I'm still at the precinct, Missy." He said. "I know I promised to be home by now, but the Donnor case has blown wide open! I have to stay here for at least another hour—or more."

Missy was excited at the news, but disappointed that he wasn't coming home on time, but, she assured Craig that there was no problem. He offered to make it up to her—something he had done often, lately. She was getting used to it and she would also hold him to his promise of "making it up to her".

Craig promised to call her prior to his leaving the precinct. "How about Chinese? He could pick up dinner when he left the station." Missy, smiling, agreed, and knowing Craig and his dedication to his job, hung up and walked to the kitchen to fix herself a sandwich.

She was sound asleep, when Craig quietly lay down next to her six hours later.

CHAPTER SEVENTY-THREE

A Bizarre Turn of Events

Sandra was now at the orphanage in Pueblo and Roseanne was back at Ft. Logan Mental Health Center—only coming home on weekends, once a month. One cold, rainy evening, Bernard came home from the hospital and Devorah greeted him with exciting news. While he and his wife were having their pre-dinner drinks, she informed her husband that she wanted to adopt another child—a boy. "I have been talking with social services, Father Ramsey and the Reverend Mother at the orphanage, and there was this little boy......" The good doctor almost dropped his drink. He stood up, looked her straight in the eye and asked if she, too, like these idiot sisters they had adopted, were crazy?

"I will not take another kid into this household! Katherine and Becky are enough!" The good doctor screamed.

Dr, Bernard, with a drawn and forlorn face, walked away, thinking, "I will not bring another child in this house to be abused."

That night, with instruction from his "loving" wife, Dr. Livingstone slept on the couch!!

Four weeks later, Devorah and Bernard sat in the Social Services office filling out the forms needed to apply for and adopt a little boy. His name was Charlie.

Why? Why, in all that is holy, would anyone give the Livingstone's another child? It's a question for all ages, and has never been answered.

Shortly after Charlie's adoption was finalized and the sweet little boy moved into the Livingstone home, the family took a trip to Disney World. It was a surprise to Katherine and Becky, since all previous summer vacations had been at Bernard's parents' home in Missouri.

What should have been an incredible week for the Livingstone children, turned into another nightmare, at least for Roseanne. It had been only a short while after Roseanne was moved back to Sacred Heart Home, that, to look good to their socialite friends and the Home, they invited Roseanne to join them on the trip.

Kathy, Becky and Charlie spent their days on the fabulous theme park rides, eating in fancy restaurants, riding the monorail and enjoying all of the Disney characters. Devorah planned, in her evil mind, to never allow Roseanne to take part in any of the activities. Instead, Devorah took Roseanne to the swimming pool where hour upon hour, with the hot Florida sun burning down on little Roseanne's light skin, both in the pool, and while sitting on the side of the swimming pool, her skin began to blister and burn.

While the good doctor, Becky, Kathy, Charlie and yes, evil Devorah would take in all of the sights of the amusement park, Devorah made sure that Roseanne sat in the lobby of the hotel, and she had "better not move! Visitors at the hotel would notice the tearful child, and stop to ask Roseanne if she was okay and why was she crying?

"You shouldn't be crying sweetheart. This is Disney World. You're in the happiest place in the world." They would say. "You should be laughing and having fun."

Did they look for Roseanne's parents? Did they contact Security? No. Roseanne, no longer able to express her feelings or ask anyone for help, and as monster mommy had demanded, just sat quietly, her skin on fire. There had never been any help before when she begged and pleaded for help. And now, as brain washed as she was she did as she was told AGAIN, and it seemed no one cared.

Roseanne returned to Dawson with third degree burns over her entire body. It was God, and God alone, who kept this child alive. Again.

Shortly after the vacation in Florida, the Livingstone's agreed to send Roseanne to the orphanage in Pueblo for good. Devorah was fed up. She could no longer stand to look at her daughter. She wanted her out of their home. She wanted her out of their lives.

Three gone—one to go.

CHAPTER SEVENTY-FOUR

Five Years to Life

It took six months to get everyone involved in the Ranch, the raid on the warehouse and Mandy Sue Donnor's murder, to court. Most of those only slightly involved in the sex trafficking and prostitution ring were found guilty and were sentenced to two to five years of jail time. Olivia Bartlett, due to her complete cooperation with the police, was sentenced to only five years in the women's prison in Canyon City, Colorado.

A jury of three women and nine men found Judge Christianson guilty of illegal smuggling and slavery, for forced sexual activity and having sex with a minor. When the jury was informed that over 100,000 young men and women are sold into sex trafficking every year, the judge didn't have a prayer. He was found guilty on three counts, and sentenced to eighteen years in the Colorado State Prison. The judge showed no emotion. His wife and three grown children never appeared in court, never visited him in jail, and never spoke to him again. Judge Christianson had committed one of the most prolific crimes known to man. No one shed a tear for him. The man who had been one of the most prominent judges serving the state of Colorado, who had been loved and respected, was now no better than the scum of the earth. His life, as he knew it, was over.

The young women found at both the warehouse and at the Ranch were either sent back to their home states and to their families, or placed in foster care. A few, were sent back to Mexico, where they had originally lived. When taken, most had been run-a-ways, living on the streets or had a pimp controlling their lives and were already prostituting themselves. Some would never change their lifestyles. They were broken souls with no hope of salvation.

Angie, due to her assisting the slain officer, Bryce Jenkins in his undercover work, was allowed to stay in the United States. She was placed in foster care until she turned eighteen years of age and returned to a local high school to finish her education. Her future looked hopeful and bright.

The Dawson Swat Team had raided the bar on Colorado Boulevard but no evidence had been found. The basement room, where the OBA members had gathered, was now just that, an empty, perfectly clean, basement room, with no trace of any illegal activity. Tyler Morris was never identified or found.

The major court cases had been the trial and conviction of Jeremy Porter, alias Jerry Boston and his counter-parts on the beatings, death, and defamation of Mandy Sue Donnor's corpse. The OBA members/police officers who had assisted Jeremy with the beatings, murder and burial of Mandy Sue were all found guilty and sentenced to twenty years. The jury took less than two hours of deliberation to convict them.

After a three-week trial, it had only taken the jury a week to finally find Jeremy Porter guilty of the beatings and the murder. If it hadn't been for the photographs taken by Bryce Jenkins, Porter may have gotten away with murder. A few members of the jury liked Jeremy, thought he was a good cop, and believed that he was working under cover for both the cops and for the OBA. Everyone involved worried that Jeremy would get off with just a light sentence. Luckily, Bryce Jenkins had come around, and realizing the error of his ways, had helped in Porter's conviction. Jeremy Porter was sentenced to life in prison with no chance for parole.

Missy Baker had sat through Jeremy's trial, some days with Craig beside her, and sometimes in tears. Jeremy had been a friend. Maybe not a "good" friend, but the two had known each other for many years and her heart broke for Jeremy's mother and sister. On one or two days of the trial, Missy had even sat with Jeremy's family, trying to console them. It was no use. Jeremy was guilty. The state's criminal lawyer had all the proof he needed to put this once good, but now evil man, away for life. There was no getting around it.

Officer Porter had at one time been a respectable, long-term Sheriffs Deputy. All who knew him loved him. Then he had accepted his first bribe. He had brought in major money, and worst of all, he had committed his most horrendous crime—yet— murder. The defense team tried their best to convince the jury that their client was insane at the time of the murder. It didn't happen. Missy cried over the loss of what once was a good man, a good officer of the law, and a friend. It was a hard trial for all concerned, but it was over.

Not that it was the proper thing to do, but Craig and several of the detectives, police officers and friends celebrated their victory. Once gathered at a local police hangout, the Downtown Bar and Grill, the men and women, held their drinks and lifted their glasses high in honor of Officer Bryce Jenkins. Even though he had strayed, he had righted himself in the eyes of his fellow officers, his family and his friends. "To Officer Bryce Jenkins", the group said respectfully. "Thank you, and may you rest in peace."

It had taken over two years, but the Mandy Sue Donnor case was closed. Craig Olson hoped that she too could now rest in peace.

CHAPTER SEVENTY-FIVE

Sandra

Becky was living in her own kind of prison. There was no hope of a reprieve. There would be no chance of parole from this prison she called home. Although there were four other people living in the house with her, four people who hated her, well, all but Charlie, but Devorah would soon take care of that, and Charlie would hate Becky too.

When Charlie was four, and Becky was ten, Devorah gave Becky fifty-cents to buy Charlie a candy bar. She told Becky to bring the candy bar home after school, and give the treat to Charlie. Since Becky never got money or a candy bar, she spent the fifty-cents on herself. That entire week, Devorah stood at the door waiting for Becky to bring the candy bar home to Charlie. When no treat ever arrived for Charlie, the young brother began to hate Becky too. Becky was now totally alone.

Becky continued to be slapped, hit on the head with a wooden breadboard and force-fed. One morning prior to leaving for school, Devorah sat down at the table next to Becky, set a box of Kellogg Corn Flakes next to her and told her to eat the entire box. Becky, as always, did as she was told. She set her mind to it. She ate the entire box and did not throw it back up like her sister Sandra had done one time. Becky had watched Sandra have to eat huge amounts of food before. Devorah would make Sandra eat breakfast on Friday mornings, consisting of an entire box of dry Malto Meal cereal, then watch as Sandra threw it up, and continued to watch as Sandra was made to eat her vomit. Then Devorah would make Sandra eat four more peanut butter sandwiches and consume 3-4 glasses of milk, immediately afterward. Sandra would not be served any more food for the entire weekend. When Dr. Livingstone would ask the sisters why they were not eating, they would say that they were "not hungry". The truth was, that each time Devorah went on a crash diet, she would make Sandra suffer, by not feeding her. It was a sick, sick situation.

That would not happen to Little Bec. She could do it and she did it, time and again—exactly as monster mommy had told her to do—eat and eat and eat. Now, who was in control, monster mommy or Little Bec?

"I'm not sure when my sister, Sandra, actually lost her mind. Roseanne told me later on in life that Sandra lost her mind completely at the orphanage in Pueblo. Sandra would constantly twirl like a ballerina down the orphanages' hallways. Roseanne and Sandra had told all of the professionals; the psychiatrists, the doctors and the counselors about the abuse at the hands of the Livingstone's. When none of them would believe my sisters, they finally stopped trying to convince anyone. The professionals believed Mrs. Livingstone to be the woman they read and heard about, and that Dr. Livingstone had saved so many children's lives, that he, too, would never turn an evil eye on a needful child. Because of our background; our real mother leaving us, her being in prison and never trying to find us when she was released, the professionals believed the Livingstone's and not three little girls. I always and forever will ask myself, why did Dr. Livingstone let this happen?"

"Several months after Sandra's move to the orphanage in Pueblo, she ran away. This time no one looked for her or ever found her. Perhaps they never cared. Sandra, insane or not, had enough sense to try and find a life for herself. Away from the torture of an adoptive mother, and she no longer wanted to live as an orphan."

"Sandra's stories are sometimes hard to believe. She is so dysfunctional and is always smoking "pot" to forget her past, I saw her later on in life, and I truly believe that everything she has told me about we sisters and our first years without our biological mother, is true. Sandra, with my help, also looked for and found the social worker in Dawson who first placed us in foster care—but Sandra decided to not look for any other people or to collect any further information on our biological mother. I, as the baby sister would start on that journey, many, many years later."

Sandra, at the age of sixteen, hitch hiked her way across the western United States, all the way from Colorado to California. No one knows for sure how she managed that trip. How did she get strangers to stop for her and take her from city to city, or how did she buy food, or where did she sleep at night? There are some things about Sandra's past that no one will ever know, and maybe don't want to know.

Upon her arrival in California, Sandra became hooked on drugs and alcohol, almost immediately. She met a man who took her into his home—if you could call it a home. It was a condemned shack with no water or heat. Sandra, so abused physically and mentally, dressed in filthy clothes, but with her face made-up, thinking she was Mary Poppins or some other famous character, would constantly go to Catholic churches and charities to beg for food and money. While still a teenager, Sandra got pregnant with her first child, precious little Chrissie. How would that child possibly survive? It would take a miracle.

During her first four years in California, Sandra gave birth to a second little girl, Anna. When Anna was only two months old, Chrissie, the big sister, always in filthy, ragged clothes, playing in the streets and suffering from starvation, got into her parent's drug bag and overdosed—it didn't take much. By an act of God, she survived, and no one ever found out. The second time Chrissie got into the bag and overdosed, the Paramedics were called. They were astounded as they entered the condemned shack. There was trash, dirty dishes and dog feces everywhere. The walls were crumbling, with large cockroaches running in and out of the walls, even when the lights were off. There was no running water and no heat.

The Paramedics took both little girls to the hospital and called the police. Both children were incredibly under nourished, dirty, sickly, and the baby had cockroach bites over her entire body. With no food, no heat, no water, and living in a bug-infested shack, social services stepped in and took over. The two little girls were placed first in the hospital, and then into foster care. Sandra was ordered to a mental health facility and her boyfriend was thrown in jail.

A month after the little girls were placed in foster care, baby Anna, only three months old passed away. All charges against Sandra and her boyfriend were dropped because the baby passed away while in foster car. However, the court placed a restraining order against the boy friend. Sandra, a few days later brought him both back with her to a sleazy hotel and while lying on the floor, with the baby, the boyfriend died of an overdose. The cycle started all over again.

The next generation of abuse, hard living, dysfunction, and drug and alcohol addiction had begun. Devorah Livingstone had done her best to destroy four human beings, and she had done an excellent job. The three remaining sisters, so completely brainwashed, and abused, started the second generation exactly how they had been taught. The next generation of abuse and neglect had begun.

Sandra made her way from California to Arkansas always hitchhiking, living out of food banks, and even applying for and getting state aid, because she had a baby. She always found a man to take her in, care for her, and get her pregnant. Sandra would have two more children. Her offspring, followed in their mother's lifestyle and would live with or marry hopeless men, some who ended up in prison. Sandra's grandchildren also, would be taken away and placed in and out of foster care or adoptive homes, just like her. Sandra's third born, Abby, would die in a car accident later in life leaving her son to be raised by Sandra, and her daughter, Izzy, to be raised by her father. Michael, the son Becky would later adopt and raise as her own son would be taken away from his abusive mother, Chrissie. The third generation of broken souls had begun. The lives of three of the four sisters had come full circle. It causes all of us to agree that Tabbatha may have been the fortunate one.

Who do we blame? Did the abuse originate from an imprisoned mother or from a couple who should have never been allowed to adopt? Perhaps the abuse originated from professionals trained to "see" or "look for" abuse in troubled children and adults, but did not. At this point, there is no longer a reason to find blame. The damage was done. The question is, could any of these now, grown women, be saved from themselves. Only God knew.

CHAPTER SEVENTY-SIX

Roseanne

Roseanne, after many months at the orphanage, was released to live in an Independent Living Center in the area. It was better than living in the orphanage, but it wasn't home. Roseanne, like her big sister, Sandra, was unhappy, unsettled, confused, angry and anxious. Roseanne, however, lived in the moment, and would not go the way of her older sister. She too, ran away. She was fifteen years old. She followed the same trail as Sandra to California. She hitchhiked her way cross-country until she found Sandra, living in horrible conditions.

Unlike Sandra, however, Roseanne tried to make something of herself. She refused to live Sandra's way of life. The original shack Sandra had lived in with her two children, had been purposely burned to the ground due to "unfit conditions", but she had found another condemned house and moved into it, yes, with her man. Roseanne, who made friends easily, quickly found a better place to live. She was not, however, immune to drug addiction. Soon, even with a job at a local hamburger joint, she, too, was addicted to drugs, especially Crystal Meth, but still managed to keep her job.

Roseanne never followed Sandra to Arkansas, as Becky would later do. She instead, worked in California for many years. She worked for years at several fast-food restaurants and her life was fairly stable, but when she got a position at a local Delicatessen that served alcohol, her life began to deteriorate. She had access to all the liquor she could drink or sneak out, and before long she was a full-blown alcoholic. No charges were ever filed, but she lost her job.

When children are treated, as the four sisters had been treated, and when you live on welfare, are always depressed and down hearted, then yes, the feeling that taking drugs and alcohol gives you is what you **think** you need. There was no one to tell them any differently. There had been no hope for little Tabbatha, and there was no help for Sandra or Roseanne. There might be help for Becky, because unknown to Becky or any of her sisters, God was about to show up in a variety of ways.

"I remember the short time I lived with my sister, Roseanne, in California, that she was so used to being beat upon, that she would beat on me—literally pound on me, more than once, especially when she was drunk! While she was hitting me, Roseanne would say, "I wouldn't hit you if you'd fight back". I could not and never would HIT MY SISTERS! I just, as always, took the beating. It was the only way of life Roseanne knew; to be hurt, or hurt someone else."

Roseanne had issues with drug addiction and alcohol abuse, due to horrible memories, but she tried harder than Sandra had ever tried to find her way in life. But, as with her other siblings, life would also deal Roseanne another bad rap.

After seven years in California, Roseanne moved back to Dawson where she got a job at the Colorado Humane Society. Roseanne had always loved animals, especially dogs, and since she handled or hid her addictions well, she was hired. She worked at that same position for almost ten years. Roseanne knowing all along that she was gay, did have one partner for many years—the only one she would ever have.

For years Roseanne's leg, due to improper medical care at the time of her injury, had caused the dormant blood clot to worsen. No longer able to handle the severe pain, she agreed with her doctors to have her leg amputated.

For fifteen years she had lived in agony—all due to her adopted father's refusal to get proper medical attention. For fifteen years, Roseanne never told a soul about her abuse or pain. She lived on legal and illegal painkillers, and now she was about to pay the ultimate price—the loss of her leg.

During this same time, the Colorado Humane Society, located in Dawson, planned to open a Non-Kill-Shelter in Pueblo, Colorado. They asked Roseanne if she would be willing to move to Pueblo and operate the shelter. She said yes. Sandra was now in Pueblo, and although they hadn't seen each often, having family close was necessary for Roseanne. Prior to opening the shelter in Pueblo, she opted first, to take the time to have her leg amputated. It was traumatizing for Roseanne, who had already been through so much, but the amputation went well. Amazingly enough, there would be no more pain and Roseanne looked forward to being in charge of the animal shelter.

As fate would have it, three months after moving to Pueblo and opening the shelter, and while two of her nephews were visiting her, Roseanne suffered a severe stroke. She had been on so many painkillers and illegal drugs, had not kept close track of her actual prescription drugs—blood thinners included—her body tried closing down. She had been in the bedroom, while her young nephews were in another room watching movies. She got up to go to the bathroom, had a stroke and fell to the floor. One of the nephews walked over her still body at least two to three times, thinking that Aunt Roseanne was asleep. He was used to sleeping on the floor himself so figured his aunt might be taking a nap. For three hours Roseanne lay, close to death, before Sandra found her. Roseanne was rushed to the hospital in Pueblo, and after a month was transferred to a nursing home in Dawson. Roseanne had suffered serious brain damage, could no longer speak fluently, and would spend the rest of her life in a tiny five by six foot cubicle, called "her" room. She had a single bed, a television and a wheelchair. She would however, have three square meals a day and perhaps one or two friends. On certain days Roseanne would remember who she was and where she lived. Her life now centered on smoking three packs of cigarettes a day and drinking her favorite orange soda. When her state aid money ran out, her baby sister, Becky was called. Becky was on the road TRYING to drive a big rig, across thirty-two states when she got the call. Becky came to her immediately, and stayed with her each and every day, even moving her to a different and nicer nursing home in Dawson. Becky would bring her orange soda and packs of cigarettes. She would play games with her, try to keep her spirits up. Even with all those years of abuse, Becky could still show love, and she loved her sister, always had, and always would. When no one else would help Roseanne, Becky did. Sandra from day one, blamed Roseanne for having a stroke in front of her children—as if Roseanne had planned it this way.

The one positive in this horrific event, the stroke, was that the nursing home doctors fitted Roseanne for a prosthetic leg.

As if the amputation and stroke weren't hard enough on Roseanne, not one of her friends ever came to visit her in the hospital or ever saw her again. She had worked so hard for so many years for the humane society and to keep those beautiful animals from being euthanized at the No-Kill-Shelter. One day, the staff decided to euthanize all of her beloved animals and closed down the shelter. The in-humane act made the Dawson newspapers, but no charges were ever filed, and the shelter closed down—forever.

Sandra also, never came to see her little sister again. Her sister's life, her speech defect, her brain damage, and an amputated limb may have embarrassed Sandra. More than that, Sandra, most likely jealous, felt that Roseanne had been more successful than she had ever been in life. Also, Sharon on any given day went from being sane to being insane—she most likely did not mean to give up on her sister. Becky tried her hardest to get Sandra and other family members to visit Roseanne, but it only happened a few times. Once again, Becky was the strong one, but Roseanne had always loved Sandra the most, probably due to the abuse, and the closeness in their ages. Becky wanted so badly for the sisters to be a family, again, but it never happened.

It was a sad, sad, day, when even the two older sisters gave up on one another.

CHAPTER SEVENTY-SEVEN

Moving On

Craig Olson spent several more weeks finalizing the paperwork on the Mandy Sue Donnor case. It had been one of the hardest cases he'd ever had to solve. But now it was over. All the bad guys were put away and the young women involved in sex trafficking and prostitution were all either back in their homes or at least safe in their home states, hopefully, getting professional help. Craig hoped that with counseling and people to love and protect them, most of the abused and broken young women would go forward and make lives for themselves.

Jeremy Porter had been the toughest suspect to crack, and Craig had felt sorry for the Sheriff's Deputy. It didn't help that Missy too, felt so badly for her friend. Jeremy had started out to be such an incredible officer of the law, and then greed, money and evil people had taken him down. Jeremy fought like a tiger to prove his innocence, but the photos that Bryce Jenkins had taken of Jeremy finally convinced him to admit to his sinful deeds. Jeremy, eyes filled with tears, had come clean when Detective Olson had informed him that Mandy Sue had been pregnant with his baby. Jeremy had sobbed at his sentencing.

Craig was sure that Jeremy had truly loved Mandy Sue. "It's a broken world we live in." Craig had said to himself. "So many broken souls. Where is God in all of this tragedy?" Craig Olson had no answers. He saw mayhem and murder every day in his job.

"It's a sad world we live in." He thought. "A very sad and broken world, but, God help us, we have to move on."

Missy kept busy with several new clients, and although she loved working with Craig, she knew they couldn't work together on every case. He was a detective and she was a Private Investigator. Their lives would always be hectic with longer than normal hours, cancelled date nights, half eaten meals, and telephone calls in the middle of the night—but she loved him, and he loved her, and she knew that this relationship would work.

Lately, they had gone to as many Sunday morning church services as they could manage. When you lived and worked, daily, in an evil and destructive world, God was the only source that seemed to keep them both sane. They had even spoken with Father Carmichael after a Sunday Mass. Father Ramsey had been on a sabbatical for several weeks—Craig and Missy did not know why, and Father Carmichael had taken his place. They spoke with the Father about their relationship and upcoming marriage plans, and he had agreed to counsel them. He also encouraged them to come to Mass a little more often. All three chuckled, realizing their schedules, but Craig and Missy promised that they would try.

Missy, on occasion would still look through the telephone book, looking for the Livingstone's. Her schedule, however, was so hectic, and she was trying in her spare time to plan a wedding. She found herself forgetting about those precious little girls. She didn't purposely forget them. It was just that life got in the way. It would be a very long time before Missy would meet up with any of them again.

CHAPTER SEVENTY-EIGHT

Becky

Becky, without her older sisters, took the brunt of Devorah's abuse for eight more years. During that time, Devorah continued to force-feed, slap and humiliate her. One lunch hour, as Becky prepared herself for the usual three or four glasses of milk and as many peanut butter sandwiches, Devorah switched from the usual, powered milk to buttermilk. She didn't tell the young girl that she had switched the milk. Becky gulped down one entire glass of buttermilk before realizing it was not the normal glass of milk. She gagged, and kept swallowing hard to keep from regurgitating. She kept choking back the horrific taste, wondering if she had been given sour milk? She also knew that if she threw up, Devorah would make her eat it, just like she had done with Sandra.

Dr. Livingstone, for some reason, came home from the hospital, early, that day. When Devorah saw her husband, she asked if he wanted a drink, and when he said, yes, she left the kitchen to make him his "usual", Scotch and water. Becky walked into the living room and told her father that her milk was sour. Hearing Becky's complaint, Devorah immediately turned into monster mommy. She pulled Becky by the hair, dragged her back into the kitchen, where she immediately dumped the entire quart of buttermilk over the child's head, screaming as she did so.

"How dare you tell your father that the milk was sour!" She screamed. "You dum-dum, stupid, fat, ignorant child. Clean yourself up! I hate you! I hate you!"

Becky had no time to reply. All she knew was that the buttermilk was dumped, and she had only had to drink one glass instead of three. It had been worth it. She felt that she had won this round with monster mommy.

These kind of daily incidents had become the "norm" for Little Bec. She would turn her mind from being Becky, which the Livingstone's called her, to calling herself, Little Bec. For some reason, when Becky thought she was "Little Bec", she could handle the beatings, the abuse and the belittling.

"I made Little Bec a precious little girl inside of me. I DID NOT have a split personality. I just learned how to cope with the abuse by becoming Little Bec. This way I learned to survive in a world that wasn't safe, and in a house where the "thing", which is what Devorah called me, could survive. I know that I was born a "precious child", but that child had to leave, temporarily, and go somewhere where the madness wouldn't get to me or find me, so I went away physically, mentally and emotionally, and became Little Bec. It helped me realize that I really was a human being, not a "thing".

"I watched my sister die, and I watched my older sisters die, not like Tabbatha, but still die. They seemed to no longer exist, unable to call on an "inner" spirit like I was doing. For some reason, perhaps spiritual, my heart was saved. Unlike Sandra, who says she has no heart, and Roseanne whose heart was so filled with hate, that she could show no love to anyone, except for her animals."

Becky admitted as she grew and became a teenager, that Little Bec would continue to live inside of her, help her to survive, handle the terror and her devastating life with the Livingstone's, until someone or something would show her once again how to survive on her own—as Becky. She longed for love, for the loving human touch of a mother and to show love herself.

On the days when the abuse was more horrific than others, Becky would hide in the basement of the Livingstone's now new, luxurious home in the eastern part of Dawson. She would close her eyes and pretend that her mother was one of those mothers from a famous television program. She would pretend that she was sitting on her mother's lap, being held, loved and cherished. She needed a "real" mom, not one like her monster mommy, to love her and protect her. When she got older, she used to wonder if the lady at the checkout counter at the grocery store might be her mom, or maybe the lady standing on a corner waiting for the bus, or her teachers might be her real mother.

As a young teenager, all she knew and felt were the scars of abuse and neglect of monster mommy. Becky would be scarred forever. She would also be afraid and live in fear for the rest of her life—all because of a monster mother she was told to call "ma'am".

CHAPTER SEVENTY-NINE

The Run-Away

Shortly after Becky's thirteenth birthday, she began to plan her escape. After many weeks of trying to remember what her real mother might have been like, she ran away from the abusive, adopted one.

"I know that whoever my biological mother was or where she might be, she would have never allowed my sisters and me to be adopted and then tortured every day. She would never have allowed us to be turned into slaves, or robots, or children who could not think for themselves. No, if my real mom was alive, I know she believed that we were protected and loved, and in a good family. If she had known about our abuse, she would have come looking for us."

"I would dream that there were cameras in our home, and that pictures were being taken of all the abuse. One day a police officer would come in and find the cameras, and Devorah would be taken to jail. I knew it was to late for Sandra or Roseanne, but I would be saved. I wanted my real mom to see how hard I cleaned house, and that it was always spotless. I wanted her to know why I was fat, that it wasn't my fault. I knew if she knew I was being slapped and hit over the head, that she would come and save me. It never happened."

"I asked God, over the cold, winter months, when Devorah would be at the Mall shopping, or away from the house, I would look out the window, watching the snow fall, and wish that He would make Devorah get hit by a car, or be in a car wreck, and die. I prayed over and over for Devorah to be killed, but I also knew that she would once again, make it home to torture me."

As far as Becky knew, God, whoever he was, had let her down—every day of her life. She was on her own to escape. She ran away from her abusive mother, three times. The first time, Becky ran to her 7th grade teachers home, just across town. But, as always, her teacher didn't believe her story and called her parents. Dr. Livingstone immediately came and got her. Becky finally asked her adopted father, one more time, "why does Devorah hate us, and why has she been so mean to us for so long?" The reply, as always was YOU DESERVE IT. Becky, had no idea what that meant.

That same night, Becky was told to get into her pajamas, and go and kiss her mother goodnight. When Becky kissed her goodnight, Devorah, slapped her across the face, hard, and said, "you don't mean it". From that time on, Becky was slapped asleep at night, and slapped awake in the morning, saying, "get up fatty" or "get up "dumb dumb".

The next time she ran, she ran all the way to California to her sister Roseanne. Roseanne hid her at a friend's apartment for a while and then the two of them tried to get to Sandra's.

Roseanne was living with a man, not as a partner, but as a provider, who promised to drive them in his vehicle the few hundred miles to where Sandra was living. On the way there, the car broke down, and the man had to work a few days picking potatoes to get enough money to repair his car and continue on. That didn't happen. Someone noticed an underage child with an older man, and the police were called. Becky was flown back to Dawson, and placed in Juvenile Hall. From Juvenile Hall, Becky was taken back to the Livingstone's but only for a short time. What Devorah did do, was give her the silent treatment from that day on.

For the same reason Sandra and Roseanne were taken to mental institutions, Dr. and Mrs. Livingstone brought Becky to Rocky Mountain Hospital for brain scans and psychiatric therapy, because, Devorah insisted that Becky, like her sisters, was also mentally unstable. After the tests, Devorah took her adopted daughter to the car and said, "part of your brain is missing, you poor mentally ill child". Becky believed every word out of monster mommy's mouth!

Becky began writing in a journal about the abuse, and called her writings "WHAT HELL IS REALLY LIKE". She wrote daily, and would hide her writings on a shelf with her record albums. Of course, Devorah, unknowing to Becky, searched her room on a daily basis and found the journal. When Becky came home from school that day, her room was destroyed, and on the mirror, in lipstick, were the words, "I hate you Becky!"

Becky knew, that like her big sister, running away was her only option, or she would die. So, she made the decision while Devorah was using the bathroom, to walk straight out the front door and walked fifteen miles to where Roseanne was now living independently in a one-room apartment.

At only fourteen years of age, Becky applied for and got a job working at McDonalds. She managed to save every cent of her paychecks, and daily planned her next escape. After several months at the fast food restaurant, and saving over three hundred dollars, she planned the day of her escape. All of McDonalds employees had been invited to an awards dinner, and were told to dress up in their finest clothes. Becky purchased a two-piece blue suit, and attended the event. The minute the event ended, Becky walked out the door of the Ramada Hotel in Dawson, called a cab, and went directly to the Dawson airport. She purchased a ticket, boarded a plane and flew to her sister Roseanne in California. Once on the ground, she counted her money—exactly $25.00. She hailed a cab with instructions to take her to her sister's home. The cab fair was exactly twenty-five dollars.

The police found her at Roseanne's and placed her in juvenile hall. After the second chance to escape, Becky was placed in a foster home in California. She ran again. The third and final time, Becky ran again to her sister Roseanne.

Life as Becky knew it—the first fourteen years—was over.

BOOK
THREE

CHAPTER EIGHTY

A Real Mother

Becky, although only eighteen years of age, began, off and on (because she was too drunk to be more diligent), to look for her biological mother. Ever since she found out that she was not the Livingstone's biological child, the hole in her heart grew deeper for her real mother—the one she had never known. She contacted the Department of Corrections in Canyon City Colorado, and received two letters, three weeks apart, from the records director. The first letter read, in part:

Becky Livingstone

...your letter was received...you did not mention your mother's name....we need her name to check our files... could she have had an alias name...

The second letter, read in part:

Becky Livingstone

...in reference to your letter...we will need more information...to locate your mother...

Somewhat disheartened at the results of her first attempts to find her mother, Becky reached out to Social Services in Dawson, and to the Sacred Heart Orphanage in Pueblo. A few letters of response came on professional letterhead while others were hand written. They read in part:

Becky

...I know your mother was in the penitentiary....but she is the only one who can answer your questions... contact the penitentiary....they can tell you when she was paroled...or

Becky

....tracing a birth mother can be very difficult....the state of Colorado seals adoption records....you may wish to petition the courts....

Becky

....perhaps Father Ramsey can be of more help to you.... he knew the Livingstone's well....he is not bound by Colorado law....or perhaps you could contact your adoptive parents for information....they too are not bound by any laws....meanwhile, good luck...

Becky was disheartened but refused to give up. For several years she wrote letters, made telephone calls and through it all began to feel more and more unworthy of a "real" mother. When children are beaten down at such a young age, they believe themselves to be unworthy of love. In Becky's case, without the nurturing of a real mother, and the horrific abuse she suffered, and also watching her sister's suffering, she felt herself to be unlovable. She was sure that she had been born "bad"!

Sandra, in one of her "sane" moments even remembered the name of a social worker that had worked with the sisters during their early years in the system. Becky somehow found an address, sent the social worker a letter, and waited daily for a response. Sandra knew as Becky waited daily for the mailman to bring her a letter, that her baby sister would never find their real mother.

"That was a long time ago, Becky." Sandra would say. "She's probably moved away or is dead. Our mother is probably dead too, or maybe she got out of jail and started a new family. Maybe she didn't ever want to see any of us again!"

"No!" Becky screamed. "I will never believe that our mother did not love or want us. Never!"

Becky would not believe any of it. She was never going to give up on finding their real mother. "Our mother would want to see us." Becky exclaimed. "I know she would want to see us if she knew where we were."

Becky waited and waited. No letter ever came. Becky was not about to give up. She checked the Internet for information on her mother's name. She tried locating her mother by her social security number. The number had been used for many years. Since Becky knew her mother had been incarcerated, she went to the Hall of Records for the Colorado State Penitentiary. Much to her surprise, as she gave the Records Clerk the information, they found not only found her mother's "booking photos", but also her mother's name, birth date, a studio photo and the reason for her incarceration. Now, Becky had a name—her mother's real name. Becky contacted the Vital Statistics Office in Dawson, and requested her own birth certificate, under the name Holmgruff— she got it. She cried! Yelling, I HAVE MY REAL NAME!

Becky looked just like her real mother.

There was, and never would be any trace of Annamaria Holmgruff again, but Becky, the now child-like adult, would never give up looking for the mother she could not remember, but she now knew who she was and that was enough for Becky.

"As I look back, over my life, and the lives of my sisters, I can not help but feel that my sisters and I were never important in anyone's eyes, or were ever protected or loved. I've always felt that I was born "flawed", or maybe I was the straw that broke the camels back; meaning that maybe, me, being the fourth child born to my birth mother (or at least I don't think there were any more children), and that I was too much for my parents to handle. Maybe there were too many mouths to feed or too many diapers to change. Maybe both father's couldn't help or didn't want to help my mother care for all of us."

"Therapists over the years told me that most likely my biological mother was also an addict or an alcoholic, hence all of us girls became addicts and alcoholics as well. I'll never know. Even as an adult, I continually blame myself for our abandonment and the abuse. Therefore, it consumes our lives, and any attempt at a normal or successful life. I hurt a lot when I think of what my sisters could have had. The different life we might have had, had we not been abandoned and then adopted into such a cruel family."

"I think often about that cold Valentine's Day when we were adopted, and I think often about Tabbatha, and her death, and that she was too fragile, as a little child, to survive, and I'm so grateful that God allowed her to die when she did. People, so many people, suspected that things were not quite right with the Livingstone's. Father Ramsey said later on in my life, that he always suspected that Tabbatha's death was not accidental, and that Dr. Livingstone was wrong, not signing the death certificate with another doctor present, or ordering an autopsy. I also wrote to one of the social workers later on in my adult life, and she told me that she knew Sandra had been abused. She also said in her letter that she knew my biological mother, but that she was sworn, by Colorado law to not give me her name or any information. I wrote to the social worker twice, and she responded each time with the same answer; "I cannot, Becky, give you any information on your birth mother, unless you get a release from the Dawson Department of Social Services, or from Catholic Charities."

Although Becky was elated at the news that she had a real identity, maybe Mrs. Livingstone had been right after all when she told her that "part her brain was missing". Maybe Becky really was a dum-dum and stupid, and maybe her biological mother really had NOT loved her. The more depressed and lost Becky became, the more she drank. The more drugs she ingested, the more she became that little girl buried deep inside her. Becky survived, only because she went inside herself and became Little Bec each time she faltered or failed.

Chapter Eighty-One

Alcohol and Drugs

It's a given that when a small child gets into trouble a parent is almost always there to either scold or love that child, depending on the situation.

Becky longed for a mother who would have, no matter what the trouble, loved her and been proud of her. Becky wanted to be the daughter that could have looked into her mother's eyes with the love only a child could give, and say the words, "mom". Becky, unlike her sisters, felt that a part of her heart and soul had died the day her biological mother gave them up. Becky felt like it was a brokenness that could never be mended.

"My search for my biological mother sent me down several different roads; some were paved with rock and stone and left a hole inside of me, so deep, that nothing could ever fill it. I've tried everything from alcohol, drugs, relationships and the innocence of my adopted son, Michael, who filled that hole temporarily. I went down the road of lost self-identity. There was the loss of a mother's nurturing and love, her smile and her warm embrace. There was the loss of a mother's comfort when a child falls down and scrapes her knee. I missed the protection of being frightened by the dark. Most of all, I missed her never-ending love for me; the child she gave birth to."

There were many reasons why Becky began her thirty years of alcohol abuse and drug addiction. She can blame most of those reasons on the fact that she was an abandoned child, but when it really comes down to it, her addiction began because of severe abuse by the hands of monster mommy.

"In the future I would have to be the strongest of the three of us, even though I was the baby: the baby that should have been taken care of in the short life I had known so far. But no, no one would or

could save me from the monster, or the damage she had caused. No one would take care of me. I would learn to take care of myself. I swore that I would not live in a dream world like my sister, Sandra, nor would I hate the world and all who lived in it, like Roseanne. I would simply go inside myself where there were no feelings, just numbness from the pain I had felt and seen for fourteen years. So, in order to feel nothing, and find peace, I found it in a bottle; a bottle of wine or tequila or beer and in a bottle of pills. This way I could be numb both on the inside and on the outside."

Becky had her first taste of liquor, while on the run, at a party Roseanne had invited her to. She was thirteen. She hated the taste, but loved the effect. The prison doors seemed to open for Becky. While on alcohol she now had feelings, something she never had with the Livingstone's. She, right or wrong, with alcohol, knew what if felt like, now, to be a human being. Alcohol and drugs would control and finish raising Becky for twenty more years. She had never made a decision in her life. Alcohol and drugs did that for her.

Sandra and Roseanne had both been drinking and doing drugs for many years, and Becky fell into the exact same pattern. It was so easy. Everywhere she went, there was booze and drugs. By the time she had lived in California for a few months, she was sloshed or high every day. She had only completed the 9th grade of middle school, and would not go back to get her GED until she was late into her thirties. Becky was going to get hired, and get fired. She was going to be in and out of detoxification centers, treatment centers, placed back into foster care and have numerous years of counseling. It would take almost twenty-five years for Becky's broken heart and soul to heal, and it wouldn't be easy, but she would survive. Her spirit, however, would never waver.

Becky spent four years, off and on, in California living with her sisters or a drunken neighbor, for whom she did favors. Becky is NOT proud of what she did. She just did what she had to do for the next drink or pill. It didn't matter to Becky that Sandra lived in filthy conditions as long as she had as much as beer, wine or tequila any young girl could drink, with drugs for dessert. It was a horrible life for a young teen, but Becky wanted to be close to her real family, to blood relatives. She so badly wanted her two sisters to take care of her, when they could not take care of themselves. Plus she had no choice. Where else would she go?

She held numerous jobs at McDonalds, and was, somehow, very good at her job. She would be hung over when she got to work, and she would go home after work, drink and do drugs, and start the next day the same way—hung over. She got so good at her job that she was trained and hired for the early morning managerial position. She wasn't always on time and some morning's customers couldn't get their coffee and breakfast exactly at 5:00am, because the drunken manager was hung over and late again! Still, she held on to her position.

After four years in California, Sandra, her boyfriend and young child and Becky, moved to Arkansas. Roseanne stayed behind.

While living in Arkansas, Becky held positions at numerous nursing homes. She had a great personality, and whether it was the alcohol and drugs, or it was the child-like characteristics of Little Bec that came out, people loved her. She never had a problem getting a position. Even without certification, directors hired her at three different nursing homes as a nursing assistant or aide. To feed her habit, she would sneak a quart of booze in to work, drink it on her lunch hour, and continue doing her work. One day, completely drunk, she left a severely mentally ill man, alone, in an unlocked room, which was completely against the rules. While Becky was "drinking" her lunch, the man escaped, got lost in the forest area around the nursing home, and after three days, was found—deceased. Becky was fired, but she could never understand why no charges were filed. She truly believes now, that God was already working in her life, and He had kept her out of prison.

At the second nursing home position, and still consistently drunk, she lifted an old lady (her favorite patient), out of her bed, and dropped her onto the floor, breaking her leg. Becky admits chuckling (although not a laughing matter), that she was fired that time too.

"I have no answers, and I have no idea why I was not charged and put in prison. I believe that God was already working on a plan for me, and being in prison was not part of that plan. Maybe he knew that I was already in prison and had been my entire life. Maybe that was it."

It was definitely not a laughing matter, but when Becky talks about her years as a drunk, some humor does come out in her stories. I guess humor really is the best medicine.

CHAPTER EIGHTY-TWO

Not a Normal Teenager

Mr. and Mrs. Craig Olson had been happily married for four years. They were engaged for two years having been in no rush to sign that white piece of legal paper. "Why ruin a good thing?" Craig had told Missy, laughing.

They had been married in a simple, but beautiful ceremony in Father Ramsey's church with two hundred family and close friends in attendance.

Missy proudly walked down the aisle on her father's arm, and was stunning in her gown of white satin. Her oldest sister had been her matron of honor, and Craig's best friend in the department had been best man. Her five-year old niece, Clarise, had been her flower girl. As the small girl walked down the aisle, spreading pink rose pedals in front of Missy and her father, Missy thought briefly of another small and precious child, from another time. Missy had met and been so taken in by her so many years before—beautiful little Becky. She smiled and wondered where Becky might be. The thought came and left quickly, however, as Missy concentrated instead on the gorgeous man standing at the altar waiting for her.

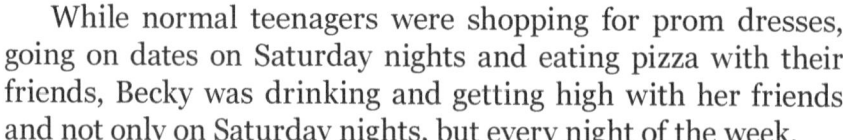

While normal teenagers were shopping for prom dresses, going on dates on Saturday nights and eating pizza with their friends, Becky was drinking and getting high with her friends and not only on Saturday nights, but every night of the week.

"I continued to drink and went from one treatment center to another. My employer at the time, McDonalds fast food restaurant, paid for one of my treatment costs, and I met a wonderful counselor,

Lois Dunkin. She, like counselors before, went above and beyond her position to help me get sober, and this time, stay sober. She was tough on me, yet I could see tears in her eyes when she would meet with me. She would also come in on the weekends and check on me. I tried to trust her, matter of fact, I trusted her so much, that I relied on her to tell me what to do, when to do it, where to go, and became completely dependent on her. I even lived with her and her boyfriend after I was discharged from the treatment center. Lois also felt I needed to be in an eating disorder treatment center. I was horribly over weight from being force-fed, and the food abuse caused by Mrs. Livingstone had led to an eating disorder as well as my addictions to alcohol and drugs."

"Lois, with help of state aid, flew me to Illinois where I lived in another treatment center, strictly for eating disorders. Once again, my decisions were made for me. All I had to do was follow directions, and do as I was told. My meals were prepared for me, and I was told when to eat. I was told when to go to group therapy, when to go to bed, and during free time, I wrote, watched television and played basketball. I lived at the treatment center for almost a year. I had not tasted alcohol, or popped a pill in a year. I returned to Colorado, feeling fairly good about myself. My previous counselor welcomed me back with open arms, even offering her basement apartment to me,"

"I was sober, but still very dependent on people to tell me what to do. I still had no idea what to do with the ramifications from the abuse by the hands of monster mommy. I still could not think for myself and I had no idea of what life expected of me. I was still an innocent child in an adult body. I had no idea how sick I really was."

"Still unable to love myself or believe that I was worthy of anyone, or have a relationship with any one, I was still lost. I did not have the skills to live in a world so cold...I needed more than a treatment center, or program. I needed mental health and emotional help, and for someone to tell me the reason for my inability to feel and to stop hurting all of the time. I knew that there was more to life than alcohol and drugs, but now that I wasn't drinking or feeling high all of the time, I was always afraid."

"I asked myself, why did I act the way I did? Why did I think unthinkable thoughts all of the time? Just who am I? What is wrong

with me? I couldn't cope with the emotions I felt, always like a ball of fire burning inside of me. It was all too much for me to handle, and my thoughts immediately turned back to drugs and alcohol."

"I stayed clean for six years and a relapse became once again, a reality!"

CHAPTER EIGHTY-THREE

Jolene

When Becky met Jolene, She was in her mid-twenties. Jolene had been recommended, after Becky had had another mental and emotional break down. It was just after she was one year sober, again, and had relapsed. She couldn't find what she was looking for in the bottom of a tequila bottle, and continued to drink to escape all of her fear and insecurities, she reached out once again for help.

"When drinking, I lived in my reality, made-up world; a world that suited me. When I sobered up, and would re-read the letters I received in search of my real mom, it would be to hard for me to handle and I would drink again. The real truth about my mother's life and about my own life was way to painful for me. I had lied to myself, all through my life, about everything, and everyone, and it had worked for me, that is until I got sober. My perception of life, the world, people, God, and this world were so screwed up, that when I would hear the truth, it would hit me like a bullet and I would be unable to cope."

Becky met Jolene Vroom, also a recovering alcoholic, when she was close to thinking about what being dead might feel like. Becky was a sick child, and she didn't have a clue as to how sick she really was. Jolene took this little girl Becky, into her care. This little girl, was broken into a million pieces, and Jolene put her back together again. Becky would actually become a human being again. Jolene not only loved Becky, but she taught Becky how to love herself, and others. Jolene loved Becky as no other human being had ever loved her.

"Firm arms embraced me every week. Jolene helped me to see what was real and what I had made reality. I lived a lie, because the truth was so far out of my reach. I made up my own reality world,

and it had worked for a long, long time. Just like the alcohol, it had worked for me for such a long time that when it also stopped working, I crashed. I was stunned and bewildered, unable to understand what was real."

"Jolene was gentle with me. She let me know the truth and was always there for me when I couldn't handle the truth and would go back into my familiar world of lies and deception. When I would chose denial because it was less painful, she had me do workshops and group therapy and workbooks for the emotionally wounded. She made sure my sobriety was solid before she worked on what had brought me to her in the first place—the abandonment by my real mom and the truth about what she had done to me and my three sisters."

"Jolene also allowed me to talk about the Livingstone's, and my "coming out". I had suspected it all along, but Jolene allowed me to say the words—I was gay. I had denied it for so long, telling myself that it could not be. It was now true and I could accept it."

Jolene gave Becky assignments on how to socialize with others and to live in the world by herself. Becky actually began to feel human and did not always have to live inside herself all of the time. Jolene pulled her out of herself and loved her like a child, because now Becky was allowed to finally live like a child, to be a child, and now she could grow up to be an adult.

Becky was scared. She didn't realize that she was now capable of loving someone. Jolene had taught her that she could now live in the real world and that the world was okay.

Jolene and Becky worked together for over five years. Jolene died very unexpectedly, and Becky did drink again, but it was the beginning of the end of Becky's horrible life. Finally, someone had gotten through to this broken soul; someone who could actually love Becky and show her how to love others. Becky wasn't completely healed, and most likely would never be completely healed, but she was on her way to a new beginning.

CHAPTER EIGHTY-FOUR

Gina, Sue and Jeannie

Becky continued to drink, but continued to hold a job, although there would be numerous positions until she became completely sober. No one could believe the jobs Becky held. She worked in a hospital gift shop, the hospital pharmacy and even worked at a local hospital laboratory doing blood draws—unbelievable, as she didn't have a license or certificate to do so. People loved her, were drawn to her, and without her knowing it, they were helping her heal.

One of the most hilarious jobs Becky ever held was when she applied for, and got her CDL license, and began to drive a big rig for a large Dawson truck line.

Becky had worked for McDonald fast food restaurants throughout every state she had fled, or moved to. She worked hard and they believed her to be management material. The other employees loved her, and she made decent enough money to live on and supply her habits. She probably worked at ten different McDonald stores in her life, always getting hired, showing great potential, but getting too drunk to work at times, and getting fired. She was even promoted to a manager at one time. While employed, the McDonald's corporation felt responsible for getting and paying for a month at an alcohol recovery treatment center, She really owed the McDonald Corporation a great deal.

When Becky obtained her CDL, and while driving her big rig through major cities through out the western states, she was horrible at turning the rig around or backing up. She would back up into walls, damage the truck, and ordered back to the training center for more driving techniques. She would run over and smash beautiful flower beds or knock over light poles and fences, and again be ordered back to the Dawson office for further training. She never did get the hang of backing up to the dock of a local department or hardware store. Each time the owner of the big rig would receive a complaint about her, he would send her back to Dawson for more training, but never fire her.

There is, however, that final straw, or last resort. On a big rig run to a major city with a load of supplies for a local manufacturer, Becky got lost. Realizing where she had made a wrong turn, she tried turning her big rig around in the local McDonald restaurant's parking lot. As she attempted to turn around, she clipped the huge Golden Arches sign. As she drove quickly out of the parking lot, finally headed in the right direction, the Golden Arches came crashing to the ground. It wasn't funny then, and thankfully, no one was injured, but it would be the last time Becky ever drove a big rig!

Becky met Gina, a woman fourteen years her senior. Gina was also dysfunctional and needy but had a big heart. It would be a relationship that although sexual in the beginning, became much more of a friendship for many years to come. Becky imagined that this woman could take care of her. Becky thought in her twisted mind that Gina might possibly be the mother she could never find.

"After six years of sobriety, I drank again! I did cocaine for the first time, and overdosed, asked the neighbor for a gun, and was about to kill myself. I had lost what meant the most to me— the six years of achievement—sobriety. My therapist placed me in a treatment center, and after thirty days, I was placed in a sober living home. Gina was the housemother on weekends. We talked a lot about our addictions and where it had taken us. Gina also had a job in a hospital gift shop, and she got me a job there too."

"I moved in with Gina, and we became lovers, but only briefly. Gina was much more to me than that. We went to AA meetings together and we became best friends and soul mates.

It was at this same time, after "blowing" her sobriety that Becky had her first taste of "shooting up". At one of the AA meetings, she had reached out her hand to Sue; just as the program suggests that they do. Sue was married and had a child and both were on the path to destruction due to Sue's continual cocaine usage. Becky had only done cocaine one time before. She had been on a beach in California and had met with a group of men visiting our country. They were doing cocaine. They had offered the drug to her, and she had tried it. Becky had no idea how she had met this group or why she had tried cocaine, since alcohol was her "drug" of choice at the time. It had been years ago, at the age of sixteen, and she only remembered it as a blur.

Sue was friendly enough, and Becky found her very attractive. Sue convinced Becky that she was really looking for help at AA, and looking for a sponsor to help get her through the Twelve Steps of Recovery. Becky and Sue became friends, even became sexually involved for a short period of time, and then Sue showed Becky how to feel good by shooting up cocaine.

Sue had to show Becky how to fill a syringe and shoot up. The dosage had been entirely to high, and Becky's body could not handle the amount and she overdosed. She fell to the floor, her eyes rolling into the back of her head, and Sue could do nothing for Becky, because she was too tweaked out herself. When Becky finally came around, the first thing she did was to grab a beer. She wondered, and then wrote later in her journal, why she had given up her sobriety for a tryst with Sue, and shooting up cocaine. She, still, had no answers.

Up to this point in her life, Becky had been in foster care, in an adopted home, in six treatment centers, four detoxification centers and a few psyche wards at local hospitals. It wasn't over yet, but God was working on her, in her, and through her. She just didn't know it.

One day, as Becky was struggling, but still staying mostly sober, she thought about another woman who had gained her trust and worked to keep her sober. Her name was Jeannie.

"In looking back at my past, it was obvious that trust was difficult for me, even impossible. I trusted that whatever anyone told me was the truth, because Mrs. Livingstone told me so many times that everything she said to me was true, especially that my real mother never loved me or my sisters. I trusted that what monster

mommy told me was true. Then in life, I found out that people lied—all of the time. It wasn't that I trusted every one, it was that I would just do what everyone told me to do, because I had been raised as a robot and as a brainwashed child in the Livingstone home. I could do nothing on my own. I could not make decisions. I could not think for myself. It was after I had been in one of the treatment centers that I thought about Jeannie again."

"Jeannie had cared for me, really cared for me, and had trusted me, just like Jolene had cared and trusted me. I was in the Mercy Hospital Rehabilitation Center, and Jeannie had been a nurse practitioner there. She cared for me a great deal, and was interested in helping me get and stay sober. I was a patient for thirty days, and I not only learned that alcoholism was a disease, but there were actually people who cared about me and getting well. Jeannie came in each day of her shift to take my vital signs, and she and I would talk about my enlarged liver, and why it was enlarged. Jeannie wanted to know all about me, and my sisters, and yes about the Livingstone's. I poured my heart and broken soul to this, I thought, angel from God. Sometimes, I was sure that Jeannie had tears in her eyes; tears just for me."

"When I was discharged, Jeannie even gave me her telephone number. She trusted that I would stay sober. When, months later, I would be drunk again, or in a blackout stage, I would call Jeannie and she would soothe me and talk to me, and assure me that I would be okay. But, like everyone else before Jeannie, and after her, I would ruin her trust in me. I would promise to quit drinking, to go straight, and instead, I would falter again, and again."

"My intentions were always good but my actions were still those of a child—a child in an adult body with no clue as to what life was all about. I had no clue what I wanted to do when I grew up—if I ever did grow up. Of course being a child carries with it certain characteristics, such as selfishness and self-centeredness, but with fear as the motivator. Would I always be a child?"

Becky asked herself, while reminiscing about the past. *"To stay alive, should I continue to drink, should I continue to do drugs?"* And the most troubling question of all, *"What is to become of me? I'm almost thirty years old, and I still have no idea who I am or what is going to happen to me."*

Becky still had no answers.

CHAPTER EIGHTY-FIVE

The Past Revisited

About eleven years after Missy and Craig had married, a decision to move to a new and larger home became eminent. They had lived in their apartment for three years before moving to a small home in the suburbs, and now had outgrown that house as well. While going through closets and drawers one day, tossing out some items and saving others for the next move, Missy ran across a brown purse that she hadn't used in years. It had been a favorite and therefore she had never gotten discarded it. She figured now was a good time.

As she went through the purse one last time, making sure there were no hidden "treasures" inside, she found, in a back pocket, and at the bottom of the zippered compartment, an old folded piece of paper. As she unfolded the small piece of paper, she realized immediately, that it was the piece of paper that she had written information on so many years before. Missy had written down the license plate number of the "silver foxes" vehicle and the badge number of the cocky police officer who had assisted in the accident and rear-ending of her old Buick on Greenway Boulevard.

She was no longer actively involved as a Private Investigator, as taking care of her family had become her priority, but her mind began to stir. She sat down on the floor next to the closet she had been cleaning and began to think, while turning the piece of paper over and over in her hand. She wondered who the police officer had been that day? She could not remember his name, wasn't sure if she had ever looked close enough to his badge to read his name, but she had taken down his badge number. She also didn't recall, or had never been introduced to the "fox", but she had also taken down his license plate number.

Why? Why, right now, at this point in her life, did she find this old white piece of paper, and why was it, or why could it be so important? The entire finding made no sense to her, but yet, her mind wouldn't let go. She stood up and took out her cell phone. She dialed Craig's telephone number.

Craig as always was happy to hear her voice. He loved his family and thanked God every day that he had found Missy—or perhaps she had found him.

"Hey, what's up, my sweet little wife?" Craig asked her. "No one's missing are they?"

"You may think that your little wife has lost it, Craig, but guess what I found?" She said excitement in her voice.

She explained to him that she had found the piece of paper and why she thought it might be important, and then asked.

"Craig, I don't know why, it's probably my PI mind kicking in, but I need to know who that silver fox guy was, and who the cop was...you know the guys involved in my rear-ending years ago. Can you find me the name of that guy who hit me, and who the badge number belonged to?"

Craig, chuckling to himself now, told her that he would look into it for her. It probably was unimportant, but knowing his beautiful wife and how her mind operated, he never put the possibility of something life shattering, out of his mind.

"Okay." He said lovingly. "Give me those numbers."

To be honest, she had peaked Craig's curiosity too.

CHAPTER EIGHTY-SIX

Michael

There would be a few more relapses in Becky's tumultuous alcohol and drug-addicted life, but for the most part, and by the time she reached her Forties, she was a recovering addict. Becky would also see her physical body go through many serious conflicts, but she would survive those as well.

Being a part of AA, and making sure she attended meetings at least twice a week, Becky learned to live by the Twelve Steps Recovery Program. The heart of the program of personal recovery is from some of the earliest survivors of the program; those who were powerless over alcohol, and whose lives had become unmanageable. They believed that a power greater than their own could restore their sanity.

Becky, through the Twelve Steps Program, and two more excellent therapists, finally realized that she could not change her life. For whatever reason, her biological mother had deserted her, but it no longer had control over her life. She also realized that she would never completely recover from the horrific abuse from Devorah Livingstone, but that, too, was beyond her comprehension or control. She could not change what she could not understand. She could not change what had happened in that "house of hell", but she could learn to forgive and forget.

Through all of the years of abuse, drug and alcohol addiction, one thing Becky could or would never forget, was that she was one of four sisters. They were blood, blood relatives—her real family! She tried often to see Roseanne, forever in a nursing home. Becky would take a bus, sometime having to transfer bus routes two or three times through Dawson to see her older sister. She loved her sister and she also felt it was her duty, as the baby of the family, to see to her wellbeing.

Sandra on the other hand, would not be as loving or caring. She would not dare see Roseanne as a victim again, so rarely visited, or spoke with her, unless Becky initiated the call.

Becky and Sandra's relationship came to a complete and screeching halt when Becky took one of Sandra's grandsons out of a filthy, unhealthy environment to raise as her own son.

"Michael Joseph was born in Las Vegas Nevada. Chrissie, Sandra's first-born child was his mother. His father (although the birth certificate does not name the father), was Paul. I took Chrissie and Paul into my home when Chrissie was seven months pregnant. They had no other place to go. I was back on alcohol when they moved in with me, so I was not the best aunt for Chrissie. Paul smoked pot all of the time, but luckily, Chrissie did not. She did, however smoke cigarettes. Chrissie did not see a pre-natal doctor until her last trimester, and then again at Michael's birth. Chrissie carried Michael to term."

"I knew nothing about Chrissie and Paul's criminal life, until the day I asked them to leave. They admitted that they were wanted felons. Chrissie and Paul also refused to clean up after themselves. They lived like my sister Sandra had always lived, in filth. I on the other hand did not live that way. I had been a robot in Mrs. Livingstone's house, cleaning each and every day."

"I didn't see Chrissie and Paul again until four months after Michael's birth."

"Chrissie, I don't believe, ever did drugs or alcohol. Instead, she was having a child every other year—each birth from a different father, five different times. The state took two of the five children. One was adopted, one lives with Sandra and I adopted Michael. None of this is actually Chrissie's fault, but as I can tell you, it's the little one's that suffer. Chrissie's first child was actually adopted by a family in Dawson, and Chrissie constantly harassed the family for money, even though an agreement had been made previously to pay for her hospital bills and an apartment. Finally, unable to shake Chrissie, the family moved far away. Luckily, this tiny baby

was adopted into a very loving home with a loving family—unlike Sandra, Roseanne, Tabatha or me."

"Michael's father, presumably Paul, was put in prison for a number of felonies. Chrissie was also a wanted felon. During this time, Gina and I had been together for three years, when I requested and was allowed custody of Michael. After his 3rd birthday, I legally adopted him, and since Gina was no longer my lover, and she loved him as much as I did, she became Michael's grandmother. No papers were actually signed in the courts for Gina, but since Sharon, the biological grandmother who wanted nothing to do with Becky, Gina would from then on be his grandmother.

"I know that both of Michael's parents were more interested in themselves than in their son. Chrissie was also a victim. Her mother, Sandra, who had been raised and tortured in the Livingstone home, had raised her. Chrissie was a victim of circumstance. Something (I believe God was talking to me), woke me one night and told me to get Michael. When I arrived at their apartment, Chrissie and Paul were being evicted (just like her mother, Sandra had been evicted so many times). Chrissie and Paul were sitting on their bed. There was trash, moldy dishes and cat feces everywhere. I asked about Michael. I found him lying on an automen, with nothing protecting him from falling. A dirty pillow was holding a bottle in place in his little mouth. Each time the bottle would fall to the floor, the 5-month old baby boy would not cry. He already knew that no one was going to come and prop the bottle back up for him. The surroundings were filthy. Cat feces covered the room, the baby bottles with curdled milk, and the soiled diapers strewn everywhere. I knew that God had sent me to save my great nephew."

"When I bent down to pick Michael up, I startled him. At first I thought he couldn't hear me, but later we found out that his little ears were so full of dirt and wax, that he actually COULD NOT HEAR!"

"I took Michael out of that hellhole directly into my house. Gina was the manager at the local hospital gift shop and I was still employed there too. I took Michael to the Emergency Room the next day, to get him a physical checkup. He just didn't seem right for a six-month old child. I was correct in my suspicions. Michael was malnourished. He was also in a "failure to thrive baby" mode, had

never had his three-month and six-month immunizations, and was considered a "special needs" child.

"I filed a petition with the courts to get temporary custody of Michael, and after a few months filed for permanent custody. I was awarded this precious little boy—someone I could love and cherish as my own. Sandra, furious with me for filing charges and taking her grandson away from Chrissie was never able to fully comprehend why I did it. Sandra did not speak to me for several years."

Michael was just what Becky needed and Becky was just what Michael needed. His parents had never held him close or bonded with him and Becky was thrilled to hold and love this beautiful little boy.

Becky did relapse when Michael was a little over three years old. She got blood clots in both her legs, causing a deep vein thrombosis, and had to have her left vein stripped. And the largest vein in the right leg removed. It was a three-hour surgery, and she barely survived. There was a good chance that a clot could have gone to her heart and the doctors placed her in the hospital for a week. While hospitalized, she was prescribed painkillers, and immediately, Becky was hooked on drugs. Again.

However, with immediate professional help, and realizing that now she had responsibility and someone who needed her, she weaned herself off of the drugs. Michael was just what she needed to learn to love and care for herself. Becky was thirty-five years old and after only one relapse, got clean and stayed clean.

Seven years after the first episode with blood clots Becky developed more clots: this time in her lungs and again in her leg. The unanswered question is, were the blood clots hereditary or were they due to the horrific beatings from her childhood. No one will ever know.

After more surgery, the state put Becky on disability. Unable to work, she would remain on disability for the rest of her life, live in state-assisted housing and on food stamps—but Becky was clean and happy. She and Michael moved into housing for single mothers with children. Here, at the Village, Becky and her son were safe. Becky would never let anyone harm her or her son, ever again!

CHAPTER EIGHTY-SEVEN

A Clue

Craig, leaned back in his rolling office chair, stretching his arms and hands high above is head. He was glad to be finishing up the case he was working on; a body found in the Platte River. It had been a fairly easy case, although all cases of death, murder or manslaughter are not easy for anyone. A homeless man, with a family, had been murdered, and another homeless man, fighting him over of all things, a sleeping bag, had killed him. The family had called the police and reported their father, although homeless, presumed missing. Craig had taken the case. The murderer had been caught, convicted and sentenced. "A broken soul, dead, at the hands of another broken soul." Craig thought, shaking his head from side to side. Another broken soul."

Craig picked up the note pad and reread what he had written down, the license plate number and the police badge number given to him by his perky, sweet little wife.

Craig had no idea of course, who the license plate number belonged to, but looking at and repeating the police badge number aloud, Craig knew immediately who it belonged to, or had belonged to—Bryce Jenkins.

Missy had always thought she had seen money change hands between the officer called to the accident so many years ago, and the man, Missy called the "silver fox". Craig presumed that Bryce Jenkins had already turned bad cop before that day, and had gotten paid to cover up a rich man's sins.

Looking at his watch, Craig realized that the License Bureau would be closing soon for the day, but he dialed the number anyway. After several rings, a message machine voice stated for him to "please hold", nothing new to anyone who ever tried to get a live person, quickly, at the Motor Vehicle Department.

After ten minutes, Craig was surprised when he got a live person on the telephone. He immediately asked for his friend Jackie Davenport, hoping to get quick answers to his questions.

"Jackie Davenport. Theft." The sweet voice said.

"Craig Olson. Missing Persons." Craig retorted, laughing.

Jackie was pleased to hear her friend's voice, and asked what he was up to, and did he realize it was 4:30pm, and she was leaving for the day?

Grinning now, he told her he was sorry, and asked who in the government work place ever got to go home on time anyhow? Jackie laughed.

Craig gave her the license plate number, and after only a few minutes, Jackie shared with him that the number in question was no longer active. "That particular plate number hasn't been renewed in over ten years, Craig." Jackie said. "But those plates were on a Cadillac that was owned by a Dr. Bernard and Devorah Livingstone."

The name immediately rang a bell. Craig knew that several years earlier, Missy had been involved with adopted children bearing that same last name, and that she had also gone to the funeral of one of those children. He knew Missy would put on her PI cap, put two and two together, and realize that the man who had been involved in her mishap years ago, was most likely the father of the orphaned sisters.

He was anxious to give her the news.

CHAPTER EIGHTY-EIGHT

Twelve Steps

There are multitudes of broken people in this world. We read about the horror of child abuse, broken homes, murder and terrorism every day in the newspapers. We only need to turn on the television and watch the nightly news to hear of a starving child found locked in a dark closet or a child or adult being raped, beaten or murdered. Becky and her sister's story are not new or unusual. What is unusual is that the sinister, evil people who do the abusing, often time get by with it—just like Dr. Bernard and Devorah Livingstone.

The horror of it all is that five or ten years of horrific abuse lead to a lifetime of pain and heartache. It was no different for Becky and her sisters. The heart, mind and soul can never forget that kind of abuse. Without professional help, and forgiveness, the abused most likely will never be normal. Becky is damaged forever, but she learned to go forward, get professional help, and make something of her life.

"I had to go forward with my life, especially after I adopted Michael. I continued to attend a Catholic church once in awhile, but mostly it was out of habit. Monster mommy made me go to church with her and father every Sunday. I found God most times in the bottom of a bottle of pills or at the bottom of a bottle of wine or beer. While down on my knees, and while strung out on pills and booze, I would plead to God for help. When one time I did the devil's drug, Crystal Meth, and I was on the brink of insanity, I again reached out to God. With help I found Him in the Twelve Steps. The Steps taught me that I could not help my own destructive self, and the Twelve Step Program showed me how God could bring me back to life and guide me through all things. I also have the Twelve Steps recovery Bible, where the scriptures coincide with the steps to recovery. My job is to

let God take care of me, because I spent so much of my life trying to take care of myself, and I know where that got me! I will live the Twelve Steps forever. I also make an attempt to go to at least one or two AA (alcoholics anonymous), or NA (narcotics anonymous), meetings a week. I have to work on Little Bec each and every day. I believe in God, Jesus Christ His Son, and the Holy Spirit. I also believe that I have a close relationship with God, and He has a close relationship with me. I tell everyone I meet, that I DID NOT FIND GOD. GOD FOUND ME! He found me through the Twelve Steps.

THE TWELVE STEPS

1. We admit that we are powerless over alcohol—that our lives have become unmanageable
2. We come to believe that a power greater than ourselves could restore us to sanity
3. We make the decision to turn our lives over to the care of God as we understand Him
4. Make a Searching and fearless moral inventory of ourselves
5. Admitted to God to ourselves and to another human being the exact nature of our wrongs
6. Entirely ready to have God remove all defects of character
7. Humbly ask Him to remove our shortcomings
8. Make a list of all persons we have harmed and become willing to make amends to them all
9. Make direct amends to such people wherever possible, except when to do so would injure them or others
10. Take personal inventory and when we were wrong promptly admitting it
11. Through prayer and meditation to improve our conscious contact with God as we understand Him, praying for knowledge of His will for us, and the power to carry that out
12. Having had a spiritual awakening as result of these steps, we try to carry the message to other addicts and to practice these principals in all our affairs

No one has to be a religious person to join in on the Twelve Steps. People see a higher power in different ways. The higher power concept is about recognizing that some forces are beyond our control. The Twelve Steps are for all people of all faiths provided that they have one thing: the desperation to change!

"I would have never been able to forgive my adopted parents for their abuse had I not found, learned and believed in the Twelve Steps. I also would never have learned to "love myself" (something I still work on daily), had I not found the Twelve Steps. I no longer hate myself nor anyone else in my life. God, through the Twelve Steps now controls my every being, (at least most of the time)."

Becky, at thirty-five years of age had found her way in life. It was by no way a perfect life. She was unable to work. She lived off of the state, and went to her "meetings" once or twice a week. She was however, a loving mother to Michael.

However, Michael, a typical teenager, got himself into a few scrapes. He wanted to spend time with his ex-con father, and Becky allowed that to happen. Becky felt she had made the right decision. Michael got caught up with the wrong crowd and stole a car. Becky worked with him and the courts to keep him out of prison and he did community service. He also got a teenage girl pregnant, and showed no responsibility for the mother or the child. He did not finish high school, but is working on his GED. He currently holds a good-paying position. Michael has a good heart, and would never hurt anyone intentionally.

Three generations had now evolved. Michael is of the third generation of child abuse and neglect, and it has taken its toll. No matter how much Becky loved him, no matter how hard she tried Michael has seen the affects of his grandmother and mother's abuse. The damage was already done before Michael entered the world. But he and his adopted mother, Becky, through love, attention and hard work are working together to teach him to be and remain a better person.

"Michael is turning from a boy into a man, and I am very proud of him. I have never loved anyone, as much as I love my son."

CHAPTER EIGHTY-NINE

A Lifelong Promise

Missy was elated with her husband's informative telephone call. He had told her that the badge number belonged to Bryce Jenkins, the murdered police officer and that the license plate number, he was pretty sure, belonged to the four sister's adopted parents.

"I cannot believe it, Craig." She said excitedly. "I now know what I'm going to do. I promised my friend Jeanine Simpson, years ago, that I would follow up on those little girls, and even though it's been a long time, I'm going to try and find them. I always thought that the" "silver fox" wasn't all he was cracked up to be too, but I hope he was a good father to those little girls.

Missy asked Craig if he remembered that one of the adopted little girls had died?

"I went to her funeral, Craig." Missy said adamantly. "Her name was Tabbatha."

Craig smiled and assured her that he remembered, but then said. "I'm not sure why finding these girls is so important to you, Missy." He continued. "I know you made someone a promise, years ago, but why is this still so important to you?"

Missy tried to explain to her husband that she wasn't sure either. "I just know that something has pulled at my heart strings all of these years. I agree with you. I don't know why it's so important. Maybe God wants me to find those little girls when He is ready for me to find them, He will show me the way, or give me a reason if I don't find them. I know that now is the time. I have to look for them, and with God's help, I **will** find them."

Missy and Craig agreed that she should start spending more time as a Private Investigator. Their sons were older and could be left by themselves. She and Craig could also use the extra money, but more importantly, she wanted to look for and find those little girls. Having a current PI license would help her in her hunt.

For more than two years, Missy looked for the Livingstone's. She browsed the Internet and genealogy websites. She spent hours in the Dawson Public Library in the Archives looking through old newspaper articles. She located old articles on Mrs. Devorah Livingstone and her famous garden parties and fundraisers, but nothing current or on the good doctor. It was like the Livingstone family had moved away from Colorado, and no longer existed.

Missy worked diligently on her quest, all the while getting her Private Investigative business up and running again. After a few years, she all but gave up on finding Becky Livingstone or her sisters, but once again she had a flourishing and profitable PI business. She and Craig set up an office in their new home in Lakewood Hills, specifically for her daily business ventures, and on the weekends they camped, hiked and fished in the beautiful Colorado Mountains.

The Olson family had always enjoyed camping. When the boys were babies, the family camped in a tent and later graduated to a camping trailer. They had traveled through most of the United States before the children had graduated high school.

After the boys had both left home, Craig and Missy volunteered on the weekends at a wilderness area for people with disabilities. It was sixty-five miles west of Dawson, close to the town of Kenosha, and they could easily drive there in an hour. They would take their camping trailer and park it on one of the thirteen available campsites. They would register campers, clean campsites and restrooms, teach fishing to disabled children, and take campers on tours of the facilities on the weekends. They would return to their Lakewood Hills home late on Sunday evening and back to their weekly careers.

As the years went by, they spent more and more time volunteering at the wilderness area. It was located in a beautiful valley and surrounded by snow-covered mountains. There were daily sightings of elk and deer, accessible hiking trails and a stocked pond and a meandering river for fishing. It was definitely God's country.

When they were both in their sixties, Craig and Missy decided to retire. They had seen their sons graduate from college, start their own careers, marry and give them grandchildren. They had worked hard on their individual careers, had decent pensions, and they looked forward to a relaxed retirement—perhaps in the Colorado Mountains.

As it happened, the board of directors for the Wilderness Disability Center offered the Olson's a managerial (volunteer), position and Missy and Craig became summer managers at the Disability Center. They volunteered the entire summer for ten to twelve days at the Center, and then spent two or three days at their Lakewood Hills home. It was a lifestyle they loved. They met so many awesome disabled people, their families and friends, and they were able to live in the mountains—something they had always dreamed of doing.

The Olson's split their time between Kenosha and Lakewood Hills for over eight years. Finally, they decided that a move to Kenosha was the right decision and they put their Lakewood Hills home on the market.

During this same time, the neighbors to the right of their home in Lakewood Hills sold their home. The new owners, a company that "fixed and flipped" houses began the remodeling process soon after the sale.

On an early spring morning, Missy, while sitting at the dining room table drinking a cup of coffee, heard a knock at the front door. She grabbed her crutch and went to see who it might be.

A short, somewhat stocky woman, with blondish/reddish/ short hair, dressed in athletic shorts and tee, probably about fifty years old, held a very small dog in her arms and was smiling ear to ear.

"Hi." The woman said. "I'm Becky. I'm sorry to bother you, but I'm working on the renovation next door. Oh," and looking down at her dog, said, "this is Little Bit...I wondered if I could borrow a wheelbarrow?"

Missy introduced herself to Becky and invited her in. She told Becky that the wheelbarrow was in the shed in the backyard, and walked her through the house to the back door.

"There." Missy said, pointing to a small shed at the back of the beautifully landscaped yard. "It should be setting right in front of the shed. There, under the plum tree."

As Missy opened the back, sliding patio door, a large black dog, lazily lying on the patio floor, gave out a small "woof", wagged his tail, but didn't move.

"This is Spook." Missy said. "He's old, a little grumpy at times, but wouldn't hurt a flea."

The stranger walked to the shed, and finding the wheelbarrow, waved back at Missy as she pushed the three-wheeled piece of equipment out the back gate.

"Please close the gate." Missy yelled. "Don't want the dog to get out."

CHAPTER NINETY

A Promise comes to Fruition

Becky came over to her neighbor, Missy, several times during the house renovation process. Each time, Becky would ask for a tool, or to use the restroom, and each time Missy would wonder about this sweet, but, strange woman.

Becky was sweet enough, very polite, and always appreciative of what Missy did for her, but still, there was something about this newly found friend that Missy could not put her finger on.

Missy shared her feelings with Craig.

"It's the PI in you my dear wife." Craig said, laughing. "Maybe she's a serial killer, or robbed a bank and is burying her treasure in the neighbor's front flower beds."

Missy popped him across the head with a loving hand, and said that he was no help whatsoever.

One afternoon, while Becky was digging up old rock and tree roots, Missy walked outside, and sat herself down on the grassy area next to the flowerbeds in the neighbors yard.

"Becky." She said sweetly. "Do you like to read? Do you mind if I give you something to read?"

Becky walked over to Missy and sat down beside her and said. "I really don't read much, Missy. My attention span is very low, and (chuckling), I'd prefer to wait for the movie! Why? Do you have something you want me to read?"

Missy told Becky that she would be right back. She got herself up to a standing position, grabbed her crutch and hurriedly walked into her front door. A few minutes later, Missy came back out to where Becky, petting Little Bit, was still sitting on the grass. Missy handed her a book, and sat down next to her.

"I'm a writer, Becky...along with other things. I wrote this book a few years ago, and I would like you to read it. I think you would enjoy it."

"I don't have any money, Missy." Becky said, sadly.

"No. No. I don't want you to pay me for it, Becky. I want you to have it. It's a gift. I wrote it. It's a very inspirational book about overcoming my disability. It's an easy read."

Becky took the book from Missy's hand, and shyly told her thanks. As Becky paged through the book, she looked at Missy and said. "So, you're a writer?"

"Yes." Missy sad.

"I'm a writer too." Becky said. "I'm not very good at writing, but I have put a lot of my feelings on paper already. I want to write a book some day. I want to tell my story."

Missy asked her if her boss would be angry if she didn't get back to work? Becky said that no, taking a break for a few minutes would be okay. "He's not paying me very good, anyway." Becky continued. "Sometimes, he doesn't pay me at all. I'm used to that. It's okay."

Becky told Missy that she was a recovering addict. "I take odd jobs when I can. My son is also working here. He needs to work several hours for Community Service, and John, my boss, is letting us both work for a few months. I'm on disability insurance, so I can't get paid very much."

The two women chatted for a few more minutes, when Becky said she needed to get back to work. She asked Missy if they could talk some more? Becky wanted to learn more about how to write a book. Missy suggested that she come to work early one day, and they could talk more. Becky told her that she didn't have her own transportation and that she rode with the boss to work. Before work, she worked out at a gymnasium, close to her house in South Dawson.

"Could you possibly drive down there and pick me up sometime? I can work out, and then you could take me to work. That will give us some time to chat."

"I can do that." Missy said. "I have to be in South Dawson next Tuesday. I could come by the Warrington Park Gymnasium around noon. We could have lunch and talk more. How would that be?"

Becky agreed. On the next Tuesday, after Missy had ended a speaking engagement at the Dawson University, she waited for Becky in the gymnasium's parking lot. Becky said she really didn't want lunch, and Missy said she had just had a huge brunch at the university, so, instead of going to lunch, the two women sat in Missy's car, chatting.

Six weeks into this newly found friendship, and after many hours spent talking and drinking coffee, Missy Baker finally realized who Becky really was...Becky Livingstone. It absolutely blew Missy's mind!

Becky had continually shared with Missy (and sometimes with Craig), that she had no idea where her real mother and father were, but that she wanted so badly to find out if they were still alive. She talked about being adopted, and how horrible her life had been. She spoke of her Catholic upbringing, Father Ramsey, the time spent in foster homes and orphanages, the alcohol and drug addiction, her employment history, and that she and her son were living on welfare. She talked lovingly about her son, Michael, admitting, however, that he too was a challenge. She mentioned in passing, that she was a firm believer in a higher power, and would not be where she was today, without Him.

One afternoon, over iced tea and cookies at the table in Missy's charming dining room, Becky told Missy that she had been one of four children, all girls, and that one of her sisters had died when she was only four years old. A light bulb went off in Missy's brain.

Flash!!

It was another turning point in Missy Baker and Becky Livingstone's life!

Missy, now in her seventies had been looking for, or thinking about a small child and her three sisters for over thirty years. The spunky Private Investigator had never stopped wondering about four little girls who had been adopted by a supposedly prominent loving family. She remembered vividly little Tabbatha's funeral and she and Becky discussed the funeral and a multitude of other things over and over.

Missy was appalled when she heard Becky's entire story. She had no idea that anyone could treat a child the way the Livingstone's had treated Becky and her sisters. She shared with Becky that she had spent years looking for the adoptive parents.

"Now, here you are. It's amazing isn't it?" She said to Becky. "I truly believe that God brought you and I together. I'm not sure why, but I believe it is fate."

Becky looked into Missy's tear filled eyes. There were no words. She had lost her biological mother when she was an infant. She had been looking for her biological mother now, for over twenty years. Maybe she would never find her. But, in the meantime, Becky was sure that God had sent her a "stand-in" mother—Missy, and a stand-in father—Craig.

Her goal to find her real mother would not end here, but, now, with someone to assist her, it would make the search so much easier. With God's help, maybe, just maybe, Becky would find closure. Whether her real mother was alive or if she is dead, Becky still needed closure.

Becky knows who her mother was—at least her name. But, that's all Becky knows. Becky also knows that she is an addict—a recovering addict, and that her duty in life is to help other addicts. She also knows that she will have good and bad days, joys and struggles, but she will continue to strive and be successful. She knows that she is a human being (even though Devorah never treated her like one); one who is trying to be a better person today than she was yesterday. She truly believes that God is not "done with her yet."

"I'm not the person I used to be. I also believe that it's not so much how we all start out in life, but how we live our lives and

continue to live our lives, that matter. I believe that I can do all things through Jesus Christ, and I pray every day that I will never lose that faith. It's what I live on every day...FAITH IN A HIGHER POWER For me that includes God the Father, His Son, Jesus Christ and the Holy Spirit."

"I WAS A VICTIM, BUT I AM ONE NO LONGER!"

EPILOGUE

There are two ways to get to the Wilderness Disability Center from Dawson. The short way is to travel west on Highway 285 directly to the Center. The two-lane highway meanders along Elk Creek through mountains lined with massive evergreen and blue spruce trees. As you get higher in elevation there are groupings of aspen trees—bright green in summer and glimmering gold, red and yellow in the fall.

The longer way to the Center is to go west on the Interstate, and travel through several mountain towns, tourist attractions and ski areas. When traveling this route, you notice, high on the mountain, the beautiful Mother Cabrini Statute and Shrine.

A year after their miraculous meeting, Missy invited Becky to visit the Center. Missy hoped that Becky might enjoy volunteering, and working with those with disabilities might be a real blessing to this damaged woman.

Since Becky had shared her story of living at the Queen of Heaven Orphanage, (the orphanage started by Mother Cabrini), Missy and Becky drove the long way to get to the Center. Upon arrival, they left the Interstate and drove the steep, unpaved road to where the beautiful, white statue, stands tall and serene. Becky began to cry.

"I don't remember anything about the Orphanage, Missy." *She said, tearfully. "I just remember what my sisters told me about it. I do remember them telling me about the nun who started the Orphanage and I remember her name was Mother Cabrini."*

It was a special stop on the way to what would turn out to be a new way of life for Becky. It was as if her life had come full circle. At a very young age she had been loved and cared for by Mother Cabrini's nuns, and now she was viewing the Statue and Shrine dedicated to the woman who had, unknown to Becky, helped start her life. Now, she was on her way to a new and hopefully, productive life.

Becky took a few minutes, knelt at the Statue of the Reverend Mother Cabrini, said a few prayers, and afterward gave Missy a hug. No words were needed.

Becky told Missy early in their friendship, that her goal in life was number one, to find her real mother, which together, the two women are currently working on. Her second goal is to do Christian Service for all who need her. The Center is the perfect place for her to do just that.

Missy, Craig, and the Center's board of directors, approved Becky and Little Bit (Becky's dog), to live in the volunteer apartment at the Center at no charge. In turn, she cleans campgrounds, restrooms and cabins, and spends quality time speaking with and assisting handicapped children and adults in their trek through the wilderness. She is a real asset to the disability community, to Missy and Craig, but mostly, Becky is an asset to herself.

Becky admits that she is a damaged, broken soul and that she was a victim of circumstance. However, that does not define who Becky is today. Her heart and soul may have been broken, but God saw to it that no one **BROKE HER SPIRIT!**

"We, all four of us, were victims, but I broke out of the pack… guarding my spirit while God protected my heart. I have had a lot of challenges to overcome, and a lot of lessons I've had to learn. I've also had to learn so many perceptions and beliefs—those I had to change on my own; my life, my belief in God and myself. I fell many times during my journey, but I never gave up and I kept going, at times, through horrible pain. Most of the pain was for my sisters, never for myself. Now, I can say that God was with me the entire way. He never left me; I just didn't realize He was there. I will not be a victim ever again. I am a warrior, and although I still cry for my sisters and any child that has been abused, anyone can find freedom, if you chose to rise above your pain. God is always with you. You must never give up. You have to be an example of courage to all you meet."

"It took me until I was an adult to learn to make decisions. I had to learn to love. I had to have empathy for the child within me who taught me how to survive. I am not just surviving today, I am living, although, one day at a time. I thank God for that, and I thank all of those people who came in and out of my life, and who knew what I needed to survive."

"I can say, truthfully, today, that I love myself! I am a grown woman. I am no longer that little girl who was so horrifically abused. That little girl has grown up and become a sensitive, loving woman. My name is Becky Harrison."

A few years ago, in a Michigan newspaper's obituary section (Sandra doesn't remember how or why she found it on the internet), there was a notice of Devorah Livingstone's death. It really had no meaning to any of the three remaining sisters except for the fact that the obituary read:

"Our beloved Devorah...married to Dr. Bernard Livingstone for 54 years...mother of Kathy and Charlie...her countless acts of charity, famous Sunday dinners, her true kindness, sweetness and goodness survive in the memory of all who knew her..."

The words written in the obituary notice meant nothing to Becky, Roseanne or Sandra, except that most of the notice was untrue! Devorah had NEVER been a kind or caring person to the Holmgruff sisters. Becky felt no remorse, no hatred, perhaps only sadness when she read the notice. That part of her life was and is over. She has forgiven the woman who gave her life and with no fault of her own left her and her sisters. She has also forgiven the woman who abused her beyond belief. The past is behind her. Becky truly believes that God, even after fifty-five years of abuse, torment and addiction; a life of pure hell has a plan for her.

Little Bec is no longer that abused little girl. Little Bec has grown up and become a strong, sensitive and loving woman. Her goal in life is to help others, just as others helped her. Will she ever be able to support herself? Maybe not. Will she ever be off of welfare and disability? Probably not. Will she ever allow anyone to abuse or torment her again? Never!

Her name is no longer Little Bec. Again, and forever, her name is Rebecca Sue Harrison. The name she was given at birth, and the co-author of **BROKEN SOULS!!**

"I am not what happened to me. I am what I choose to become!"
Carl Gustaf Jung

About the Author

Barbara Roose Cramer lives in Littleton, Colorado with William, her husband of fifty-two years. She has three sons, seven grandchildren and one great grandson. She is a paraplegic due to polio and has used a wheelchair for sixty-six years. She is a paralympian gold medalist, a retired bookkeeper, and avid quilter and she and her husband are managers of the Wilderness on Wheels Foundation, located in Grant, Colorado. BROKEN SOULS is her fourth publication.

Printed in the United States
By Bookmasters